The War in Heaven

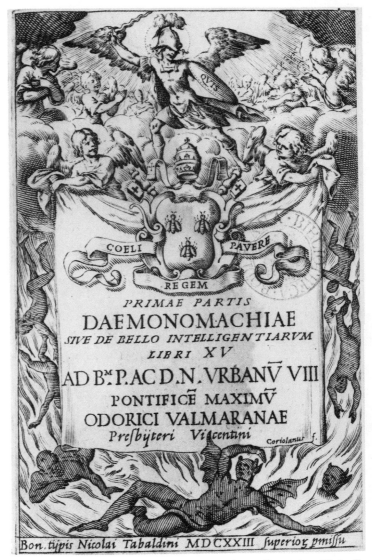

Title page to Valmarana's *Daemonomachiae*, illustrating Michael's victory over Satan, by permission of the Bodleian Library, Oxford.

→ THE WAR IN HEAVEN

Paradise Lost and the Tradition
of Satan's Rebellion

STELLA PURCE REVARD

Cornell University Press

ITHACA AND LONDON

First published 1980 by Cornell University Press.
Published in the United Kingdom by
Cornell University Press Ltd., 2–4 Brook Street,
London W1Y 1AA.

International Standard Book Number 0-8014-1138-6
Library of Congress Catalog Card Number 79-23297
Printed in the United States of America
*Librarians: Library of Congress cataloging information
appears on the last page of the book.*

For MAE HILL PURCE

Sit memorasse satis, repetitaque munera grato
Percensere animo, fidaeque reponere menti.

Contents

Preface

The war in Heaven ended for the loyal angels after two days. I envy their lot, for after two decades I have had to negotiate my own peace. I became interested in the "problem" of Milton's war in Heaven following Arnold Stein's critical reappraisal of book 6 of *Paradise Lost* in the 1950s. It became apparent to me then that it was impossible to deal with the critical issues of Milton's battle in Heaven without knowing more about its intellectual background. My first approach to this background was through an investigation of the theological history of Satan and his fall, from the early Christian period to the seventeenth century, focusing particularly on the interpretations of Satan's motivation among the patristic and Renaissance Protestant theologians. Chapters 1 and 2 of this book trace this historical background.

Although knowledge of the theological tradition is primary to an evaluation of Milton's treatment of Satan's revolt, there are still other important background materials to be considered. The war in Heaven that Revelation 12 describes could be interpreted not only as Satan's first war of insurrection but as all subsequent wars. Hence it had particular meaning for Milton's England, which considered both the Gunpowder Plot of 1605, against which all England was united, and the Civil War of the 1640s, which divided England into accusing factions, as conspiracies or wars led by the archvillain Satan. In exploring the political and social implications of the new "wars" in Heaven that raged in seventeenth-century England, I have not attempted to write a

history of Satanism or to trace Milton's political stances from the
1620s to the 1660s (although these issues are not without relevance), but to assess rather how the seventeenth-century political
scene might have affected Milton's presentation of Satan's conspiracy in books 5 and 6 of *Paradise Lost*. While theological,
political, and social traditions exerted considerable influence on
Paradise Lost, the literary tradition exerted still more, since the
war in Heaven first became an epic battle in the hexaemeral
poems of the sixteenth and seventeenth centuries which preceded
Milton's epic. To this literary tradition, however, scholars have
given little attention, for the poems that comprise it, many of
which Milton undoubtedly knew, are not readily accessible. Yet
without a knowledge of the literary tradition, it is not possible to
assess what is new in Milton's treatment of Satan's revolt and
what is borrowed from predecessors. My work on the various
traditions of Milton's war in Heaven began as a doctoral dissertation at Yale University, but my investigations were not completed
until 1975, when, on sabbatical leave from Southern Illinois University, Edwardsville, I was able to consult the original editions
of the Renaissance epics and dramas on the war in Heaven.

Portions of this book have appeared in somewhat different form
under the following titles and are used by kind permission of the
respective journals. Chapter 2 appeared as "Satan's Envy of the
Kingship of the Son of God," in *Modern Philology* 70 (February
1973): 190–198, © 1973 by The University of Chicago; chapter 3
as "Milton's Gunpowder Poems and Satan's Conspiracy," in
Milton Studies 4 (1972): 63–77; chapter 4 as "The Warring Saints
and the Dragon," in *Philological Quarterly* 53 (spring 1974): 181–
194. Some of the material from the following articles has been
reworked and is used in various sections of the book, particularly
in chapters 1, 5, 6, and 7: "Milton's Critique of Heroic Warfare in
Paradise Lost V and VI," *Studies in English Literature* 7 (winter
1967): 119–139; "The Dramatic Function of the Son in *Paradise*

Lost," *Journal of English and Germanic Philology* 66 (January 1967): 45–58; "The Renaissance Michael and the Son of God," in *Milton and the Art of Sacred Song* (Madison: University of Wisconsin Press, 1979); "Neo-Latin Poems on the War in Heaven," in *The Third Acta Conventus Neo-Latini Turonensis,* forthcoming.

I wish to thank the staffs of the following libraries for assistance with various aspects of this book: Yale University Library, Amherst College Library, Washington University Library, Newberry Library, Bodleian Library, British Library, Biblioteca Nazionale of Florence, and Biblioteca Nazionale of Naples.

I am grateful to friends and colleagues (many of them Milton scholars whose work is cited in this book) who over the years have offered encouragement and support. J. Max Patrick and Roger Sundell helped this book on its way when they asked me to write a paper on Michael for the Tercentenary Conference on Milton at Milwaukee in November 1974. Scott Elledge was helpful in suggesting that I send my manuscript to Cornell University Press. Balachandra Rajan not only read my manuscript with care but also was instrumental in reshaping it. He suggested that I compose the first and final chapters, on which he has generously offered criticism. Gertrude Drake looked over my Latin translations and offered suggestions. Helen Goode helped with the Spanish translation. I owe thanks for conscientious work on a difficult manuscript to my typists: James Havranek, Linda Hartman, and Mary Diedam. I appreciate also the efforts of editors at Cornell University Press who helped prepare this manuscript for publication.

My greatest debts are to Irene Samuel and Louis Martz. Professor Samuel, my first teacher of Milton at Hunter College, both by her own splendid example and by her encouragement led me to persevere in Milton studies. To her I am also grateful for reading this manuscript with sympathy. Professor Martz directed my dissertation at Yale University and was the one who first suggested that I explore seventeenth-century pamphlet literature as background for Milton's war. I am happy he can now see the long "war" ended, for he never lost interest in the book he hoped would come from the dissertation.

My husband, Carter, and my children—Stephen, Geoffrey, Vanessa, and Lawrence—have looked on with patience as this became, in true seventeenth-century style, a twenty-year war. My mother, Mae Hill Purce, to whom this book is dedicated, has been an inspiration for it, as for all my endeavors. Such comrades-in-arms have made easier the long and tedious havoc of battle. With John Milton at one's side too, one can never despair of winning the better fortitude.

STELLA PURCE REVARD

Oxford, England

The War in Heaven

The War in Heaven
and the Critics

Him the Almighty Power
Hurl'd headlong flaming from th' Ethereal Sky
With hideous ruin and combustion down
To bottomless perdition, there to dwell
In Adamantine Chains and penal Fire,
Who durst defy th' Omnipotent to Arms.

[1.44–49]

When Milton began the narrative of *Paradise Lost* with the flaming fall of Satan from Heaven, it became almost inevitable that he should return to recount fully the events that had preceded it. It was inevitable not only because Adam and Eve needed to know intimately the history of the enemy they would face or because narrated wars had become almost pro forma in epic since Demodocus had told of the Trojan horse in *Odyssey* 8 or Aeneas of the sack of Troy in *Aeneid* 2, but more truly because Milton and his contemporaries regarded the war of Satan's expulsion as so vital a part of the cycle of history it began that without it the whole could not be understood.

Through the early books of *Paradise Lost* Milton builds toward the war in Heaven by repeated allusion. Whenever he speaks of the war, as Addison has observed, his imagination is "so inflamed with this great Scene of Action, that ... he rises, if possible, above himself."[1] At intervals different characters recall the "im-

---

1. In his commentary on *Paradise Lost* Addison makes much of the fact that Milton raises the reader's expectation and prepares him for the war by several passages in the early books. See Joseph Addison, *Criticism on Milton's "Paradise Lost."* From *The Spectator*, Saturday, March 22, 1712, ed. Edward Arber (Westminster, 1903), p. 92.

pious War" and "Battle proud," always from their own special points of view. By such glimpses Milton keeps the war before us, never permitting us to dismiss it as mere past history, and piques our desire to know what actually occurred. Was it the "Glorious Enterprise" that Satan eulogizes, giving us the first glimpses of that battle he is never permitted to narrate (though, like Aeneas, he is its defeated "hero")? Why does it provoke such different reactions in Moloch, Belial, and Mammon, who either wish to resume the battle or want to escape it forever? In Hell or in Heaven the war is treated as unforgettable. Death, meeting his father at Hell's gate, taunts him for his "proud rebellious arms" (2.691), and Sin recalls her distress at the rout of the rebel troops. In Heaven the angelic chorus celebrates the war as proof of the Son's heroism, when with his thunders he overthrew the "aspiring Dominations" (3.392). And, finally, when Satan and Gabriel prepare their arms in book 4, this encounter is treated by Milton both as a postlude to the war in which they first met and as a prelude to its narration. Each reference moves us closer to what Milton seems to regard as a major event of the poem.

Yet critics do not usually regard the war in Heaven as a major event of *Paradise Lost*. With books 11 and 12, it has been least the subject of literary analysis and inquiry, more often thought of as a digression than as an integral part of the poem. Dr. Johnson set the tone here, as in other matters, when he dismissed the episode as a "favourite of children, and gradually neglected, as knowledge is increased" and complained that the war itself suffered from "incongruity," the chief source of which was "the confusion of spirit and matter."[2] On the last point at least, critics have come to Milton's defense—C. S. Lewis most notable among them—and have explained that what Johnson took for incongruity was not ineptly managed poetic fiction but deliberate design. Still, however, the stigma of confusion and incongruity clings to the episode and seems to justify its neglect.[3]

2. Samuel Johnson, "Milton," in *Lives of English Poets* (London, 1906), 1:133.
3. A. J. A. Waldock, for one, is not fully satisfied with Lewis's defense of

Curiously enough, this was not always so. Early eighteenth century critics found much to admire in the war, describing it as forceful and skillfully contrived, a real climax in the action. For the first time in *Paradise Lost,* they felt, Milton had the opportunity to compose true epic, with war scenes patterned on Homer and Virgil that fully met the classical standard. Addison felt that Milton's particular gift for the sublime was fittingly exercised by a heavenly war. "It required great Pregnancy of Invention, and Strength of Imagination, to fill this Battel with such Circumstances as should raise and astonish the Mind of the Reader; and, at the same time, an Exactness of Judgment to avoid every thing that might appear light or trivial." Homer's method with supernatural warfare had been, Addison comments, to order his battles so that each surpassed the others in intensity. Milton, meeting the Homeric challenge, orders his "Fight of the Angels . . . with the same Beauty."

> It is usher'd in with such Signs of Wrath as are suitable to Omnipotence incensed. The First Engagement is carried on under a Cope of Fire, occasion'd by the Flights of innumerable burning Darts and Arrows which are discharged from either Host. The second Onset is still more terrible, as it is filled with those artificial Thunders, which seem to make the Victory doubtful, and produce a kind of Consternation even in the Good Angels. This is follow'd by the tearing up of Mountains and Promontories; till, in the last place, the Messiah comes forth in the Fulness of Majesty and Terrour. The Pomp of his Appearance, amidst the Roarings of his Thunders, the Flashes of his Lightnings, and the Noise of his Chariot Wheels, is described with the utmost Flights of Humane Imagination.[4]

Richardson in his commentary on *Paradise Lost* takes a similar

---

Milton's design for corporeal spirituality (*A Preface to Paradise Lost* [London: Oxford University Press, 1942], pp. 105–111). Although Waldock concedes that "Johnson was incorrect in assuming that Milton was only trying to find 'the best solution to a technical problem,' " he argues that Johnson was right to complain of the incongruity in the war in that Milton is grossly inconsistent in applying the theoretical bases he lays down (*Paradise Lost and Its Critics* [Cambridge: Cambridge University Press, 1947; reprinted Gloucester, Mass.: Peter Smith, 1959], pp. 106–111).

4. Addison, *Criticism on Milton's "Paradise Lost,"* pp. 93–94.

point of view on the war in Heaven, gauging Milton's success
therein by whether his battle scenes equaled Homer's in imagination and variety of invention. It is to Milton's credit, says
Richardson, that he excels even Homer. "Here will be seen a
Battle-Picture, Such as No Pen Before, nor any Pencil has shown
to the World. . . . all the Incidents are so Great and Surprizing that
the Reader cannot be Tyr'd Unless the Multitude and Weight of
the Ideas oppress the Mind."[5] If the eighteenth-century critics
found anything to criticize in the war, it was only the punning of
the rebel angels on the second day, levity that appeared improper
in the high seriousness of the epic context.[6]

It is hardly surprising that the war narrative should fall into
disrepute in the nineteenth century, when different notions of the
heroic prevailed and magnificent war scenes no longer seemed
requisite for the true epic. Hazlitt dismisses the war in Heaven as
neither a "climax of sublimity" nor "the most successful effort of
Milton's pen."[7] Disaffection with the war continues into the
twentieth century; Grierson in the late thirties sums up the general critical unease with the episode. As an imitation of Homer, it
seemed both unsuccessful and inappropriate in a Christian poet:
"When it comes to the actual physical combat one feels that after
all these are not Homeric combatants, men or gods, but angels
contending with the Almighty; and the battle scenes become
purely decorative, not enhanced by the invention of artillery and
the interchange of jibes and jokes."[8] Arnold Stein's suggestion in
the 1950s that Milton was writing not serious epic narrative but

5. J. Richardson, Father and Son, *Explanatory Notes and Remarks on Milton's "Paradise Lost"* (London, 1734; reprinted New York: Garland, 1970), pp.
258–259.

6. *Milton 1732–1801: The Critical Heritage,* ed. John T. Shawcross (London
and Boston: Routledge & Kegan Paul, 1972), pp. 102, 124 (anonymous criticism).
Addison also condemns this passage as the silliest in the poem (p. 30).

7. *Milton Criticism: Selections from Four Centuries,* ed. James Thorpe (London: Routledge & Kegan Paul, 1951), p. 106. Walter Savage Landor, however,
takes another view: "Milton's epic battle is worth all other battles in all other
poets," from "Southey and Landor," *Imaginary Conversations,* in *The Roman-
tics on Milton* ed. Joseph A. Wittreich, Jr. (London and Cleveland, 1970), p. 573.

8. Herbert J. C. Grierson, *Milton and Wordsworth* (London, 1937; reprinted
1950), p. 118. Some later critics such as J. B. Broadbent (*Some Graver Subject*

antiepic or mock epic, therefore, becomes one solution to the problem. Stein was attempting to reclaim book 6 for the twentieth century when he characterized it as Milton's "great scherzo... epic comedy, even on its physical level—elevated to the epic by magnificent imaginative power, made comic by controlled excess."[9] In once more admiring Milton's epic inventiveness, as the eighteenth century had done, Stein restored a lost sensibility. But in finding value in those ironic and punfilled passages of book 6, which some eighteenth-century critics had merely deplored, in suggesting that these change the epic war to mock epic, Stein radically altered the modern apprehension of the war. But he thereby returned an important section of *Paradise Lost* to critical attention.

Side by side with the return of critical interest in the war in Heaven has come a renewed interest in the central episodes of *Paradise Lost* for their structural or numerological importance. Scholars exploring the structure and numerological system of the poem have argued that its central episodes, far from being mere digressions, contain some of the most important thematic material in *Paradise Lost*. By locating these episodes centrally, Milton planned that they should receive central attention. Milton's redivision of the poem in 1674 into twelve rather than ten books was designed, urges Arthur Barker, to focus attention upon books 6 and 7, the war in Heaven and the Creation, "with evil on the one hand frustrated, and on the other creation and recreation."[10] This redivision, Joseph Summers also observes, permits the dramatization at the center of "the divine image of God's ways at their most providential."[11] Victory of heavenly good over hellish evil

---

[London, 1960], pp. 219–223) also find Milton's imitations of Homer unsuccessful: "these conventions accumulate so wearisomely that they overwhelm their own point" (p. 220).

9. Arnold Stein, *Answerable Style* (Minneapolis, 1953), pp. 20–23.

10. Arthur Barker, "Structural Pattern in Paradise Lost," *PQ* 28 (1949): 1–30; reprinted in Barker, *Milton: Modern Essays in Criticism* (New York: Oxford University Press, 1965), p. 152.

11. Joseph H. Summers, *The Muse's Method* (Cambridge: Harvard University Press, 1962; reprinted Norton Library, 1968), pp. 112–115.

here occurs dramatically to fix this important theme upon the reader's mind. So closely contrived is Milton's design, insist the numerological critics, that the victory occurs not just generally at the center, but at the exact mathematical apex, reckoned by number of lines, when the Son ascends (in 1667 *ascended* is the central word) into his chariot of victory.[12] Hence it is not merely the victory of good that lies at the poem's center, but the Son's ascendancy over Satan. To the climax of the war in Heaven, it seems, Milton has accorded supreme symbolic significance with *Paradise Lost,* thereby extending to the entire episode structural and thematic importance of the highest order.

Analogous to the numerological reading, yet quite distinct, is the typological reading of the war, which has also received its share of attention. Jon S. Lawry in *The Shadow of Heaven* and William G. Madsen in *From Shadowy Types to Truth* both read Raphael's narrative as a "shadowing" or "foreshadowing" episode. Lawry sees it as prefiguring not only the fall itself, but also significant moments in earthly history: the defeat of Pharaoh, Jesus' triumph over demons, his Resurrection, and his return on the Last Judgment. Madsen, exploring the entire question of typology, views the war most particularly as foreshadowing the Christian struggle on earth preceding Christ's ultimate return at the millennium. These readings of *Paradise Lost* are supported in large measure by the Protestant interpretations of Revelation (the whole text, but most especially the twelfth chapter) by such biblical exegetes as John Napier and Joseph Mede. The entire millenarian movement in seventeenth-century England has, as both

12. For a summary of the numerological position, see Alistair Fowler's edition of *Paradise Lost* (London, 1971), pp. 22–25. Also see Galbraith Miller Crump, *The Mystical Design of Paradise Lost* (Lewisburg, Pa.: Bucknell University Press, 1975) pp. 68–147; John T. Shawcross, "The Son in His Ascendance: A Reading of *Paradise Lost,*" *MLQ* 27 (1966): 388–401; John T. Shawcross, "The Balanced Structure of *Paradise Lost,*" *SP* 62 (1965) 696–718; William B. Hunter, Jr., "The Center of *Paradise Lost,*" *ELN* 7 (1969): 32–34; Gunnar Qvarnström, *The Enchanted Palace* (Stockholm, 1967); Maren-Sofie Røstig, *The Hidden Sense* (Oslo, 1963). For an analysis of the numerological approach, see Balachandra Rajan, "*Paradise Lost* and the Balance of Structures," *UTQ* 41 (1972): 219–226.

Katherine Firth and Christopher Hill argue, special significance for Milton.[13]

Graphic interpretation of Revelation and the war in Heaven adds yet another dimension to the war, as Roland M. Frye has demonstrated with his study of the iconography of the battle of the good and bad angels. By analysis and by illustration Frye has sought to determine how the pictorial traditions of the Middle Ages and Renaissance might have affected Milton in his poetical description of armed angels in celestial combat.[14] Painters and poets alike, as we shall see when we come to consider the hexaemeral poems of the Middle Ages and Renaissance, were fascinated by the warlike Michael and his duel with the Dragon-Satan.

While the work of modern critics and scholars has assured us that books 5 and 6 are significant parts of *Paradise Lost*, it has not provided a consensus on the meaning of the war or its place in the poem.[15] As introductions and commentaries to books 5 and 6

13. Jon S. Lawry, *The Shadow of Heaven* (Ithaca, N.Y.: Cornell University Press, 1968), pp. 199–212; William G. Madsen, *From Shadowy Types to Truth* (New Haven: Yale University Press, 1968), pp. 85–113; Katherine R. Firth, *The Apocalyptic Tradition in Reformation Britain, 1530–1645* (Oxford: Oxford University Press, 1979); Christopher Hill, *Milton and the English Revolution* (New York: Viking, 1978), pp. 279–284.

14. Roland Muscat Frye, *Milton's Imagery and the Visual Arts* (Princeton: Princeton University Press, 1978), pp. 43–64.

15. For a useful summary of the different critical approaches to books 5 and 6, as well as a review of their major critical and scholarly cruxes, see the Cambridge edition of *Paradise Lost*, books 5–6 (Cambridge University Press, 1975), ed. Robert Hodge and Isabel G. MacCaffrey. No attempt will be made at this point to review fully twentieth-century scholarship on the war in Heaven. Most of the leading critical books have chapters on the war, and there are full-length articles devoted to various critical readings. Many are responses to Stein's important chapter in *Answerable Style*. B. A. Wright (*Milton's Paradise Lost* [Southampton: Camelot Press 1962] characterizes the war as a satire not only on epic battle, but on war in general. Helen Gardner (*A Reading of Paradise Lost* [Oxford: Clarendon Press, 1965]) reads it as a parable of the deepening tragedy of human history, William G. Madsen (*From Shadowy Types to Truth*) as a parable of patience, Stanley Fish as one of Christian heroism (*Surprised by Sin* [New York: St. Martin's, 1967]). Joseph Summers (*The Muse's Method*) treats the war as a meaningful lesson for angels, mortals, and readers alike. James Holly Hanford's early article "Milton and the Art of War," *SP* 18 (1921): 232–266, and Dick

testify, along with the continuing number of critical readings or scholarly explications of the war, questions on the very basic nature of Satan's revolt continue to be raised. Satan's motivation has not yet been settled, nor has the place of the Son as both inspirer and defeater of Satan's warfare. Smaller matters also, such as the use of Hesiodic reference or the appropriateness of modern artillery to celestial battle, continue to perplex readers and critics alike. In undertaking a full-scale study of the war in Heaven, I cannot hope to solve all its problems. But I shall attempt at least to provide a sound background against which they may be appraised. When Milton wrote of the war in Heaven, he was not writing something unique or previously unattempted. In the sixteenth and seventeenth centuries other poets had composed poems about Lucifer's rebellion, and many had even employed epic conventions to describe it. Therefore, as we approach Milton's war, it is useful to look first at the literary background. Source studies, such as Grant McColley's or Watson Kirkconnell's, have identified contemporary analogues (Vondel's *Lucifer* and Valvasone's *Angeleida* are the most famous of these) to the war in Heaven. By examining some of the epics and heroic dramas by Milton's contemporaries and predecessors from a literary or critical point of view (in the past they have more often been the subject of source study), we may be able to assess what

---

Taylor, Jr.'s, later one, "The Battle in Heaven in *Paradise Lost*," *Tulane Studies in English* 3, (1952): 69–92, offer important insights—Hanford on the war in Heaven as the epitome of war in general, Taylor on the war as developing the themes of obedience, free will, and Christian liberty, as well as those of hierarchy and pride. Articles and books elaborating other approaches include the following: William McQueen, "*Paradise Lost* V, VI: The War in Heaven," *SP* 71 (1974): 89–104; Jason Rosenblatt, "Structural Unity and Temporal Concordance: The War in Heaven in *Paradise Lost*," *PMLA* 87 (1972): 31–41; Stella Revard, "Milton's Critique of Heroic Warfare in *Paradise Lost* V and VI," *SEL* 7 (1967): 119–139; Kitty Cohen, "Milton's God in Council and War," *MS* 3 (1971): 159–184; Jackie Di Salvo, "'The Lord's Battells': *Samson Agonistes* and the Puritan Revolution," *MS* 4 (1972): 39–62; Austin C. Dobbins, "The War in Heaven," in *Milton and the Book of Revelation* (University, Ala., 1975); Michael Murrin in "The Language of Milton's Heaven," *MP* 74 (1977): 350–365, explores some of Milton's models and the alternate claims that the war is comic or sublime.

Milton intended in designing a "epic" war in Heaven.[16] Was he merely following convention, or was he criticizing or perhaps even parodying convention? By devoting a large section of this book to the exposition and analysis of the contemporary poetical background to the war in Heaven, I hope to evaluate by comparison the tone and intention of Milton's war. Basic to any consideration of the war in Heaven must be a definition of the kind of war Milton intended to place at the center of his poem. Should we read his war as serious Homeric imitation, as the eighteenth century did, or as mock epic, as we are urged by Stein and those who follow his view?

The question next in importance to that central one of Milton's intention must be its theological meaning. Problems of theology and characterization merge in an episode where the main persons are God, the Son, Satan, and the rebel and loyal angels (individually, as with Abdiel, or en masse). Milton's theology has received a good deal of attention in recent years, both as it has been explored by scholars like Kelley, Patrides, Hunter, Adamson, and others and as it has been attacked by Empson and those critics who follow him.[17] Many of the most basic questions about the theology of *Paradise Lost* involve issues and motives central to books 5 and 6. Most of those major issues raised by Milton's God in book 3 have their genesis in these books, for they begin the story as we know it. Therefore it is reasonable to direct our attention to books 5 and 6 when we query, as William Empson has done, the motives for God's and Satan's behavior. Why precisely

16. Austin Dobbins has recently argued the view that the primary source for the war in Heaven is not Homer or classical literature but the Bible (*Milton and the Book of Revelation*, pp. 26–27). Hence it is imperative to examine once more the "literary" tradition of Milton's war.

17. A. J. A. Waldock, before Empson, raised a number of questions about the theology of books 5 and 6, being among the first to contend that the "rebel angels appear to have been kept in the dark about a number of... facts" ("*Paradise Lost*" *and Its Critics*, pp. 71–73). John Carey, in *Milton* (London, 1969), argues, as Empson first did in *Milton's God* (London, 1965), that God in a sense provokes the rebellion of Satan (pp. 81–89). Empson also asserts that God has withheld convincing Satan of his "credentials" until it is too late (p. 95).

23

does God choose to elevate the Son to kingship at the moment he does, knowing, as he must, that the anointing of the Son will spark Satan's resentment and cause his rebellion? Why is the elevation spoken of as the "begetting" of the Son (how is his divine origin intimately bound up with the origin of his kingship)? Why does Milton depart from the usual theological account to make envy and not pride the prime force that moves Satan to revolt? Despite the work done on Satan's motivation by Grant McColley, Arnold Williams, and Allan H. Gilbert, these and other questions remain perplexing and suggest that Miltonists would profit from a more thorough account of the pride and envy that first move Satan. To investigate Satan's pride fully one must begin with its origin as a leading motive among the early church fathers, its cumulative growth during the patristic period, and its survival into the Renaissance to affect Milton's characterization of Satan, not only in book 5 when it chronologically first appears, but also in book 1 where it receives its first narrative mention. To account for Satan's envy of the Son one must follow a still more abstruse path, for as a motive it originates in the patristic period but lacks real theological importance until the Renaissance, when it becomes closely involved with the question of Satan's entire relationship to Christ. Thus it is perhaps even more important than pride in elucidating the grounds for Satan's rebellion and so in answering the claim of Empson and others that in his objection to the Son Satan had a reasonable case against God. Both motives merit, I believe, the detailed explication they receive in chapters 1 and 2.

Just as important a theological issue as Satan's relationship to God is the Son's; in *Paradise Lost,* books 5 and 6 are crucial to understanding that relationship. During the 1950s and 1960s the work of such scholars as C. A. Patrides, William B. Hunter, Jr., and J. H. Adamson (as well as the continuing work of Maurice Kelley) has contributed much to our understanding of the nature of the Son's relationship to the Father, not only as explicated in the theological treatise *De doctrina Christiana,* but also as presented in *Paradise Lost,* particularly in these central books, 5, 6, and 7.[18] In books 5 and 6 there is the important scene of the Son's ordination to kingship, dramatized by Milton as parallel to the celebration of his future Incarnation, that had already been presented in book 3; then there are two intimate colloquies of Father and Son; and finally there is the Son's ascent into the chariot, meant not only to effect his victory over Satan, but also to reveal the nature of his divinity. As Empson has raised questions about God's so-called provocation of Satan, he has also queried God's promotion of the Son, charging, in fact, that the entire war is engineered by God as the means for the Son to ''win his spurs.''[19] Since, in a gross sense, this is precisely what does happen (God does control the order of events, the Son does ''win his spurs''), it becomes all the more needful to look closely at character and motive in the light of traditional theology, of the theology Milton expounds in *De doctrina,* and of the theology of divines and thinkers of Milton's own time. To understand the subtle implications of the relationship of the Son to the Father will be to understand more fully a war provoked by the Father's elevation of the Son and won by the Son as he emerges to express the Father's omnipotence.

If it is important to look closely at the theological and poetical backgrounds to the war in Heaven, it is also well not to ignore its social and political spheres, especially in the world of the seventeenth century, where religion and politics were so closely allied. Milton's political stance on the war in Heaven has for a long time been somewhat of a puzzle to readers. In his own life he supported rebellion and was on the side of the revolutionaries (of the devil's party, as William Blake or the English Royalists would say—meaning different things by it, of course); but in literature he seems to have turned ''royalist'' and upheld King Messiah and

18. See William B. Hunter, C. A. Patrides, and J. H. Adamson, *Bright Essence: Studies in Milton's Theology* (Salt Lake City, 1971); Maurice Kelley, *This Great Argument* (Princeton, 1941), and ''Introduction'' to *Christian Doctrine,* vol. 6 of the *Complete Prose Works of John Milton* (New Haven, 1973).

19. Empson, *Milton's God,* pp. 95–97.

the divine right. To examine some seventeenth-century background on rebellion seems helpful, then, for, as recent studies of Milton's politics have indicated, the political paradigms of the seventeenth century were different from our own.[20] Hence we shall look not only at the political scene closest at hand—views of rebellion held by those of Milton's own party who opposed Charles's "bad" kingship—but also at some larger, more basic views on conspiracy and insurrection held by Englishmen of both parties throughout the century. By so doing we shall come to see that in his outline of Satan's conspiracy and war in *Paradise Lost* Milton took the conventional seventeenth-century view against devilishly inspired insurrection; yet he could also support the special cause that urged loyalists to God to resist the imposition of a Satanic tyranny. It is remarkable how relevant the seventeenth-century political scene is to the world of war and rebellion Milton depicts in books 5 and 6.

Not only is it interesting to investigate some of these different backgrounds, I believe, but it is also basic to any critical understanding of the war. As I suggested at the beginning, Milton made the war in Heaven a part of his story of Adam and Eve and their fall because traditionally it had been a part, as we shall see, of that story. He was responding to a complex theological and poetical tradition, which I hope to elucidate more fully than has been done heretofore. He was not just writing epic for epic's sake, as eighteenth-century critics assumed. Nor was he merely anticipating the mock heroics of Dryden or Pope. Tradition not only made him take the war seriously but gave him the license to make it an integral and vital part of his story of man and the origin of evil. Contemporary attitudes toward the Scriptures that "describe" the war (Rev. 12:7–9), moreover, made it possible for Milton to

20. Both Jackie Di Salvo, " 'The Lord's Battells,' " and Boyd M. Berry, *Process of Speech* (Baltimore: Johns Hopkins University Press, 1976), read the war in Heaven as a political allegory. Joan S. Bennett, "God, Satan, and King Charles: Milton's Royal Portraits," *PMLA* 92 (1977): 441–457, also explores the relationship between Milton's poetical and political attitudes.

extend its application beyond what theological and poetical traditions had bequeathed to him and make it a metaphor for the contemporary world. If we approach the war in Heaven, therefore, knowing and responding to the political, religious, and poetical traditions Milton was aware of, we may come to understand it not just, as the eighteenth century urged, as a fine piece of Homeric imitation or, as the mid-twentieth century exhorted, as mock epic within epic, but as a finely wrought episode in its own right that reflects many traditions and lends manifold meaning to the whole of *Paradise Lost*.

CHAPTER I

Pride as Intellective Sin

The first cause of the war in Heaven in *Paradise Lost* is intellective. The war begins in the mind of Satan at that moment when he resolves to leave "unworshipp'd, unobey'd" the throne of God; and pride (repeatedly named from book 1 on as Satan's main characteristic and leading motive) is the force that makes Satan so resolve. Pride it was, says the narrator, introducing Satan to us, that "cast him out of Heav'n" (1.36–37);[1] "Pride and worse Ambition threw me down" (4.40), cries Satan, remembering on Mount Niphates his former state. Because of pride, states Raphael finally in book 5, Satan could not bear the sight of Messiah anointed and "thought himself impair'd" (5.664–665). With these pointed references to pride, Milton not only builds a dramatically effective motivation for Satan, but also bows to a long and complex theological tradition that had named and anatomized pride as Satan's leading motive and as his sin. To understand Milton's use of pride in *Paradise Lost,* then, it is well to become intimately acquainted with that tradition, which begins in Old Testament times and is not complete until the time of such latter-day fathers as Anselm and Aquinas.

I

The tradition of the prideful, malicious spirit who refuses to serve God has its first and fullest flowering in the fourth century

---

1. Citations of *Paradise Lost* and other poems are to *Complete Poems and Major Prose,* ed. Merritt Y. Hughes (New York: Odyssey Press, 1957).

with the Nicene fathers in general and Augustine in particular. But it begins much earlier. The Satan of the Old Testament, however, is quite a different personage from the later Satan. As he appears in Zechariah, 1 Chronicles, and Job, he is neither a demon nor an opponent to God, for, as a tester rather than a tempter of man, he functions to accuse man of evil or to bring evil upon him.[2] He is not connected with the evil spirits of the desert referred to in Deut. 32:17; Isa. 13:21; or Isa. 34:14, nor with the brutish gods of the pagan peoples.[3] The notion that these evil spirits or demons were celestial in origin, formerly good creatures turned wicked enemies to God and man, arises late in Old Testament history. Some books of the Apocrypha (the Testament of the Twelve Patriarchs, the Book of Jubilees) and two key books of the Pseudepigrapha (Enoch and the Secrets of Enoch) refer to evil spirits devoted to the destruction of mankind. The Testament of the Twelve Patriarchs (137–107 B.C.) cautions against the workings of Beliar, the spirit who leads men astray. The Book of Jubilees (135–105 B.C.) similarly warns of Mâstêmâ, and the Wisdom of Solomon (ca. 50–10 B.C.) blames Satan and his temptation of Eve in the guise of the serpent for bringing evil into the world.[4] Enoch and the Secrets of Enoch supply more information about these demons. These books were highly relied upon by the early

2. See Hastings, *Encyclopedia of Religion and Ethics* (New York, 1912), vol. 4, S.V. "demons and spirits (Hebrew)"; Schaff-Herzoz's *Encyclopedia of Religious Knowledge* (New York, 1882), vol. 1, S.V. "devil"; and R. H. Charles, *A Critical and Exegetical Commentary on the Revelation of St. John* (New York, 1920), 1:324.

3. See Stephen Herbert Langdon, "Semitic," in *The Mythology of All Races*, vol. 5 (Boston, 1931). See chap. 12, pp. 352–374 ("The Devils, Demons, Good and Evil Spirits"). Langdon tells us that the demons who inhabit the deserts were originally thought of as animal spirits. Further he says: "Under their leader, Azâzel or Iblis, they rebelled against the gods, and angels drove them to the waste places of the earth. They have the power to change their forms in the twinkling of an eye, and rarely appear visible to man, although animals can detect them.... The Jinn have animal forms, and appear as snakes, dogs, cats, swine, and infest the waste places of the desert" (p. 352).

4. See R. H. Charles, *The Apocrypha and the Pseudepigrapha of the Old Testament in English, with Introductions and Critical and Explanatory Notes to the Several Books* (Oxford, 1913). See Issachar 6.l; Jubilees 10.8; Wisdom of Solomon 2.23–24.

Christian fathers, but later were banned by Hilary, Jerome, and Augustine. Enoch, the earlier (which dates in some sections to the second century B.C.), attempts to explain why the evil spirits hate man.[5] Formerly angels, they came to earth tempted by the beauty of women. In an account, based no doubt on Genesis 6, Enoch tells how the angels led by Semjâzâ lust after the daughters of men and take them for wives, fathering the race of giants.[6] The angels then teach men to use metals, make weapons, and practice all types of enchantment, magic, and wickedness. God, displeased with the evil rampant upon earth, proclaims the Deluge to Noah and sends Raphael to punish Azâzêl, chief among the erring angels, by binding him and casting him into darkness. Azâzêl's punishment is not only eternal exile from light, but also eventual destruction on the Day of Judgment by being cast into the fire. His primary offense was the propagation of evil arts among men: "To him," proclaims God, "ascribe all sin" (En. 10:8).

5. An account of the background of the Book of Enoch is found in Charles, *Apocrypha and Pseudepigrapha*, 2:163–185. The Book of Enoch was known to the church fathers but was lost sometime after the fourth century and was not discovered in its entirety until late in the eighteenth century.

Grant McColley ("The Book of Enoch and *Paradise Lost*," *Harvard Theological Review* 31 [1938]: 21–38) points out that part of the manuscript of Enoch was available to Milton in the seventeenth century through Syncellus's *Chronographia*, published in Paris sometime after 1650. McColley argues that this version of Enoch is a direct source for many of the references and some of the names of angels in *Paradise Lost*. These references and names, however, are to be found outside Enoch, especially in the writings of the fathers, notably Origen, who *did* know Enoch.

The demonology of Enoch seems to have influenced the New Testament. R. H. Charles points out that many of the concepts are the same and even lists a number of parallel passages. A few of these are:

Jude 6—"the angels which left their own habitation . . . reserved . . . great day"	Enoch 12:4—"the Watchers . . . who have left the high heaven"
Rev. 13:14—"deceiveth them that dwell on the earth"	Enoch 54:6—"leading astray those who dwell on the earth"
Matt. 25:41—"prepared for the devil and his angels"	Enoch 54:4, 5 "chains . . . prepared for the hosts of Azâzêl"

6. In Enoch 15 the giants are referred to as evil spirits who cause destruction on earth. The union of angels and women (spirit and flesh) is responsible for the birth of these evil spirits (demons) who later inhabit the earth.

The Secrets of Enoch, the companion book that dates perhaps as late as A.D. 70, agrees that the corruption of the earth was the work of angels, but it makes these spirits angels *already* lapsed from God.[7] As a fugitive, the devil tempts Eve and thereby brings evil into the world. He had fallen when as an angel he had directly challenged the eminence of God.

> And one from out of the order of angels, having turned away with the order that was under him, conceived an impossible thought, to place his throne higher than the clouds, that he might become equal in rank to my power.
> And I threw him out from the height with his angels, and he was flying in the air continuously above the bottomless.
>
> [Secr. Eno. 29:4, 5]

The accounts in both Enoch and the Secrets of Enoch have great impact. The former seems to have been preferred by Jewish commentators and the earliest Christian fathers. Justin Martyr, the second-century Christian father, concludes that evil entered the world when the angels abandoned what God had committed to them, the care of the human race, in favor of the deluding love for women, thereafter propagating, as it were, the works of evil.[8]

For Clement of Alexandria, the specific sin of the angels was not so much the dereliction of their duty toward men as a forgetfulness of angelic attitude toward God: the angels "renounced the beauty of God for a beauty which fades, and so fell from heaven to earth." The desire for women, says Commodianus, taking the argument one step further, actually contaminated the celestial nature. Corrupted by lust, defiled, the angels *could no longer return to Heaven*. Therefore they denounced God and he judged

7. The Book of the Secrets of Enoch is also called the Slavonic Enoch or 2 Enoch. It was composed by a Hellenistic Jew, probably in Egypt, but the only manuscripts are those found in Russia and Serbia in the late nineteenth century. The Secrets of Enoch is referred to and used by Origen, Clement of Alexandria, and Irenaeus. See Charles, *Apocrypha and Pseudepigrapha*, 2:425–430.

8. Justin Martyr, *The Second Apology of Justin for the Christians*, in Ante-Nicene Christian Library: Translations of the Writings of the Fathers down to A.D. 325, ed. Reverend Alexander Roberts and James Donaldson (Edinburgh, 1867–1872), 2:75–76.

them.[9] Whereas Enoch sees the angels' sin as their divulgence of God's secrets to man, the early Christian fathers stress that the angels corrupted themselves in coming to earth. They sinned against their own created natures, against what God intended them to be; thus they sinned against God.

Later fathers give little credit to the notion that angelic lustfulness was anything but a minor incident in their fall. Rather, they seek out other motivations. The New Testament provided little information. That a fall had occurred, both Jude 6 and 2 Pet. 2:4, books influenced by Enoch, testify in speaking of the angels who kept not their first estate and suffer the penalty of everlasting exile. That the devil or Satan (now *the* adversary, rather than just an adversary, as is frequent in Old Testament usage) exists, Jesus acknowledges in calling him the father of lies (John 8:44) and in testifying to his fall like lightning from Heaven (Luke 10:18). That he is the enemy who seeks as a roaring lion to devour mankind (1 Pet. 5:8), the prince (John 12:31) or god of this world (2 Cor. 4:4), and the tempter of Eve in the serpent (Rev. 12:9), texts throughout the New Testament attest. But of his status before his fall and of his motivation for that fall, nothing direct is said. It is no wonder, then, that fathers of the second century turned from the New Testament to the Old in search of passages that might elucidate the nature of Satan before his fall. In poetic passages from Isaiah (14:12–15) and from Ezekiel (28:12–18), they found descriptions of the expulsion of an extraordinary being from Heaven.[10] Ostensibly these passages narrated the ruin of the kings of Babylon and Tyre, cast down because they in their impi-

---

9. Clement of Alexandria, *The Instructor,* in *The Ante-Nicene Christian Fathers: Translations of the Writings of the Fathers down to A.D. 325,* American reprint of the Edinburgh edition, revised and chronologically arranged, with brief prefaces and occasional notes by A. Cleveland Coxe (Buffalo, 1885–1896), 2:274. Commodianus, *Ante-Nicene Christian Fathers,* 2:203. Philo Judaeus also attributes the fall of the angels to lust (*Works,* Trans. C. D. Yonge [London, 1900]), as do many other early fathers.

10. Isaiah 14: 12–15.

How art thou fallen from heaven, O Lucifer, son of the morning! *how* art thou cut down to the ground, which didst weaken the nations!

For thou has said in thine heart, I will ascend into heaven, I will exalt my

ous ambition had defied God and sought to place their thrones above his. The two great second-century fathers of Christianity, the Greek Origen and the Latin Tertullian, however, saw in them reference to a greater being. They maintain first that the extravagant language of the accounts points unmistakably to their concealed meanings. No mere earthly kings could be spoken of with the name Lucifer or cherub. Referring to Ezekiel's account, Tertullian remarks: "This description, it is manifest, properly belongs to the transgression of the angel, and not to the prince's: for none among human beings was either born in the paradise of God, not even Adam himself, who was rather translated thither; . . . No, it is none other than the very author of sin who was denoted in the person of the sinful man."[11] Origen argues in a

---

throne above the stars of God: I will sit also upon the mount of the congregation, in the sides of the north:

I will ascend above the heights of the clouds; I will be like the most High.

Yet thou shalt be brought down to hell, to the sides of the pit.
Ezekiel 28:12–18:

Son of man, take up a lamentation upon the king of Tyrus, and say unto him, Thus saith the Lord God; Thou sealest up the sum, full of wisdom, and perfect in beauty.

Thou hast been in Eden the garden of God; every precious stone *was* thy covering, the sardius, topaz, and the diamond, the beryl, the onyx, and the jasper, the sapphire, the emerald, and the carbuncle, and gold: the workmanship of thy tabrets and of thy pipes was prepared in thee in the day that thou wast created.

Thou *art* the anointed cherub that covereth; and I have set thee *so*: thou wast upon the holy mountain of God; thou hast walked up and down in the midst of the stones of fire.

Thou *wast* perfect in thy ways from the day that thou wast created, till iniquity was found in thee.

By the multitude of thy merchandise they have filled the midst of thee with violence, and thou hast sinned: therefore I will cast thee as profane out of the mountain of God: and I will destroy thee, O covering cherub, from the midst of the stones of fire.

Thine heart was lifted up because of thy beauty, thou hast corrupted thy wisdom by reason of thy brightness: I will cast thee to the ground, I will lay thee before kings, that they may behold thee.

Thou hast defiled thy sanctuaries by the multitude of thine iniquities, by the iniquity of thy traffick; therefore will I bring forth a fire from the midst of thee, it shall devour thee, and I will bring thee to ashes upon the earth in the sight of all that behold thee.

11. Tertullian, *The First Five Books against Marcion*, bk. 2, chap. 10 in *Ante-Nicene Christian Fathers*, 3:305–306.

similar vein that it would be illogical to speak of a prince of Tyre as being "amongst the saints" and "without stain" or to describe an earthly king as the morning star, Lucifer. Further, says Origen, the New Testament will corroborate this assertion, for Jesus speaks of Satan falling like lightning from Heaven, his testimony without doubt elucidating the prophesies of both Ezekiel and Isaiah but referring particularly to Isaiah's description of the lightninglike fall of Lucifer. "Nay, even the Saviour Himself teaches us, saying of the devil, 'Behold, I see Satan fallen from heaven like lightning.'... He compares him to lightning, and says that he fell from heaven, that He might show by this that he had been at one time in heaven, and had had a place among the saints, and had enjoyed a share in the light."[12]

In their inquiries into and speculations about the nature of that supernatural being called Satan, Tertullian and Origen seem to have two concerns: first, to explore the mystery of how Satan, an evil being, could have originated in God and, second, to assert that God, nonetheless, is blameless for the creation of evil. Tertullian uses Ezekiel's account to point out that the evil of Satan occurs by choice and not by creation. "Now, whence originated this malice of lying and deceit towards man, and slandering of God? Most certainly not from God, who made the angel good after the fashion of His good works. Indeed, before he became the devil, he stands forth the wisest of creatures; and wisdom is no evil. If you turn to the prophecy of Ezekiel, you will at once perceive that this angel was both by creation good and by choice corrupt."[13] Tertullian makes much of Ezekiel's praise of the

---

12. Origen, *De principiis*, bk. 1, chap. 5, in *Ante-Nicene Christian Fathers*, 4:259: "Most evidently by these words is he shown to have fallen from heaven, who formerly was Lucifer, and who used to arise in the morning. For if, as some think, he was a nature of darkness, how is Lucifer said to have existed before? Or how could he arise in the morning, who had in himself nothing of that light?... In this manner, then, did that being once exist as light before he went astray, and fell to this place, and had his glory turned into dust, which is particularly the mark of the wicked, as the prophet also says; whence, too, he was called the prince of this world, i.e., of an earthly habitation: for he exercised power over those who were obedient to his wickedness."

13. Tertullian, *First Five Books against Marcion*, p. 305.

"cherub's" goodness, employing it to observe that Satan once was "irreproachable," "formed for good by God, as by the good Creator of irreproachable creatures, and adorned with every angelic glory." Origen maintains that Satan's creation was totally good, for Isaiah's Lucifer was in nature first a creature of light. Both fathers absolve God of any disposition of evil toward Satan, explaining that evil could come into existence only spontaneously. Tertullian explains: "For God would in nothing fail to endow a being who was to be next to Himself with a liberty of this kind. Nevertheless, by precondemning him, God testified that he had departed from the condition of his created nature, through his own lusting after the wickedness which was spontaneously conceived within him."[14]

What evil is in essence and how it could have been created spontaneously from good remain mysteries that Tertullian and Origen prefer to leave largely unexplored. Neither do they attempt to reconcile the many contradictions that result from imposing a definite personification—be it Isaiah's Lucifer or Ezekiel's cherub—upon the shadowy and elusive evil spirit named in the late Hebrew and early Christian Scriptures. These problems remain for later fathers. But what Tertullian and Origen accomplished by giving Satan personality was to supply Christianity with a clear identification for its "evil factor," which in the course of history was to be vital. For Christianity, then, Satan became the angel, created *in good* by God, indeed created in the height of perfection, who fell *by his own choosing* when in presumptive aspiration or egotistical pride he sought to exalt himself above God. The two salient features of this portrait—that Satan was created good and that he fell by choice—are the very ones, it is significant to note, that Tertullian and Origen markedly emphasize. Moreover, they are the very features later fathers name first when they must refute doctrines alien to Christianity, which concern the nature of the "evil factor."

Principal among these alien doctrines was Manichaeanism,

14. Ibid., p. 306.

which originated in the East and by the fourth century was rapidly winning adherents in the Roman world. Grounded in clear-cut dualism, Manichaeanism asserted that the "evil factor," Satan, was created from a kingdom of darkness over which the God of Light had no authority or control. Satan thus was generated in evil from the beginning and exercised power over evil, in opposition to God, which threatened the very existence of good. If such a doctrine did not call into question the goodness of God (since God was not credited with the generation of Satan), it did unequivocally reject his omnipotence. The Christian fathers were obliged to assert that God had created Satan, if they were to argue God all-powerful, and that he had created him originally good, but self-Perverted, if they were to argue God all-good. Whereas no verse in the New Testament describes Satan's original goodness, certain verses do seem to support the Manichaean contention that Satan was created evil. Both the Gospel of John and the First Epistle of John call Satan a murderer from the beginning, one who stood not in the truth. In order to answer the Manichaean claims that evil is a real power, born of cosmic darkness and engaged in perpetual struggle with good or light, in order to explain the perplexing statements made in the New Testament about Satan and his authorship of evil, the Christian fathers had to undertake some subtle philosophical explorations.

The scene of inquiry had shifted from the entry of evil into the world to its primal entry into existence. Little direct exegesis of Isaiah and Ezekiel is undertaken; the logical debate is rather with the Manichaean doctrine that evil came into existence as evil and with the New Testament verses that seem to support this contention. The testimonies of Isaiah and Ezekiel to the original goodness of that author of evil, Satan, serve as touchstones whereby the goodness of God in his creative plan may be affirmed, and as such they are invaluable. Cyril of Jerusalem undertakes to explicate the paradox implicit in the New Testament verse, I John 3:8, that the devil sinned from the beginning.

> The devil then is the first author of sin, and the father of the wicked: and this is the Lord's saying, not mine, *that the devil sinneth from*

the beginning: none sinned before him. But he sinned, not as having received necessarily from nature the propensity to sin, since then the cause of sin is traced back again to Him that made him so; but having been created good, he has of his own free will become a devil, and received that name from his action. For being an Archangel he was afterwards called a devil from his slandering: from being a good servant of God he has become rightly named Satan; for "Satan" is interpreted *the adversary.* And this is not my teaching, but that of the inspired prophet Ezekiel.[15]

Two things are concerned here: first, the relationship of Satan to the evil he creates and, second, the relationship of God, as author of Satan, to the evil Satan has brought into being. For what Cyril and later fathers point out is that evil is a secondary, not a primary creation; it begins as a willful act or choice of Satan, not as a quality contained in his being engendered as a creature by God. Thus evil may be said to begin with Satan, although Satan (as Cyril points out, with evidence from Ezekiel) does not begin with evil.

Manichaeanism has as a principal tenet that evil as the opposite of good is in truth the opposing equal to good. But the Christian view holds the subordination of evil to good; in terms of Satan and his domain over evil, the Christian fathers argue first that Satan, being a creature of God, is subordinate and, second, that Satan's evil, as a product of Satan, has no real validity as the opposite of good. Basil contends that it is absurd to speak of evil as an equal power.

> In reality two rival principles of equal power, if engaged without ceasing in a war of mutual attacks, will end in self destruction. But if one should gain the mastery it would completely annihilate the conquered. Thus, to maintain the balance in the struggle between good and evil is to represent them as engaged in a war without end and in perpetual destruction, where the opponents are at the same time conquerors and conquered. If good is the stronger, what is there to prevent evil being completely annihilated.[16]

15. Cyril of Jerusalem, *Lecture 2*, in *A Select Library of Nicene and Post-Nicene Fathers of the Christian Church*, 2d ser., ed. Philip Schaff and Henry Wace (New York, 1890–1900), 7:9.
16. Basil, *The Hexaemeron*, homily 2, in *Nicene and Post-Nicene Fathers*, 2d ser., 8:61.

If it is illogical to pose evil as a self-sufficient power equal to good, it is equally illogical, continues Basil, to pose it as derived from good. God, who is total good, cannot produce its contradiction.

> It is equally impious to say that evil has its origin from God; because the contrary cannot proceed from its contrary. Life does not engender death; darkness is not the origin of light; sickness is not the maker of health. . . . Certainly that evil exists, no one living in the world will deny. What shall we say then? Evil is not a living animated essence; it is the condition of the soul opposed to virtue, developed in the careless on account of their falling away from good.[17]

While Basil affirms evil's existence, at the same time denying its existence as a truly animated essence, he has left entirely vague the manner in which this nonanimated essence has come into being. Gregory of Nyssa approaches the problem of evil by recognizing that since evil is basically a paradox, an essence that in the finest sense cannot be said to exist, its genesis may best be investigated through analogy. The analogy he chooses is that of blindness: "As we say that blindness is logically opposed to sight, not that blindness has of itself a natural existence, being only a deprivation of a preceding faculty, so also we say that vice is to be regarded as the deprivation of goodness, just as a shadow which supervenes at the passage of the solar ray." Satan's blindness, however, is not a physical blindness but a moral one; he chooses to shut his eyes to goodness as to light and so to become blind to goodness: " . . . since the above-mentioned power was created too, and could choose by a spontaneous movement whatever he liked, when he had closed his eyes to the good and ungrudging like one who in sunshine lets his eyelids down upon his eyes and sees only darkness, in this way that being also by his very unwillingness to perceive the good, became cognisant of the contrary to goodness." Hence Gregory implies that Satan chose evil

17. Ibid.

not as he would choose a vital quality, but as he deprived himself
of a vital quality, sight, and thus denied himself its virtue. Now,
having once chosen this deprivation, he is no longer naturally
attracted to good; indeed, as Gregory posits, he is repelled by it.

> For when once he, who by his apostasy from goodness had begotten
> in himself this Envy, had received this bias to evil, like a rock, torn
> assunder from a mountain ridge, which is driven down headlong by
> its own weight, in a like manner he, dragged away from his original
> natural propension to goodness and gravitating with all his weight in
> the direction of vice, was deliberately forced and borne away as by
> a kind of gravitation to the utmost limit of iniquity.[18]

The evil of Satan in its final dimension is a forceful and frightening
power, but, as Gregory has emphasized, it has developed not in a
spontaneous and inexplicable manner, but in an orderly and logical one.

Augustine, who in many ways is the most sophisticated of the
fourth-century theologians exploring the nature of Satan and his
evil, seeks to discover not only how but also why Satan turned
against God and good. Like Origen, Tertullian, Cyril of Jerusalem, and others, he affirms the perfection of Satan's origin
and quotes Isaiah and Ezekiel to support this view. Yet, says
Augustine, Satan in being created perfect was not alone; he was
only one of a host of angels—some who maintained the perfection
of their creation and others who fell. Perfection implies created
goodness, not immutability, goodness that must be upheld by free
choice. Immutable good is achieved only through God's grace
and only after the creature has been confirmed in good. Although
mutability is a necessary quality in all created beings, it does not
dispose or preordain the being in evil; it merely permits evil to
come into existence. Such was the quality of Satan's condition,
explains Augustine, before he became evil, and thus the perplexing verse from John (1 John 3:8), "The devil sinneth from the
beginning" may be explained.

18. Gregory of Nyssa, *The Great Catechism,* chap. 6, in *Nicene and Post-
Nicene Fathers,* 2d ser., 5:481.

what the blessed Apostle John says thus becomes intelligible: "The devil sinneth from the beginning,"—that is, from the time he was created he refused righteousness, which none but a will piously subject to God can enjoy. Whoever adopts this opinion at least disagrees with those heretics the Manichees, and with any other pestilential sect that may suppose that the devil has derived from some adverse evil principle a nature proper to himself. These persons are so befooled by error, that, although they acknowledge with ourselves the authority of the gospels, they do not notice that the Lord did not say, "The devil was naturally a stranger to the truth," but "The devil abode not in the truth" [John 8:44], by which He meant us to understand that he had fallen from the truth, in which, if he had abode, he would have become a partaker of it, and have remained in blessedness along with the holy angels.[19]

To explain why Satan became immutably bad and not immutably good, Augustine studies the nature of the misery the fallen angels endure and deduces that "they are miserable because they have forsaken Him who supremely is, and have turned to themselves who have no such essence."[20] The original sin of Satan, he speculates, must accordingly have involved a turning from God and a turning to self. Turning from God harms a creature, he points out, only if the creature derives, as did all the angels, his power and strength from God. The angels could not turn to them-

19. Augustine, *The City of God*, bk. 11, chap. 15, in *A Select Library of Nicene and Post-Nicene Fathers of the Christian Church*, 1st ser., ed. Philip Schaff (Buffalo, 1886–1890), 2:213: "As for what John says about the devil, 'The devil sinneth from the beginning,' they who suppose it is meant hereby that the devil was made with a sinful nature, misunderstand it; for if sin be natural, it is not sin at all. And how do they answer the prophetic proofs,—either what Isaiah says when he represents the devil under the person of the king of Babylon, 'How art thou fallen, O Lucifer, son of the morning!' or what Ezekiel says, 'Thou hast been in Eden, the garden of God; every precious stone was thy covering,' where it is meant that he was some time without sin; for a little after it is still more explicitly said, 'Thou wast perfect in thy ways?' And if these passages cannot well be otherwise interpreted, we must understand by this one also, 'He abode not in the truth,' that he was once in the truth, but did not remain in it. And from this passage, 'The devil sinneth from the beginning,' it is not to be supposed that he sinned from the beginning of his created existence, but from the beginning of his sin, when by his pride he had once commenced to sin."

20. Augustine, *City of God*, bk. 12, chap. 6, 2:229.

selves as source of their powers, for not they but God had created them. Their happiness consisted in turning to God, their misery in turning away from him. Augustine is careful to note that "departure from God would be no vice, unless in a nature whose property it was to abide with God."[21] But since departure from God is contrary to the created nature of angels, it vitiates that nature, and this damage is what we may call vice or evil. Like Basil and Gregory of Nyssa, Augustine affirms that evil has no true existence of itself. He defines it, however, not as a blindness to the goodness of God, but as a vitiation of the goodness that God the Creator has imparted to the creature himself. Evil in the finest sense is not an all-threatening foe to God and his goodness, but foe only to the soundness or wholeness of the creature.

> Therefore the vice which makes those who are called His [God's] enemies resist Him, is an evil not to God, but to themselves. And to them it is an evil, solely because it corrupts the good of their nature. It is not nature, therefore, but vice, which is the contrary to God. For that which is evil is contrary to the good. And who will deny that God is the supreme good? Vice, therefore, is contrary to God, as evil to good. Further, the nature it vitiates is a good, and therefore to this good also it is contrary. But while it is contrary to God only as evil to good, it is contrary to the nature it vitiates, both as evil and as hurtful. For to God no evils are hurtful; but only to natures mutable and corruptible, though by the testimony of the vices themselves, originally good. For were they not good, vices could not hurt them.[22]

Augustine recognizes, of course, the basic contradiction in the idea that a good creature should allow itself to be vitiated by an alien quality. Having noted that the preoccupation of the wicked is with self and not with God, Augustine poses the theory that the preoccupation with self initiated the vitiation of good in the first place. According to Ecclesiastes, "pride is the beginning of sin" (Eccles. 10:13); pride, reasons Augustine, caused the angels to

21. Ibid., bk. 11, chap. 17, 2:214.
22. Ibid., bk. 12, chap. 3, 2:227.

prefer their own will to the will of God, despite the fact that God's will would have worked for the good of their created nature, whereas adhering to their own will could only damage it.

> That the contrary propensities in good and bad angels have arisen, not from a difference in their nature and origin, since God, the good Author and Creator of all essences, created them both, but from a difference in their wills and desires, it is impossible to doubt. While some steadfastly continued in that which was the common good of all, namely in God Himself, and in His eternity, truth, and love; others, being enamored rather of their own power, as if they could be their own good, lapsed to this private good of their own, from that higher and beatific good which was common to all, and, bartering the lofty dignity of eternity for the inflation of pride, the most assured verity for the slyness of vanity, uniting love for factious partisanship, they became proud, deceived, envious. The cause, therefore, of the blessedness of the good is adherence of God. And so the cause of the others' misery will be found in the contrary, that is, in their not adhering to God.[23]

Augustine was not the first to assign pride to Satan; both Ambrose and Gregory of Nazianzus had described it as Satan's sin. Moreover, pride can easily be traced to the "aspiration" to set his seat above God's that infected Isaiah's Lucifer or to the "iniquity" that caused Ezekiel's cherub to lift up his heart because of his beauty. Yet pride, not as a mere quality of evil, but as *the* prime spur of evil, was not anatomized before Augustine. Augustine explained not only how pride could vitiate a creature's innate goodness, but also how pride began—that is, as the desire for private good above the common good and the choice of self, not God, as the source of beneficence. Pride commences in the exaltation of self in place of the exaltation of God and ends ironically in the cutting off of self from the true source of its being. Pride thus directs the choice that vitiates primal goodness and confirms the creature in evil. For Augustine pride presents the genesis of evil as a logically understandable moment, not as a haphazard occurrence or forever inexplicable mystery.

23. Ibid., bk. 12, chap. 1, 2:226.

After Augustine's anatomy of pride, Satan can acquire still more qualities of a personality rather than a mere cipher of evil. John Cassian, a contemporary of Augustine's, speculates on the mental state that led Satan to think himself the author of his own "private good." Satan's occupation with his beauty and splendor triggers within him a presumptuous belief in his own powers.

> For as he (viz., Lucifer) was endowed with divine splendour, and shone forth among the higher powers by the bounty of his Maker, he believed that he had acquired the splendour of that wisdom and the beauty of those powers, with which he was graced by the gift of the Creator, by the might of his own nature, and not by the beneficence of His generosity. And on this account he was puffed up as if he stood in no need of divine assistance in order to continue in this state of purity, and esteemed himself to be like God, as if, like God, he had no need of any one, and trusting in the power of his own will, fancied that through it he could richly supply himself with everything which was necessary for the consummation of virtue or for the perpetuation of perfect bliss. This thought alone was the cause for his first fall.[24]

The emphasis for Cassian is on psychological rather than philosophical truth. The pride that causes Satan's fall, as Cassian has told it, has the anthropomorphic touch of pure, self-deceptive vanity. As pride becomes a type of moral deception, the confirmation in evil becomes a type of moral collapse. Satan has allowed himself to construct a falsely based opinion of himself and his own powers, involving himself by degrees more and more in untruth until, unable to extricate himself and psychologically befuddled, he falls to complete evil. "On account of which being forsaken by God, whom he fancied he no longer needed, he suddenly became unstable and tottering, and discovered the weak-

---

24. Cassian, *The Institutes of John Cassian*, bk. 12, chap. 4, 11:281. "And that we may understand the power of its [pride's] awful tyranny we see that angel who, for the greatness of his splendour and beauty was termed Lucifer, was cast out of heaven for no other sin but this, and, pierced with the dart of pride, was hurled down from his grand and exalted place as an angel into hell" (p. 280).

ness of his own nature, and lost the blessedness which he had enjoyed by God's gift."[25]

2

Theologians, in continuing to be fascinated by the creature Satan, who not only could create evil in others but could cause it to come into being initially in himself, discover other problems in the notion of cosmically oriented evil. Some are puzzled by the nature of Satan's original goodness. Gregory the Great, for example, conceives that the fall of Satan must have been from the highest to the lowest, and, taking Isaiah and Ezekiel as well-established authorities, he emphasizes the perfection of Satan's original state as chief—and therefore most glorious and most beautiful—of the angels.[26] John of Damascus visualizes Satan's original state as total light and his subsequent evil as total deprivation of light or complete darkness. He points out that in choosing evil Satan was the first to put out goodness, which is the light of the mind, thereby rejecting the state the Creator had first put him in and producing darkness in himself of his own free will.[27]

Yet the greatest puzzle to theologians after Augustine was not how good could become evil, but *specifically* how Satan in becoming evil could be said to have aspired to become like God. If the text from Isaiah is followed strictly, we must allow that Satan's sin was not merely that he wished to be separate from God, exalting his "throne above the stars of God," but that he wished

25. Ibid, p. 281.

26. See Gregorius Magnus, "Moralium, Lib. XXXII—In Caput XL B. Job," Caput 23, *Opera Omnia,* in *Patrologia Latina,* ed. J. P. Migne, vol. 76 (Paris, 1878), pp. 664–665. "Prima et nobilior creatura fuit angelus qui cecidit."

27. John of Damascus, *Exposition of the Orthodox Faith,* bk. 4, chap. 20, in *Nicene and Post-Nicene Fathers,* 2d ser., 9:94, 20. "Is the devil, then, evil? In so far as he was brought into existence he is not evil but good. For he was created by his Maker a bright and very brilliant angel, endowed with free-will as being rational. But he voluntarily departed from that virtue that is natural and came into the darkness of evil, being far removed from God, who alone is good and can give life and light" (p. 94).

to be equal to or like God, ascending "above the heights of the clouds, to be like the most High." First, theologians propose, the wish to be like God may be understood in two ways: to resemble him in goodness or to equal him in powers. The desire to resemble God in goodness is natural and to some degree admissable. The creature may seek to imitate God's goodness, though he may never hope to attain it. But the desire to equal God in power is irrational, since such a goal is clearly impossible. Isidore of Seville reasons that Satan must have desired the second, to equal God in power: only if he had grasped for the impossible can we understand the magnitude of his sin and the severity of his irreversible punishment.[28] Hugh of Saint Victor adds that Satan wished not only equality, but superiority and in those terms committed the unforgivable sin.[29]

Anselm and Aquinas dissent on this matter. Satan, they say, could not have wished directly for equality with God, for as a rational and perfect being he would have known that this was impossible. He must therefore have wished for the authorized imitation of God's likeness, but the manner he chose for his imitation must have been an unauthorized one. Thus his wish for resemblance became, as the wish for equality would have been, impossible to attain. Anselm's explanation of Satan's behavior is actually an expansion of the Augustinian concept of "private good"; that is, in aspiring to be like God Satan wished for some good for himself that he would not owe to God. He wished to be directly responsible for an increase in his own beatitude. In wishing for this responsibility, he was denying the authority of God's will over his own will, and in wishing that his will triumph over God's will, he was in fact wishing to be greater than God. There are two ways, Anselm explains, in which Satan has erred here: first, in maintaining his will independent from God's will and,

28. Sanctus Isidorus, *Opera Omnia*, in *Patrologia Latina*, vol. 83 (Paris, 1862), p. 555.

29. Hugo de S. Victor, *Opera Omnia*, in *Patrologia Latina*, vol. 176 (Paris, 1880), p. 83.

second, in wishing with his will something the will of God did not wish for him. Anselm calls this wish of Satan's the desire for that which is not just, and this desire produces the act of injustice that is Satan's rebellion.[30]

Aquinas, before considering the nature of Satan's aspiration, places the sin of Satan in the perspective of spiritual sin. There are only two sins that spiritual beings are by nature capable of committing: pride and envy. Whereas in their falls devils may be said to be guilty of all sins in that by tempting men to all sins they become guilty *by association,* in their original state angels can sin only with their intellect. Thus they are drawn *by affection* to those purely intellective sins, pride and envy.[31] Aquinas has focused upon the basic, innermost movements of mind as they pertain to the relationship of a creature to self and to his Creator in order to define the essence of sin. Like Anselm, Aquinas sees the initial moment of sin in Satan's desire to be like God.

> Without doubt the angel sinned by seeking to be as God. But this can be understood in two ways: first, by equality; secondly, by likeness. He could not seek to be as God in the first way: because by natural knowledge he knew this was impossible: and there was no habit preceding his first sinful act, nor any passion fettering his mind, so as to lead him to choose what was impossible by failing in some particular; as sometimes happens in ourselves. And even supposing it were possible, it would be against the natural desire; because there exists in everything the natural desire of preserving its own nature; which would not be preserved were it to be changed into another nature....
>
> To desire to be as God according to likeness can happen in two ways. In one way, as to that likeness whereby everything is made to be likened unto God. And so, if anyone desire in this way to be Godlike, he commits no sin; provided that he desires such likeness in proper order, that is to say, that he may obtain it of God. But he

30. Anselmus, "Dialogus de Casu Diaboli," *Opera Omnia,* in *Patrologia Latina,* vol. 158 (Paris, 1864), pp. 332–360.

31. Thomas Aquinas, "Part I, Question LXIII," in *The "Summa Theologica" of St. Thomas Aquinas,* trans. Fathers of the English Dominican Province (London, 1920–1925), 3:144, 146.

would sin were he to desire to be like unto God even in the right way, as of his own, and not of God's power. In another way one may desire to be like unto God in some respect which is not natural to one; as if one were to desire to create heaven and earth, which is proper to God; in which desire there would be sin. It was in this way that the devil desired to be as God. Not that he desired to resemble God by being subject to no one else absolutely; for so he would be desiring his own not-being, since no creature can exist except by holding its existence under God. But he desired resemblance with God in this respect,—by desiring, as his last end of beatitude, something which he could attain by virtue of his own nature, turning his appetite away from supernatural beatitude, which is attained by God's grace. Or, if he desired as his last end that likeness of God which is bestowed by grace, he sought to have it by the power of his own nature; and not from Divine assistance according to God's ordering.[32]

Aquinas's view represents still another refinement. Satan is guilty of intellective opposition to God, but according to Aquinas this opposition is not a conscious wish for injustice, but an almost unconscious contrariness of disposition. Satan does not sin in wishing to be like God; he sins by having this wish *in an improper order*. This very small detail—the principle of proper order—determines what will be in a creature the genesis of beatified grace or of sinful and ultimately damning pride. Aquinas has defined how pride came to be.

3

Many of Milton's views on Satan and his sin are founded, sometimes directly, sometimes indirectly, on traditions first enunciated by the Christian fathers.[33] In choosing to tell the story

32. Ibid., 3:148–150.
33. For further background on Milton's Satan, see Frank S. Kastor, *Milton and the Literary Satan* (Amsterdam, 1974). See especially Kastor's discussion of the councils of the early church. "The authoritative teaching of the Catholic Church is based, for example, upon a single section of the Decrees of the Fourth Lateran Council: 'Diabolus enim et alii daemones a Deo quidem natura creati sunt boni, sed ipsi per se facti sunt mali' " (pp. 8–9).

of Satan as that of an angel aspiring beyond his sphere, Milton has chosen (at least by implication) to adhere to those figurative interpretations of Isaiah 14 and Ezekiel 28 that the fathers of the Catholic church, beginning with Tertullian, have established. Actual echoes of these texts in *Paradise Lost* are few but strategic. The very first reference to Satan's revolt (1.38–40), that "aspiring / To set himself in Glory above his Peers, / He trusted to have equall'd the most High," paraphrases those very lines from Isaiah that made Tertullian and Origen assert that it was an angel, not a man, who in the name of Lucifer so aspired above his station. Even Satan's first words to Beelzebub argue his Luciferan heritage: "But O how fall'n" (1.84). And his actions and plan in book 5 are those of Isaiah's Lucifer when he withdraws to the North (5.689) or aspires to the Mount of the Congregation (5.732, 766). Actually the name "Lucifer" is used only twice by Milton, first when his overornate citadel of the North is designated as "The Palace of great *Lucifer*"(5.760), and next when Raphael refers to him after his fall, "Know then, that after *Lucifer* from Heav'n / (So call him, brighter once amidst the Host / Of Angels, than that Star the Stars among) / Fell" (7.131–134). Yet these few references are enough; Milton has used them as touchstones to make his readers recollect the tradition of Lucifer as the angel of light.

But Milton is indebted in a more subtle way to the patristic heritage. *Paradise Lost* as a whole is a study of the apparent victory of evil over good, when "death" is brought into this world, and "all our woe." And truly Milton, like the fathers before him, found he could not undertake an examination of evil's entry into the world without also investigating its primal entry into being. Accordingly, the war in Heaven is not merely a dramatization of an Old Testament-inspired myth, offered for the sake of historical narrative or moral exemplum, but an anatomy of the genesis and progress of evil, designed to demonstrate (alas, also to forecast) how evil comes to be. Milton reveals his grounding in the patristic tradition by his emphasis on evil as the product of the conscious "mischoice" by a good creature, and in fact he has Raphael introduce Satan to his hearers at the exact moment of "mischoice."

It is one of the odd paradoxes of *Paradise Lost* that, though the history of Satan's rebellion is told, the prelapsarian Satan does not appear. Never is the "good" Satan shown; never do we even see him in the throes of conflict. Whatever we are told of Satan's motivation comes ex post facto. Though still in Heaven, Satan is fallen intellectually as we first glimpse him resolving to leave the throne of God unworshipped and unobeyed. Since so much of patristic philosophy has concerned reconstruction of the character of the "good" angel, and since the image of unfallen splendor is essential to the portraits from Isaiah and Ezekiel, one naturally questions why Milton has not described the brightness of the loyal Lucifer and thence delineated his darkening through pride.

We should remember, however, that the beginnings of Satan's story are not in book 5; the revolt is actually set in an intricate framework. From the moment the reader sees the flaming fall of the rebel angels in book 1 and still more insistently in book 4, during Satan's soliloquy on Mount Niphates, the question is asked, though Satan shrinks from the answer, why Satan chose to revolt against God. Why, when his position and favor were so high, did he seek to be higher? What in God's goodness, in *his own* original goodness, predisposed him to evil? Satan, agonized by guilt, cannot bear to contemplate his prelapsarian state. If we, as readers, would know the perfect angel who was Satan, we cannot know him directly; we must see him in another character.

It is no accident that the prelapsarian Adam enters the drama between the time Satan contemplates the loss of his perfect state and the time Raphael recounts that loss. Nor is it an accident that Satan spontaneously sees himself in Adam. A definite parallel exists between the two. Adam in book 4 stands where Satan only recently had stood: perfect, preeminent, exercising great command and sway, yet required to obey God. Adam represents, in the truest sense, not merely universal man, but the universal created being, newly formed and striving with all his perfect consciousness to understand the Creator who made him. Like the heavenly Lucifer and like all newly made creatures, he confronts an immense creation and an inapproachable Creator whom he feels he must revere, but whom he finds a limitless enigma. It is therefore entirely to the point to consider Adam's dilemmas in books 4 and 5 in their most universal light, for Adam's struggle for understanding is not his alone, but the struggle in which all creatures are involved and the one Satan has only recently failed.

For this very reason, Milton shows us Adam in books 4 and 5 grappling with the problems of the "universe," for first and foremost a creature must assess correctly his relationship to God, if he is to succeed in any other relationships in his experience. In his initial utterance in *Paradise Lost,* Adam speculates about the nature of God.

> Sole partner and sole part of all these joys,
> Dearer thyself than all; needs must the Power
> That made us, and for us this ample World
> Be infinitely good, and of his good
> As liberal and free as infinite,
> That rais'd us from the dust and plac't us here
> In all this happiness.
>
> [4.411–417]

What Milton is illustrating here in Adam is that any creature made by God, in fact by reason of his perfect creation, must recognize and affirm the goodness of his Creator. Adam is speaking as the angels speak in praising God, as Satan himself must have spoken, for even in his lapsed state Satan has retained the reason to affirm that it was God who created what he was "in that bright eminence, and with his good / Upbraided none" (4.44–45). The Nicene fathers had particularly emphasized that in creating all good God had bestowed reason on his creatures so that they could recognize the creative goodness in God; as Augustine had pointed out, Satan once recognized the truth, although he did not thereafter abide in it.

Having recognized God's goodness, the creature must learn how to abide in it, to be a "part" of it through his own response. Satan himself acknowledges that this was his difficulty; for, as he cries out on Niphates: "all his good prov'd ill in me" (4.48). Augustine had put it simply that the happiness of a creature consisted in his ability to understand the derivation of his being and the growth of his happiness thence. The first step, Adam knows, toward responding to God is the expression of thanks: "let us praise him, and extol / His bounty" (4.436–437). But this Satan also had known: "What could be less than to afford him praise, / The easiest recompense, and pay him thanks, / How due!" (4.46–48). The second step Adam can acknowledge without fully understanding; he knows that to approach God he must be obedient. Yet what obedience is and wherein it consists beyond the external form of abstinence from the tree, he does not know. This second step, obedience, Satan had construed as the irrational submission of self, for it is his repeated complaint that this is what God *exacts* from all creatures. And, if obedience is submission, Satan refuses absolutely to obey. Thus in the spiritual quest to know God Satan has refused to take the crucial "second" step in fear that obedience will impair his sense of self.

Adam, though uncomfortable about the prohibition of the tree, has not turned away from obedience as a *means* to know God. He recognizes the tree, correctly, as a symbol: "the only sign of our obedience left / Among so many signs of power and rule" (4.428–429), and as such he feels that he and Eve ought not to resent its presence, since it in no way interferes with the pattern of their life in Eden. But, not fully reconciled, he must urge Eve not to "think hard" the "easy prohibition." In puzzlement, he looks upon the tree as something negative, something he is not to do, and finds it difficult to comprehend how mere restraint can in any way be construed as a positive, rewarding act. By restraint he will certainly retain his relationship to God. But does restraint alone further or fulfill a creature in this relationship? Thus Adam parallels the state of the prelapsarian Satan. Like Satan, he understands only in a limited way how he must act toward God. Beyond expressing his thanks, beyond restraining his disobedience, he comprehends little of how he is to become a part of that infinitude of goodness that is God.

Herein is the importance of the role to Raphael. To some, Raphael is merely a narrator of fabulous formless wonders beyond the ken of human beings. To others, he is the voice of duty, teaching through exemplum that Adam must avoid disobedience. But Raphael is also the intellect who responds to Adam's puzzlement, who not only unravels the genesis of the newly created earth and unties the knots of domestic quandaries, but also meaningfully answers Adam on how he may approach the infinitude of good in his Creator. Raphael knows that Satan had refused to know intimately the good of God and had shut himself away from it. If Adam is to succeed, he must understand why Satan has failed; he must come to see why Satan refused to obey. He must relive Satan's mental struggle—but relive it triumphantly. And, because his teacher Raphael had succeeded in like mental adventure, we may know that Adam is being led in the paths of light.

If we understand that Raphael's counsel of Adam describes dilemmas common to all prelapsarian intellects, his several long speeches may be related all the more pointedly to Satan's revolt. Raphael has addressed himself to the problem of how the abstract good of the Creator may be assimilated by his creatures. Operating by analogy, he defines abstract good in terms of the tangible needs Adam may recognize. Adam knows that, after Creation, life in plant and animal must be nourished in order to continue. From Adam, Raphael has drawn this image of God as the "Nourisher," for in inviting the angel to share the dinner fruits Adam refers to God as a "Nourisher, from whom / All perfet good unmeasur'd out, descends" (5.398–399). Raphael's elaboration of the chain of being illustrates Adam's conception of God and shows, as well, the dependence of the myriadness of creation upon the oneness of God.

O *Adam*, one Almighty is, from whom
All Things proceed, and up to him return,
If not deprav'd from good, created all
Such to perfection, one first matter all,
Indu'd with various forms. . . .

[5.469–473]

As Augustine had asserted, the property of created beings is to abide in God, from whom they have proceeded and by whom they must therefore be sustained. Since they have been created in God's good, they cannot separate themselves from it without vitiating their created natures. But, explains Raphael, this system whereby creature is linked to Creator implies not only his sharing in the good of God, but also his sharing in the collective good of all other beings. All creatures are interdependent: sustained by God, they are also related to and sustained by one another.

whatever was created, needs
To be sustain'd and fed; of Elements
The grosser feeds the purer, Earth the Sea,
Earth and the Sea feed Air, the Air those Fires
Ethereal. . . .

[5.414–418]

In the ONE UNIVERSE, survival depends on the interrelatedness of parts. this is why Raphael's analogy of the plant is so significant, for the plant is not only an illustration of the unity of nature, here organic nature with which Adam is familiar, but also an illustration of the continuity of parts, differing in degree one from another.

So from the root
Springs lighter the green stalk, from thence the leaves
More aery, last the bright consummate flow'r
Spirits odorous breathes. . . .

[5.479–482]

On the simplest level this is a plea for the creaturely community of spiritual and corporeal life, in that Raphael is explaining that what is fit for man (as nourishment) in one form is fit in a more sublime form for angel.

> flow'rs and thir fruit
> Man's nourishment, by gradual scale sublim'd
> To vital spirits aspire, to animal,
> To intellectual, give both life and sense,
> Fancy and understanding, whence the Soul
> Reason receives. . . .
>
> [5.482–487]

On a higher level this symbolizes the oneness of the total creation, unencumbered by dividing contraries of body and spirit. Finally, this is an argument for the importance of the part within the whole. Indeed, only in relationship to the whole does the part—be it root, leaf, flower—have meaning; for neither root, leaf, nor flower can *function* without respect to the other parts. Moreover, the functioning together of the parts of the plant may be likened to the functioning of the universe, having been infused in its creation by vital living force or goodness. As the root is a functioning part of the plant, transmitting life to the leaves and flower, it has meaning, has life; as man functions as part of the creation, he lives to partake of and re-create in himself the vitalizing goodness of God. Only the *entire* plant, not the dependent parts, has life. By emphasizing the oneness of a living creation, sustained in good by God, Raphael has instructed Adam of the danger when a part of that creation chooses separate or "private good" for itself in violation of the good for the continuing whole. Adam thus may understand why the choice of the dissenting part, Satan, proves disastrous; as readers we also are led to understand how the sinless Lucifer came to make his choice.

As he begins his narrative of Satan's revolt, Raphael sets the scene, so to speak, by drawing for Adam another image of the inviolability of creation. Heaven is pictured in terms of the one-

ness of the circle whose center is God. The angels, called from the
ends of Heaven, stand before God in their Hierarchies, Orders,
and Degrees, "in Orbs / Of circuit inexpressible . . . Orb within
Orb" (5.594–596). "Heav'n's great Year" itself has brought forth
this day from its perfect cycle. All individual parts function in
flawless order with respect to the great whole, but each part has,
Raphael implies, remarkable flexibility of individual reference.
The analogy of planetary orbit is drawn to illustrate this principle.
The angels do not stand mute and motionless about the throne of
God, frozen in rigid, changeless orbs, but spend that day "In song
and dance about the sacred Hill, / Mystical dance" (5.619–620),
likened by Raphael to the dance of the planets in their orbits, a
phenomenon Adam has observed.

> Mystical dance, which yonder starry Sphere
> Of Planets and of fixt in all her Wheels
> Resembles nearest, mazes intricate,
> Eccentric, intervolv'd, yet regular
> Then most, when most irregular they seem.
>
> [5.620–624

The part, here exemplified by the planet, may range in intricate,
individual pattern, just as the part of the plant could grow and
change. But within its movement, its change, the planet *must*
remain related to its orbit, for if it breaks its orbit it ceases to be a
part of the circuit of creation and becomes a meaningless mass of
matter lost in chaos. Only as it remains within its orbit does the
planet remain *truly itself* yet at the same time express the harmony of creation. So too, says Raphael, the angels in their dance
and accompanying song symbolically portray that harmony that
can result only when the part rejoices to fulfill its role.

> And in thir motions harmony Divine
> So smooths her charming tones, that God's own ear
> Listens delighted.
>
> [5.625–627]

55

The song of the angels, the dance of the planets are not perfunctory displays, as the singular word "delighted" will tell. God
has implanted within each individual part of his creation the potential, not the edict, to flourish. If the flower blooms, if the
planet dances, if the angel sings, it is because it chooses to do so,
and the moment of its flourishing is a moment of spontaneous
delight.

Milton has let us know that there is much in Heaven in which to
delight. The festivities of the angels that Raphael describes are
the archetypes of the communion of joy he celebrated on earth
when he partook of Adam's and Eve's simple feast. Creature
joins with creature to affirm their part in the oneness of creation.
The angels turn from the mystical circuit of their dance and the
tables are set, Milton tells us, "all in Circles as they stood"
(5.631). All aspects of angelic life are related to their perfect relationship to God, the circle in which we first saw them arrayed.
And from this relationship all is given. God appears, as he did to
Adam and as Raphael commended him to be, the Nourisher of all
things living, "th' all bounteous King, who show'r'd / With copi-
ous hand, rejoicing in thir joy" (5.640–641). The feast of the
angels, as well as celebrating their communion with one another
and their sustenance from the creative oneness of God, also celebrates their willingness to flourish. In all delights, from the beginning of the angelic day to its conclusion with the onset of twilight
and its "grateful" change, the angels are left free to ordain their
pleasures. At evening they are dispersed either to choose their
resting place in camps "by living Streams among the Trees of
Life," where "Pavilions numberless" appear or else to wake with
those "who in thir course / Melodious Hymns about the sovran
Throne / Alternate all night long" (5.650–657). Whichever the
choice, order and cycle are maintained.

"But not so wak'd / *Satan*" (5.657–658). Thus Milton has
Raphael introduce Satan to Adam as the sole angel who, refusing
the grateful rest of twilight, wakes not to rejoice in song. By his
fallen name only does Raphael designate him, for the glory of his

person is gone and his name has been blotted out in Heaven. Yet the memory of the glory of his place survives, for once he was "of the first, / If not the first Arch-Angel, great in Power, / In favor and pre-ëminence" (5.659–661). In his place, the archangel functioned as a part of the vast creation and steadied and maintained the entire system. Having great place within the functioning universe, he himself was great. But, ironically, Satan is depicted in the moment of deserting his place of power and greatness. So he imperils his own glory in denying the role that nourished it and endangers the universe when he as renegade part withdraws from the whole. In terms of the universe, of course, Satan's act is not irreparable (for God has power within himself to renew and uphold his threatened creation), but it is disastrous to self. Irreparably, as he removes himself as part of God's creation, he vitiates his own nature.

It is one of Milton's most remarkable paradoxes that the very decree that "causes" Satan to revolt might have been, had Satan listened to it carefully and without the blinding fury of his pride, the means to stay his revolt. For in the decree God is stating that ruin will result when a creature, a part, separates himself from the creation, the whole. God has named the Son to kingship so as to make manifest visually and symbolically the union upon which the vitality of his creation depends. The angelic essence must, if it is to retain its vigor, abide in God and, as Augustine has noted, look to be one with him. The Son is the means to achieve this union, for to look to the Son as king is to look to be united with God "as one individual Soul / For ever happy" (5.610–611). It is an exercise of the angels that they understand the decree as a furtherance, not an impediment, to their desire for union. If, knowing God as a loving Creator, they see his decree as perverse, then they willfully misunderstand the universe and their part in it. The mistake must be willful, for it must represent the conscious demand of self over that of Creator.

If a creature has demanded that he himself and not the Son be the means for his union with God and his attainment of bliss, that creature is fragmenting the natural order to heavenly union, which exists and functions for his own good. In rejecting the Son, moreover, as a vital "part" of God, he impairs the function of his own "partship" with the Father, since alteration of one relationship in the universe alters correlative relationships. Denial of the Son as the instrument of God's will thus perforce effects denial of the Father: "him who disobeys / Mee disobeys, breaks union" (5.611–612). And breaking union with God so reorders a creature's place in the scheme of the universe that those creaturely powers transfused by God, as he transfused life to the creature, must be weakened and distorted as the creature removes himself from their source.

The fall into darkness, so much a part of the patristic imagination as a metaphor for primal sin, is described by God in the final words of his decree.

> Cast out from God and blessed vision, falls
> Into utter darkness, deep ingulft, his place
> Ordain'd without redemption, without end.
>
> (5.613–615]

What is described here, however, is not the threat of a vengeful God who swears to extinguish his angel's brightness if he disobeys. God foretells that Satan will close his eyes to blessed vision, and that eclipsing of light will result in the fall into darkness. Milton's God does not urge Satan into disobedience; like the God of the Nicene fathers he cannot urge evil in a good creature. It is Satan who step by step withdraws into the darkness he has been forewarned will come upon him when he separates himself from God and denies himself the light of God's presence. For Milton damnation is synonymous with separation, and in this he also follows patristic doctrine. Had Satan understood God's words to the angels as a paternal warning of the dangers of alienation and a loving plea to seek the blessings of union through the Son, he would neither have resented the Son's function as king nor have resolved upon the separation from God that effects his damnation.

Yet why does Satan so resolve? For to separate from God is something that he with his superior angelic understanding must know to be disastrous. Envy and pride move him, we are told, with the thought that he was "himself impair'd." From the fourth century on, pride was the motive most frequently named, and Milton in his elaboration of Satanic motive does not dissent. But does Milton mean by pride that intellective disorder that was anatomized by fathers such as Augustine and Aquinas? We have had ample opportunity to study Satan's pride in the first four books of the epic. In book 1 Satan is said to regard Hell "mixt with obdurate pride and steadfast hate" and to speak, "vaunting aloud, but rackt with deep despair" (1.58, 126). As he surveys his troops in Hell, he holds himself, "above the rest / In shape and gesture proudly eminent" (1.589–590). Seated upon the throne in Hell, in his coronation speech he "his proud imaginations thus display'd" (2.10). In his manner of address to others, pride repeatedly takes precedence: to Death (2.680) when he first encounters him at Hell's gate "with disdainful look"; to the Monarchs of Chaos (2.968) as he pleads his cause "turning boldly"; to Gabriel (4.885) after he is discovered in Eve's bower, "with contemptuous brow." Pride is the inward driving emotion that so overpowers Satan as to become his dominant and manifestly prime characteristic. But is it, in the instances thus cited, the cause of his sin or the symptom of his sin? The beginning of sin must be the reason's mischoice and not the emotions' misdirection, however strongly the emotions may be said to sway the reason. The cause of sin is intellective. Thus pride, as designated in book 5 as the motive for Satan's sin, must be quite different from the pride designated in book 1 as his compulsion, for in the first it is a defect of the reason, in the second, of the emotion; in the first, a cause; in the second, an effect. In the beginning Satan controls pride's emergence, but thereafter pride controls Satan.

In book 5 pride involves for Milton, as it did for the fathers, a serious confrontation of Satan's mind with the nature of God. Throughout book 5 Milton has led us to understand that if a creature of God will thrive in God's creation, he will rejoice in his "partship" and will regard his highest happiness as that of moving ever closer to oneness with God. Satan, having witnessed Messiah's coronation, is moved not with love but with envy, not with a sense of "oneness" but with a sense of separation or pride. His state to him seems *impaired,* and the scene designed to beatify has left him distressed. How then does he react? He seeks to elevate the state he feels has been depressed; he attempts to raise himself as he has seen Messiah raised so that he will bring himself once more into a sense of "oneness" and "order" within Heaven. Yet he seeks this elevation not from God but from self. In all this, however, he never seeks to abnegate God's power, for the mainspring of his world still to his mind is God. God is that height by which he measures his own, God the sublimity that must mete out his own blessedness. God, who has raised Messiah, must finally be called upon to sanction Satan's selfraising. Only from Messiah does Satan depart—from that being whose height threatens his own: God, as Satan knows, is all-present in the universe, and to depart from him would be to negate his own basis for being. In departing from Messiah, Satan seeks to repair the depression he feels has been caused by Messiah's elevation; his is a logical, if mishaken, undertaking. Satan does not set out to revolt against omnipotence, to challenge the power of his Creator; for such an act, as Anselm and Aquinas asserted, Satan would have known was absurd. He seeks something permissible and desirable: the happiness of being raised toward God. Yet he chooses *not* to see that such happiness is available by being exalted in the Messiah and attempts to generate his own "happiness" in his flight to the North and his institution there of an alternate elevation. Why Satan refuses the Son and how his refusal takes the form of envious imitation, however, I shall defer for discussion in chapter 2.

What is of moment here is that Milton has made Satan's flight to the North a dramatic illustration (according to the Augustinian principle) of election of ''private good.'' To Satan his own elevation upon the diamond mount is that ''good'' he embraces for himself, having denied the elevation of the Messiah, the ''good'' God intended for him. He spurns the angelic ''self'' God wishes for him and grasps *with pride* for that other self of his own making. Pride is, we clearly see, that intellectual refusal to allow the Creator who formed him to continue to nourish his being. As Satan falls, pride becomes not just the instant of intellective mischoice but the wedded component, the daughter of Satan's personality. So, as the allegory of book 2 explains, Sin springs from the brain of Satan as he wishes for the second self, separate from God. And together they generate what only generation abstracted from the Creator can produce: Death. Yet there is another offspring of the heavenly hierarch with his pride, for the second self wished for also springs forth: the adversary, the foe of God, the Satan. Satan's first ''uncreation'' is his own demonic person.

Satan, of course, does not foresee the full implications of his actions, though when he does he chooses not to repent, even as he first chose separate good. When hopes of happiness through his own ''good'' are frustrated, he admits only the unwisdom, not the undesirability, of his acts (4.58–72). His wish to soar in happiness through his own powers is a perverting chemical that has mutated his nature, destroying the fabric of sound intellect. Wishing happiness from self makes Satan no longer able to experience happiness from God. Satan has become a being who is ''unable'' in his very nature, and this ''unableness'' is aptly illustrated when he persists in seeking elevation after the ''goal'' of elevation— being one with God—has disappeared. In the final sections of book 5, Milton moves on to consider directly the paradox defined by Anselm and Aquinas: Satan's challenge of God's omnipotence. Like these Scholastics, Milton shows that Satan could not have proposed from the first to contest with omnipotence, since his perfect intellect would have told him such a contest was impossible. He first *withdraws* from God, seceding, as it were, from Messiah's rule. But hardly has he arrived in the North before he assembles a power that, by the end of book 5, plans to return and besiege God's throne. How does Milton resolve this contradiction?

It is not Satan but God (in conversation with the Son) who first proposes that in seceding from him Satan is in effect attempting to nullify God's omnipotence. With irony, God exposes Satan's intention: "Nearly it now concerns us to be sure / Of our Omnipotence" (5.721–722). God's irony, to be sure, points up the absurdity of an angel's attempting to replace God. It also shows the absurdity of Satan's notion of partial secession. If God is omnipotent, is it possible to secede from a part of his rule, that delegated to the Messiah? Is such secession not indeed a challenge? To propose to negate a part of God's rule is to assume a prerogative of God and so to affect an equality with God: God has seen that Satan's possession of the "quarters of the north" entails more than a plea for separation. Satan's magnific throne is no harmless imitation, but a throne designed to "equal" God's. As Aquinas noted, imitation of God is desirable and a good; but imitation of God *in an improper order* (and such is Satan's raising of a rival throne) is not a good but a challenge to God's omnipotence. God sees also that Satan, having separated himself from God and having attempted to simulate equality, must next reach for supremacy. For to aspire to supremacy is merely to insist upon those very principles of power and right that first prompted the impulse for separation. So God reveals:

> Nor so content, hath in his thought to try
> In battle, what our Power is, or our right.

[5.727–728]

Now the progress from separation to contest, which God has so outlined, Milton casts into the dramatic action of the remainder of book 5. On the one hand, Satan is himself moving inwardly from

separatist to activist; on the other, he is impelling the one-third of
the angels whom he has drawn off from sympathizers into soldiers. It is the first of these movements we shall analyze as we
examine the final scene of book 5, in which Satan appeals to his
angels for support. Satan *begins* to argue against Messiah by
proclaiming one of the truths of Heaven: that he and all his hearers are free, a doctrine no one attendant at his first speech would
dispute.

> Ye will not, if I trust
> To know ye right, or if ye know yourselves
> Natives and Sons of Heav'n possest before
> By none, and if not equal all, yet free.
>
> [5.788–791]

Satan does not here reflect, however, upon the reason for the
heavenly freedom, although no doubt he has been told. Freedom
exists in Heaven so that the allegiance of angels may be uncom-
pelled, the product not of a constrained necessity, but of minds
and wills left unconstrained so that, inspired by love, they might
freely choose. But for Satan the word freedom, so introduced,
does not long remain untrammeled with necessity. The government of Heaven, he asserts, is founded upon the paradox that
freedom exists despite inequalitites in rank; all therefore—to take
Satan's statement one step further—are unequally free. And this,
says Satan, is not unjust, for "Orders and Degrees / Jar not with
liberty, but well consist" (5.792–793). Next, however, Satan
proposes that, if inequality may exist in order, it cannot in freedom; all must be "equally free." Yet Satan's definition of
"equally free" in fact contradicts all that he has before argued
about the state of Heaven. None can be free if the state of
monarchy is assumed over them by one whom they "think" their
equal, or even if in fact any law or edict is placed above them.
Satan argues that a creature is not free unless he is *without* order.
Thus the godly paradox of freedom subsisting well in order is
turned into the Satanic contradiction of freedom without order.

But even in so arguing freedom begins to be constrained. It no longer has the sense of the uncommitted will or mind that may choose its own disposition. It begins to become proscribed duty. Satan's angels are "free" to deny the Messiah, "free" to govern themselves, "free" to choose not to serve, but "not free" to choose any alternative. Implicitly, Satan has told them what to do with their freedom, and in so advising and regulating has indeed deprived them of freedom.

Of course Satan has created the illusion of equalitarianism. That he has done this with a rhetorical turn rather than by a logical argument is significant. The adverbial "equally" free has become the nominal "equals" in freedom. That this change in phrase has produced an absurdity does not go unchallenged. Here, however, it is the humble angel Abdiel, not God Almighty, who points out the error. Quite simply, Abdiel asserts that the angels cannot be the equals of the Messiah, for they were created by him. Up till this point Satan has been intent on defining "legalistic" freedom—that is, the range he is allowed to pursue by virtue of his order and place within society. Deliberately he has avoided the question of his personal or creaturely relationship to God or Messiah. But with Abdiel's challenge, no more may he avoid it. If he denies his legal responsibility to Messiah, he must also deny his creaturely one. The surprising thing here, however, is not that Satan denies Messiah as creator, but that he denies God with him. He proclaims himself and the angels,

> self-begot, self-raised
> By our own quick'ning power, when fatal course
> Had circl'd his full Orb, the birth mature
> Of this our native Heaven, Ethereal Sons.

> [5.860–863]

The doctrine of spontaneous generation is not in itself illogical. Feasible in the abstract, there is no reason why in a given universe or system things might not be ordered in that way. But in God's universe they were not, and Satan *knows* they were not.

As Augustine long ago noted, this denial of God would be no vice except in a creature who, made by God, had a nature whose property it was to abide in God. In book 4 Satan in a fallen state so recognizes his nature: that God had "created [him] what [he] was / In that bright eminence" (4.43–44); why then at the height of his angelic powers in book 5 should he know or acknowledge less? It must be that Satan consciously lies and with his lie deliberately embraces the absurdity.

Now, however, we must ask why a perfect creature should embrace an absurdity. Satan, if he did not *at first* know that what he proposed was impossible, does at last know it. If he chooses to continue, it must be because the "evil" unleashed within him when he separated from God now constrains him to change alienation from Messiah into contest with God, even though he knows such a contest is an absurdity. It may be, as well, that the moment he defined freedom in terms of necessity he bound himself to act in compliance with that definition. But ultimately, I think, we must see Satan's act in terms of his having been brought, unwillingly, to the persuasion that God may not be separated from Messiah, as Satan had originally asserted. God has decreed that he and Messiah are one in government as in act of creation. Satan belatedly must face the truth of that connection. He is subject to the rule of God through Messiah because he is the creature of God through Messiah. Therefore he must bow to Messiah as to God or deny God with the denial of Messiah. There are no alternatives. But, of course, to assent to Messiah's rule would mean to abandon those angelic prerogatives (to govern, not to serve) he has only now promulgated. Satan is trapped. His leap in logic from denying the Son as agent of creation to pronouncing himself self-begot illustrates as much. With his next move, he forsakes logic altogether. No longer singling out Messiah as an adversary, he proposes to attack God and try him as his equal. In this he follows exactly the path God has predicted he would take. He swears to raise his "own right hand" against God, and by his own "puissance" to attempt the highest deeds. To the Almighty Throne, which he left in stealth, he will return in strength, "to begirt [it] ... besieging," not beseeching (5.868–869).

It is one of the supreme ironies that the throne of God, which was first shown us by Raphael circled with celebrant angels, is now to be begirt with ambitious armies. Yet in a way it is no more surprising than that Satan, who began as the rational angel who dissents, should now appear as the mad militarist. Careless of reason, negligent of argument, Satan rushes headlong, vaunting his dual absurdities: that contest with the Almighty is feasible and that such a contest is one he means to win. However strange this ultimate course of rebellion that Satan pursues, we must understand that Milton, like the church fathers, saw the genesis of this folly in Satan's misdirected desire to be like his Creator, in his wish for "dubious" good.

CHAPTER 2

"Envy and Pale Ire"

Envy has always been the "alternate" sin of Satan's soul. Had not Aquinas said it was the only sin besides pride of which angels were capable by "original nature"?[1] Moreover, when Milton in book 5 of *Paradise Lost* comes to dramatize Satan's revolt, it is envy to which he gives first mention.

> yet fraught
> With envy against the Son of God, that day
> Honor'd by his great Father, and proclaim'd
> *Messiah* King, anointed could not bear
> Through pride that sight, and thought himself impair'd.
> [5.661–665]

But it is clear that Milton in naming envy as Satan's "first" sin is not concerned with an abstract anatomy of angelic sinfulness in the way Aquinas is. It is envy conceived on a very special occasion—the announcement of the Son's exaltation—and directed toward a particular person—the Son himself—that concerns him. And, in delineating envy as an important motivation for Satan's revolt, Milton parts company with the patristic tradition and adheres to theological opinion closer to his own time.

The devil's envy, it is true, is a theological issue as old as the figure of Satan himself. What the early Christian fathers meant when they alluded to Satan's envy, however, was his envy of

---

1. Aquinas, "Part I, Question LXIII," in The *"Summa Theologica"* of St. Thomas Aquinas, 3.146–147.

man. Traditionally Satan tempted man because he was envious of
the favors God had bestowed upon him. So the apocryphal book
(Wisd. of Sol. 2:24) recounts: "by the envy of the devil death
entered into the world." So also says the second-century Christian father Irenaeus, who emphasizes that Satan's envy of the
goodness in God's creation of man made him wish to spoil it.[2]
And, finally, so narrate the popular Books of Adam and Eve,
which tell the story of how Satan's envy was provoked when God
ordered him to worship his latest handiwork, man.[3]

Envy of Satan for the Son is a subordinate note throughout
early Christianity, perhaps because the fathers felt that to give
Satan too prominent a place as the envious rival of the Son was
only to encourage the elements of Manichaeanism and Arianism
already dividing Christianity. The third-century Christian father
Lactantius, however, had elaborated on Satan's role as the rival
of the Son and had proposed that the rivalry was motivated by
envy.[4] Lactantius recounts that the Son and Satan were produced
"almost" on parallel occasions, the Son, however, generated first
and greatly superior to the second being, Satan. In the Son the
perfections of the Father were produced and sustained; in the
second being, however, "the disposition of divine origin did not
remain." But Lactantius goes on to say that the lapse of the
second being was directly caused by the envy that arose within
him for the perfections of the first being. Evil comes into existence as Satan envies the Son. "Therefore he [Satan] was infected with his own envy as with poison, and passed from good to
evil; and at his own will, which had been given to him by God
unfettered, he acquired for himself a contrary name. From which

2. Irenaeus, *Against Heresies,* bk. 4, chap. 40, in *Ante-Nicene Christian
Fathers,* 1.524.
3. "Vita Adae et Evae," 13–16, in Charles, *Apocrypha and Pseudepigrapha,*
2:137. For a discussion of Satan's envy see Arnold Williams, "The Motivation of
Satan's Rebellion in Paradise Lost," *SP* 42 (1945): 253–268.
4. Kathleen Hartwell in her book *Lactantius and Milton* (Cambridge, 1929)
studies many of the similarities between Lactantius and Milton and cites among
them the use of the theme of Satan's envy of the Son. She points out that Milton
knew Lactantius and mentioned him twice in his prose and seven times in his
commonplace book.

it appears that the source of all evils is envy. For he envied his predecessor, who through his stedfastness is acceptable and dear to God the Father."[5]

Lactantius's views did not prevail in the face of the opinion of fourth- and fifth-century fathers such as Augustine, who maintained that Satan fell through pride and illustrated this contention by elaborating on the portraits of the aspiring "angel" in Isaiah and Ezekiel. But when these portraits from Isaiah and Ezekiel came under the scrutiny of Protestant theologians, who denied that they referred to the figure of Satan, the motivation of pride was likewise reexamined. Both Calvin and Luther look upon the patristic Satan with suspicion; both regard the elaborate accounts of his fall as fables created by commentators. Calvin, especially, would have it that the fall of Satan was one of God's mysteries into which human curiosity should not pry, asserting that the brief allusions to it in the New Testament provide Christians with sufficient information "to vindicate the majesty of God from every calumny."[6] Calvin and Luther maintain that the prophets Isaiah and Ezekiel in their highly poetical and extravagant manner merely intend to censure the arrogance of the kings of Babylon and Tyre. Without question, says Calvin in interpreting Isaiah 14, it is the king of Babylon and not Satan who aspired beyond his sphere, who wished to sit upon God's throne—that is, to rule over the people of God and God's temple. Any other reading, insists Calvin, would make "inane fable" of Scripture.[7]

Protestant theologians generally follow Luther and Calvin in

---

5. Lactantius, *Divine Institutes*, bk. 2, chap. 9 in *Ante-Nicene Christian Fathers*, 7:52–53.

6. John Calvin, *Institutes of the Christian Religion*, bk. 1, chap 14, trans. John Allen (Philadelphia, 1936), 1:193. He also comments, "That we ourselves, therefore, may not dwell upon unprofitable subjects, let us be content with this concise information respecting the nature of devils; that at their creation they were originally angels of God but by degenerating have ruined themselves, and become instruments of perdition to others. This being useful to be known, it is clearly stated by Peter and Jude. 'God,' say they, 'spared not the angels that sinned, and kept not their first estate, but left their own habitation'" (1:163–164).

7. Calvin, "In Isaiam," in *Opera Omnia,* ed. Guilielmus Baum, Eduardus Cunitz, and Eduardus Reuss, 36 (Brunswick, 1888): 277.

this reassessment of the Old Testament texts and Satan.[8] The motivation of pride, however, continues to be the prominent one even in Protestant circles. Some churchmen merely seek to find evidence elsewhere in the Bible that pride was Satan's principal motivation. Such seventeenth-century commentators as Thomas Adams and John Boys reason that since Satan tempted Eve by appealing to her pride, he must have been urging her to repeat his own presumption.[9] Others such as Joseph Caryl argue that the "folly" of which God accuses the angels in Job must have been pride.[10]

Despite this entrenched orthodoxy in some commentators, there is a strong desire in others to reevaluate the causes of Satan's fall. Taking as a guide Calvin's and Luther's emphasis upon the New Testament, they seek New Testament texts that illuminate the character of Satan. Ironically enough, it is John 8:44, which had been used by the fourth- and fifth-century Christian fathers to explicate Satan's pride, that now supplies evidence of his envy. In this text John speaks of the devil abiding not in truth from the beginning. Truth cannot be, argue the Protestant commentators, an abstract term denoting some vague state of Heaven against which Satan revolts. The truth of God can be none other than the Son of God, for only he is the eternal Word. Therefore

8. In explicating these texts, the annotation attached to the Geneva Bible makes no allusions to their traditional association with Satan. The marginal notes concisely identify Lucifer as Nebuchadnezzar and the "anointed cherub" as the king of Tyre. Even in so long a work as William Greenhill's commentary on Ezekiel (1650) there is no hint that the "anointed cherub" had been interpreted as Satan. Milton himself in *De doctrina Christiana* omits Isaiah 14 and Ezekiel 28 from the texts cited for elucidation of Satan's character and history.

9. Thomas Adams, *An Exposition upon the Second Epistle General of St. Peter,* revised and corrected by James Sherman (London, 1839), p. 275. Also John Boys, *Workes* (London, 1629).

10. Joseph Caryl, *An Exposition with Practical Observations Continued upon the Fourth, Fifth, Sixth and Seventh Chapters of the Book of Job* (London, 1671), p. 138. "We may hence learn, first, *What the sin of Angels was,* God charged his Angels with folly; the possible sin, which God saw, and still sees, in the nature of Angels, was the actual sin of Angels. Pride and self-confidence were the sins of Angels, and these are the most proper sins of Angels, Angels cannot fall into every sin."

Satan's not abiding in the truth must signify that he revolted against the Son of God while he was in Heaven, and that revolt caused his downfall.

The seventeenth-century divine Thomas Goodwin considers that Satan's "original" sin must be closely connected with that sin he inspired in the Jews: the rejection of the truth that is Christ.

> In John viii. 44, 45, (see also 25, 28, 32, 36) Christ lays open both the devil's sin and that of the Jews: They received not the truth Christ delivered them, and in their belief sought to kill him; and this truth was Himself, "even the same he told them from the beginning," the Messiah, the Son of God, whom when they had crucified, "they should know, that it was he," some to their hardening: this he calls *the truth,* which the disciples should know, and whereby the Son should make them free indeed: As for Satan, he was "their father the devil who abode not in the truth," the first that set himself against this great truth of Christ's person, and would not be subject to God, nor accept, embrace, and continue in this first truth, but quit heaven rather; whence as a hater of God and Christ and mankind, he virtually became the murderer of them all.[11]

It was not new, of course, to cite Satan as the one who provoked the Jews against Christ. What is unusual in Goodwin's account is that what had been long identified as Satan's major offense in this world also hypothetically becomes his original offense—not opposition to God alone, traditionally ascribed to him, but opposition to the Son. From the beginning Satan has refused to accept Christ.[12]

11. Thomas Goodwin, *The Expositions of That Famous Divine Thomas Goodwin, D.D. on Part of the Epistle to the Ephesians, and on the Book of Revelation* (London, 1842), p. 352.

12. Peter Sterry, a Cambridge Platonist, reasons similarly but uses different texts for illustration. He cites those New Testament verses that Calvin and Luther had approved as reliable evidence of angelic fall: 2 Pet. 2:4 and Jude 6. He argues that the "principle" referred to in Jude 6 that the angels deserted was their state or being in Christ. "We are made by, and in Christ, Col. 1. By Christ, as our Immediate Principle, and Pattern; In Christ as our proper Habitation. The Original Sin of Devils, which infected Mankind, is plainly set down to be this: *Jude 6.* They kept not their first State, in *Greek* Principle: but left their own Habitation" (Peter Sterry, *The Rise, Race, and Royalty of the Kingdom of God in the Soul of Man* [London, 1683], p. 199).

According to most Protestant theologians, there are two reasons Satan opposed the Son: first, he resented the Son as a person who possessed a superior nature; but, second, he envied the office the Son held in Heaven or was to hold on earth. Martin Luther, in analyzing the first of these motivations, remarks that implicit in Satan's initial conception of evil was a strong antipathy for the good. The Son's good as a quality of his person was first apparent to Satan and his angels, and it was resentment of this goodness of person that provoked their revolt: "some proud angels, displeased by the meekness of the Son of God, wanted to place themselves above Him."[13]

Jacob Boehme, a German Neoplatonist of the early seventeenth century, also exposes Satan's rejection of the Son's meekness. The Son, according to Boehme, is the "Heart of God," and as such he is a peculiar manifestation of God's love. But Satan refuses to see aspects of divinity in the softness and beauty of this "Heart." The Son's meekness he merely regards as antithetical to his own strength. "He would not set his imagination therein [on the Son's meekness], and therefore he could not be fed from the Word of the Lord, and so his light went out."[14]

Other theologians, however, argue that Satan was led to revolt not by some general resentment of the Son, but by anger over the announcement of the Son's Incarnation. Satan held high office in Heaven, was the head of principalities of angels; learning that the Son now to be incarnated would set up a supreme kingdom upon earth, Satan felt his own lordship over the angels threatened and demeaned. He envied, moreover, not only the Son's great kingship, but also the favors God had chosen to bestow through the Son upon man and not upon the angels. As man was to be exalted, reasoned Satan, the angels would be despised. Martin Luther, citing Bernard as an authority, speculates that Lucifer had fore-

13. Luther, *Works,* ed. Pelikan (Saint Louis, 1957), I:112.
14. Jacob Boehme, "Of the True Eternal Nature," chap. 4 in *Concerning the Three Principles of the Divine Essences,* trans. John Sparrow (London, 1910), p. 60. For elaboration on Boehme's influence on Milton, see Margaret L. Bailey, *Milton and Jacob Boehme* (New York, 1914).

knowledge of the coming Incarnation of the Son and resented the fact that the Son was to take on human rather than angelic form. "This provoked his [Lucifer's] insolence against God. He was aware, of course, that he was a creature more beautiful and excellent in appearance than man. This also aroused his envy of mankind; he begrudged man the high honor of God's assumption of human nature. This vexed him and his companions. They became envious when they learned that God would despise them and assume human nature. Therefore Lucifer and his hosts fell and were driven out of heaven."[15] Zanchi, a sixteenth-century theologian, concurs with Luther's view, remarking that the angels' sin, for which they fell, was the sin of envy for the gift of grace the Son was to confer on mankind.[16]

Although he takes Zanchi as one of his authorities, Thomas Goodwin differs somewhat from his account. True, Satan envied the gift to man, but what he primarily resented was the power of the kingdom Christ was to hold upon earth and the necessity that he too recognize and bow to Christ's authority: "the sin of the fallen spirits was, refusing subjection to this king; and that thus they 'kept not their first estate but left their own habitation,' voluntarily quitting the station God had set them in, and leaving their dwelling in heaven, to go and set up an opposition-kingdom here below."[17] Satan's envy in this account is logically motivated (he envied the office as well as the person of the Son); his action also assumes a logical direction. Consumed with envy for Christ's kingdom but unable to challenge it directly, Satan leaves Heaven to establish *his own* kingdom. Scripture, moreover, which frequently refers to Satan as the king or god of this world, amply and fully supports the view that Satan left Heaven with the design of setting up a rival kingdom elsewhere.[18]

Much of the theology of the seventeenth century is predicated

15. Luther, *Works*, 22:103.
16. Hieronymus Zanchius, "De peccato Angelorum," bk. 4, chap. 2, in *Opera Theologica* (1605), 30:169–171.
17. Goodwin, *Expositions*, p. 351.
18. See John 12:31; 2 Cor. 4:4; Eph. 6:12; Col. 2:15; John 16:11.

upon a contrast of Christ and Satan as rival kings, ruling over opposed kingdoms. Theologians, however, take care to point out the difference in the origin and nature of their kingships. Christ is never understood as a figurehead opposed to Satan. His is no mere "hereditary" title, even though some theologians would call him, as the church father Theodoret of Cyrrhus had, "a king before all ages."[19] Most theologians concur that the office of king is one Christ has achieved by the peculiar merits of his person and one he exercises for a specific functional purpose. One view of Christ's kingship is that it is a kind of overflowing of divine authority and that its particular direction is toward checking the illegitimate authority Satan would advance. Another is that kingship is a type of supreme manhood within Christ; he is fit head for humanity because he excels as man. William Bates expresses a composite of these views.

> He is qualified for the kingly office, by the union of the two natures in him. He must be God to conquer Satan, and convert the world. As eminent an act of power was necessary to redeem, as to create; for although the Supreme Judge were to be satisfied by humble sufferings, yet Satan, who usurped the right of God (for man had no power to alienate himself) was to be subdued: having no just title he was to be cast out by power. And no less than divine power could accomplish our victorious rescue from him.[20]

The theologians see the Son's kingship as an essential part of his nature, in which is bound up intimately his divine essence as well as his power to command allegiance from all creatures. Thus the moment in which the Son is invested with kingship is significant because it is both the moment when his divinity is manifested to all creatures and a moment when by being appointed to royal power and authority he incurs the envy and wrath of Satan, who yearns to possess that power. In connecting the announcement of

19. Theodoretus, in *Nicene and Post-Nicene Fathers,* 2d ser., 3:318.
20. William Bates, *Select Works of the Rev. William Bates, D.D.* (London, 1825), 1:69.

the kingship with that of the Incarnation, most theologians are stressing how the Son's promotion to kingship *in Heaven* looks forward to his promotion to that office on earth, when he will incidentally displace Satan from the usurped throne on earth.[21] Yet there is something essentially illogical in having Satan envy the Incarnation and thus fall from Heaven by reason of that envy. Calvin comments on the frivolity of the notion that Satan in Heaven should have envied the Son of God's becoming human; for, necessarily, the need for the Son's Incarnation would not have become manifest until after Satan's own fall and the subsequent fall of man.[22]

Some seventeenth-century theologians are cautious, therefore, about interconnecting these three events: the announcement of the Incarnation, the exaltation of the Son, and Satan's incipient envy of the Son's kingdom. For them, the exaltation of the Son is referred to in the second psalm and in the first chapter of Hebrews, where God is said to "beget" the Son, that is, to "raise" him to favor. Unlike patristic doctrine, Protestant interpretation did *not* view the second psalm as describing the eternal generation of the Son. John Owen, a seventeenth-century divine, says that modern theologians believe the psalm refers not to the Son's generation, but to "some outward act of God toward the Lord Christ, on the occasion whereof he has been declared to be the Son of God, and so called." Owen remarks, however, that there is a variety of theological opinion concerning *which* occasion is being commemorated.

> Others therefore take the words to express only an occasion of giving this name at a certain season to the Lord Christ, when he was

---

21. The seventeenth-century theologian John Lightfoot (*Horae Hebraecae et Talmudicae: Hebrew and Talmudical Exercitations upon the Gospels of St. Luke and St. John* [London, 1859], 3:97) comments that Satan fell from Heaven (as described in Luke 10:18) at the moment when the Son began his ministry, that is, proclaimed his kingdom.

22. Commentary on Gen. 3:1. J. M. Evans in his book *"Paradise Lost" and the Genesis Tradition* (Oxford, 1968), p. 255, and before him Arnold Williams, "The Motivation of Satan's Rebellion in *Paradise Lost*," *SP* 42 (1945): 257, comment on Calvin's repudiation of this widespread concept.

revealed or declared to be the Son of God. And some assign this to the day of his incarnation, when he declared him to be his Son, and that should be so recalled, as Luke i. 35. some to the day of his baptism, when he was again solemnly from heaven proclaimed so to be, Matt. iii. 17. some to the day of his resurrection, when he was declared to be the Son of God with power, Rom. i. 3. and Acts xiii. 33. some to the day of his ascension, whereunto these words are applied.[23]

In Owen's opinion, the exaltation is a movable "date." He points out that theologians in his time have assigned it to a number of different occasions: the Incarnation, the Baptism, the Resurrection, and the Ascension. The second psalm refers to a moment of special favor; which moment, however, remains largely a matter of conjecture. Therefore, if we may take Owen as representing contemporary opinion, we may assume that the occasion of the Son's exaltation or investiture with kingship was regarded differently by different theologians; it was not inflexibly fixed at his Incarnation and, as Owen has contended, may be assigned to any moment, at or after the Incarnation, when the Father granted special favor to the Son.[24]

If Milton's interpretation of the second psalm is seen in this light, it remains clearly within the confines of seventeenth-century orthodox opinion. Milton is certainly following theologians like Owen when he denies that the second psalm refers to

23. John Owen, *Works*, ed. Thomas Russell (London, 1826), 24:147–148.
24. Also see Peter Sterry, *The Teachings of Christ in the Soule* (London 1648), Sterry cites the second psalm as a proof text of the Son's exaltation to kingship by God, in recognition of his truth and goodness and his eminence over all. "Christ hath the Office of a *King, Psal.* 2.6. God saith, *I have set my King upon my holy hill of Sion.* Christ is a King of God's making, and appointing; the King of Saints; a King in his Church, which is the true mount Sion.... / *Jesus Christ* is higher by the head, than all the Creatures; / ... thus is Christ crowned King by the Godhead. And by this Title hath he the Law of all Truth, and Goodnesse in his own Breast. For he is an absolute, supream King.... God calls Christ, *my King;* a King in my likenesse, in my stead (pp. 6–7)." Sterry does not specify the time of the Son's appointment to kingship, but he does say that Moses addressed the Son with the title *king.* One therefore concludes naturally that the Son held this office before his Incarnation (p. 7).

the eternal generation of the Son, connecting it instead with an occasion of the Son's exaltation. In *De doctrina Christiana,* he differs from Owen only in being more specific about the exact occasion the psalm refers to; that is, not merely to the Son's being named and honored as son (probably at some time connected with his earthly ministry), but to his being exalted to kingship.[25] "From the second Psalm it will also be seen that God begot the Son in the sense of making him a king, Psal. ii. 6, 7: *anointing my king, I have set him upon my holy hill of Sion.* Then, in the next verse, having anointed his king, from which process the name "Christ" is derived, he says: *I have begotten you today.*"[26]

Paradise Lost is yet more specific than *De doctrina* concerning the time and occasion to which the second psalm refers. The second psalm is directly echoed when the Father in Heaven anoints the Son as king; and Milton has made the investiture quite

25. In his article "Milton on the Exaltation of the Son: The War in Heaven in *Paradise Lost,*" *ELH* 36 (March 1969): 215–231, William B. Hunter, Jr., maintains that there are doctrinal distinctions between *Christian Doctrine* and *Paradise Lost* on the subject of the Son's exaltation or "begetting" by the Father. Professor Hunter argues that in *Christian Doctrine* the "changes at the exaltation took place in time only at the resurrection . . . in *Paradise Lost* they are applied to the Son throughout the poem, long before his incarnation" (p. 221).

26. Milton, *Christian Doctrine,* trans. John Carey, in *Complete Prose Works of John Milton* (New Haven: Yale University Press), 6:207. In differentiating the metaphorical from the actual begetting of the Son Milton closely follows Calvin's exposition of the second psalm and of Heb. 1:5. Calvin argues: "As to Christ's being begotten, briefly speaking, I take it that in this verse it has to do with his relationship to us. Augustine's subtle reasoning, according to which *today* means in eternity or perpetuity, is frivolous. Of course, Christ is the eternal Son of God, because he is the wisdom of God begotten before time. But this has nothing to do with our verse, which expresses the truth that men know Christ as the Son of God because the Father has revealed him as his Son. Similarly, the *declaration* mentioned by Paul in Rom. 1:4, was, so to speak, a kind of outward begetting which the secret and inward begetting which went before, was beyond human knowledge; it was above our understanding, until God gave us visible evidence of it. . . . Now, at the beginning of the psalm, he is put at God's right hand; which means, as I have said, that he is given a position second only to the Father. What we have here is a metaphor which signifies that Christ is the Father's agent and his head ambassador who exercises his power, so that the Father reigns by his hand. No angel was ever honored in this way. Christ therefore is exalted far above the host of angels." Calvin, *Commentaries,* in *The Library of Christian Classics,* ed. and trans. Joseph Haroutunian and Louise Smith (Philadelphia, 1958), pp. 178–179.

separate from the later celebration of the Son's future Incarnation. Distinctly, in *Paradise Lost,* the occasion of the Son's coronation also becomes the occasion that sparks Satan's envy. But, again, one must remember that Milton is citing *an* occasion of the celebration of the Son's kingship as *the* occasion for Satan's revolt is perfectly orthodox in terms of seventeenth-century Protestant theology. Theologians had agreed, as we have seen, that Satan opposed the Son from the beginning; they further agreed that if this opposition was founded on a personal antagonism, it was provoked to open action by the announcement of "a" kingdom that the Son had or was to have. Milton differs again only in that in *Paradise Lost* he is specific about which kingdom Satan envied and *at which time* he envied it.

Yet one must mark in *Paradise Lost* what care Milton takes to make Satan's envy of the Son, and thus his revolt, solely and completely a heavenly matter. Although to the reader Milton clearly forecasts the future opposition of the Son and Satan, never does he make Satan aware (while in Heaven) that his "rival" for heavenly power is predicted to thwart his ambition for kingdom elsewhere. Satan is witness only to the Son's being named as heavenly king, not to his appointment as earthly Savior; moreover, he becomes envious of God's gifts to Adam only after he has lost the favors of Heaven. And never in *Paradise Lost* does Satan see the Son as the means for future favors to be bestowed on Adam. Milton's emphatic denial that envy of the Son's coming Incarnation in any way influenced Satan either in his initial revolt or in his attempt against Adam is all the more remarkable in that Protestant theologians so frequently speculated that it had. We may take it then, I believe, that in depicting Satan's envy in books 5 and 6 Milton was determined that it be directed to the present, to Heaven's affairs alone, and to the Son's person as heavenly king.

As a result, Satan's envy in *Paradise Lost* is connected intimately with his feeling concerning the Son as a manifestation of God. It is an issue instinct with intense personal emotion. Envy and pride assuredly are both "spiritual" sins, but they are meant to be, as Milton implies, sharply differentiated. Pride arises when a creature values his own self-will above the will of his Creator; envy arises when one creature willfully resents the person or the accomplishments of another. Of course, Milton shows that Satan's pride and his envy are interinvolved (pride makes Satan reject the envied Messiah), but basically the two impulses are derived from different sources.

If we cannot assert with full persuasion that without the Son there would have been no envy (Satan might have found another to envy), we can say that envy as we know it takes its quality from the fact that is *is* directed against the Son. When the Son at last enters the war at the end of book 6, he states emphatically that even from the beginning Satan and his rebels have been arrayed against him personally: "mee they have despis'd, / Yet envied" (6.812–813). Therefore, to understand this reaction we must attempt to assess what it is in the Son that has caused this dual reaction of hate and envy. Protestant theologians had merely attested the presence of personal antagonism; they had not explored its cause. Milton in his description of the Son's nature implies, I believe, which qualities spurred Satan's resentment. If we as readers remember our own introduction to the Son in book 3, our clear first impression was of the Son's radiance. He was described as being "beyond compare," for in him were expressed visibly the two qualities "Love without end, and without measure Grace" (3.142). Although this description refers to the Son in a later phase of his development, it is worth recalling. Even in book 5 it is the Son, "in bliss imbosom'd," who sits beside the Father and expresses his radiance; it is the Son as he takes on the splendor of the kingly role whom Satan envies. For us, the Son's radiance has much to do with the innate personal quality of his divinity and with the functional quality of love that unites all creatures under his headship. His radiance is the physical manifestation that, as the seventeenth-century preacher would have expressed it, he is suited for the kingly role in being divine and in being the perfect head for all creatures. The Son's kingship then would merely be the normal functioning and expressing of his person or, to modify this definition, the expressing of the dual components of his person: love and grace. Such a kingship seems to ask that the creatures under it respond personally, that they adhere to the Son as they see within him the symbol and means of divine love and care. When Abdiel later elaborates on that function of kingship that is care, he asserts that the Son made all the angels, set them in their degrees, and by virtue of these two acts is become the head to whom they may adhere. Indeed, God himself assigned as the ultimate purpose of the Son's vicegerency the adherence of the angels to one another and their ultimate happiness thereby. The kingship of the Son then comes into existence merely as the function of uniting love.[27]

But the point is that Satan sees the Son's radiance not as love, but as a splendid and enviable quality; he connects the radiance, moreover, not with his person, but with his office. He sees it not as inspiring happiness and union, but as infecting with envy and disunion. Satan thus begins, I believe, with a rejection of the Son's person and with it the refusal to adhere to anyone in love. Love is the Son's dominant characteristic, and it is to this that Satan must first react—must either embrace or deny. That Satan denies the love in the Son is symptomatic of all that follows, indeed of his very repeated avoidance of creaturely communion, manifest most strikingly, perhaps, in his refusal to regard Adam and Eve as anything other than means to his revenge (see 4.358–

27. Throughout his sermons Peter Sterry describes the love and the loveliness of person by which the Son draws all to himself in a unity of spirit. Because his person is synonymous with the principle of love, the Son is the natural habitation for angels and man. "Propriety begets Love; for both Love and Propriety have their life and root in Unity. There is nothing so much thine own, as God, as Christ, as the Spirit" (*Rise, Race, and Royalty of the Kingdom of God,* p. 199). All things are naturally drawn to Christ who, in making them impressed them with his pattern and so draws them by his beauty. Sin, as Sterry defines it, is the state of being blind to the beauty of Christ (see p. 213, also *Teachings of Christ in the Soule,* pp. 27, 39). Milton appears to share many of Sterry's views, for he shows clearly in book 5 that Satan's sin is a result of his spiritual blindness to the Son and his beauty.

392). It is the very basic nature of his sin, and secondary only perhaps to that impulse for "separate good" that divided him in pride from his creator God. It may be useless to argue whether envy of the Son caused Satan to reject the love in the Son or whether the refusal to love allowed envy to appear in the first place. But I think it is clear that the envy in Satan is born as he perceives the radiance of love in the Son and desires it for himself.

To put the Son's radiance within reach of his desire, Satan resolves that it is something outside the Son and not inherent in him; that in fact it is a bestowed "part" of his kingship, the result of, not the antecedent to, kingship. Ironically, of course, it is the most personal part of the Son, the part he can "share" only if the creature joins with him in love. Having disdained any notion of "sharing," of accepting the person of the Son, Satan determines to separate "radiance" from the being who first possesses it. Viewing it as ancillary to the Son's kingship, he grasps for the kingship that will make it his. We might say that Satan has formulated his own account of the method to attain kingship. His first premise is that kingship *can* be readily transferred from person to person—that it is not inherent. He denies that the Son's radiance is the grounds by which he deserves his title. No qualifications for kingship are needed, no extraordinary "virtue" of person. Satan argues instead that kingship in Heaven is purely an appointed office In granting it to the Son God has conferred a hereditary, not a deserved, title upon him.[28] If a king has powers, moreover, they are powers that result from his office, not from his person. Satan has created a kind of mystique of kingship; the office alone, he seems to suggest, possesses a kind of magical charm. Thus it is to

28. In book 3 (lines 309–312) God has proclaimed the opposite view: that the Son's exaltation is conferred because of merit rather than birthright. If merit in book 3 is described as what exalts the Son to his future earthly throne, merit also, according to the same principle, must have exalted him to his throne in Heaven. Satan avidly embraces the principle of merit when, as in book 2, he is justifying his own advancement to kingship: "Mee through just right and the fixt Laws of Heav'n / Did first create your Leader" (2.18–19).

be desired for itself and by virtue of title alone will endow its possessor with power and radiance that are high and beautiful and awe-inspiring. Thus Milton has made Satan's resentment of the Son's person inseparable from his desire for his office.

Next Milton will show how, in revolting from God, Satan step by step is attempting to discredit and dissolve Messiah's kingdom and substitute his own. Intimately involved in his sin, as the theologians have suggested, is his refusal to accept the authority of the Son and his seeking to found his own kingdom elsewhere. What Milton will show us, however, is that the selfsame image Satan employs to undermine Messiah's kingdom will be the image by which he will construct and define his own future state. Of course Satan's rationale of kingship is radically different from Messiah's. First of all, he alters the function of kingship; no longer does it "serve" to unify God's creatures by conveying the love and care of God to all. Satan's kind of kingship exists only to transmit the care and service of others to itself. Thus the king is in a way created by the servitude of those under him, who surrender their wills to his authority. He, lonely and isolated, builds his authority and radiance at the expense of those below him and widens the gap between himself and his subjects.

The Satanic "idea" of kingship appears in *Paradise Lost* in two ironically opposed ways: first in Satan's own ambiguous denunciation of Messiah and second in Satan's very dramatic action and stance as leader of the angels and as their yet "untitled" king. Satan from the beginning implies, first to Beelzebub and then to the assembly of angels gathered in the quarters of the North, that Messiah is no more than a figurehead appointed by God to "rule over" them, a presence and a name whose true power is derived from the usurped privilege of his subjects. Satan calls him, true, "our King / The great *Messiah*" (5.690–691), but the very implication of his giving that name is to question its validity. The actions of Messiah, as Satan "represents" them, are ceremonial and pompous, for, says he, Messiah intends "speedily" to pass through their hierarchies "triumphant, and give Laws" (5.693).

When Satan addresses the angels, he emphasizes the distance Messiah has put between himself and his subjects. Having "ingross't" all power to himself and having "eclipst" not only the angelic titles but the angels themselves, he will further exact "Knee-tribute yet unpaid, prostration vile" (5.782). Satan is arguing here that Messiah has both too much power and too little, or that his power, based upon an arbitrarily granted title, is of the sort that may be replaced. Thus indeed his very critique of the kingship of Messiah leads to the positing of another's kingship—his own.

Neither in book 5 nor in book 6 does Satan call himself a king. As the "deposer" of Messiah, he cannot seem to claim a title, when he had denounced Messiah for replacing the "democracy" of Heaven with a monarchy. In fact, Satan's repeated use of the term *Messiah,* the anointed one, may suggest that Satan is sneering at the notion of a royally valid anointment. But the bases of Satan's kingship, a kingship that in Hell he will assume by name as well as action, are being defined in Heaven even as Satan is busily denying the acceptability of Messiah's assuming the same bases for rule. Ironically enough, Satan's kingship is patterned not on the *real* kingship of either Messiah or God, but upon the *misconstructed definition* of kingship by which Satan has denounced Messiah. What Satan denies to Messiah, he assumes to himself. Since Satan has refused to know what Messiah truly is, however, the thing he creates is a distortion of his own envy. Satan's kingdom, indeed, is as much the child of his envy as his daughter Sin is the child of his pride. And in each case the child is at first fair appearing, but inherently monstrous.

Our final task, then, will be to look closely at Satan's kingdom, this "child" of his envy. It has been often remarked in Milton criticism that Satan's "creations" are modeled upon the originals of God, that Satan is an assiduous, if not successful, imitator of the Almighty. Yet, while no one would argue against the general theory of Satanic imitation, it is not entirely satisfying to view Satan's majestic thrones and palaces merely as inadequate duplications. It is not that Satan's kingdom falls short, but that it is inherently different from that of Messiah. Its superficial likenesses serve only to point out the deep irony of dissimilitude. True, as Milton tells us, that royal seat in the North, to which Satan has withdrawn, suggests imitation of the "Mount whereon / *Messiah* was declar'd in sight of Heav'n / The Mountain of the Congregation called" (5.764–766). But does the mount of Satan truly resemble the mount of Messiah in any way other than that both are elevated and both seem bright? The reader recognizes instantly that more closely parallel than the Mount of the Congregation is that raised throne of Pandemonium adorned like Ormus with "*Barbaric* Pearl and Gold." Satan's mount in the North derives its dazzling light from the ornament of diamonds and gold; it lacks the holy irradiating light that pours forth from God's throne. Moreover, Satan sits "rais'd"; he is not like God "Thron'd above all highth" (3.58). The mount thus is in itself symbolic of the finite kingship Satan is putting on, the ornament of a "figurehead" authority that can be transferred from one person to another. Satan is assuming the "magnificence" he supposes attached to office; and, as his compeer Mammon asks, "What can Heav'n show more?" (2.273). Yet it is clear that what Satan here imitates is not what Messiah and his kingdom truly signify, but what Satan "thinks" they signify. Messiah's realm is radiant with light of creative love, not ablaze with artifice; and it is not confined, as is Satan's, to the precincts of the North or closed within Hell's gate but embraces all of creation. Satan in his very first impulse of rebellion, as he shuts out God, the Son, and two-thirds of the angels, has created a kingdom different in kind from Messiah's limitless, timeless realm. No truer contrast exists than that between their defining terms "darkness visible" and "brightness invisible"; for, as a kingdom of darkness cannot be generated directly from a kingdom of light, neither can Satan's throne be derived from true imitation of Messiah's.

Thus the impulse of envy to "duplicate" the quality and thing it envies inevitably results in distortion and ironic transformation.

What Milton may be saying is that the envious mind is incapable of duplicating accurately; what it produces is an image of *its own* diseased longing. (True and dynamic imitation, which we will find in the Son, has little to do with the impulse to duplicate but springs from the desire to complement and serve.) Seeking for radiance, Satan attains magnificent ceremony; seeking for height, he attains an isolation in the depths of Hell that separates him from his subjects; seeking to be a king, he blots out all memory of the former king, so that the name, indeed the very existence, of Messiah or Son is never mentioned by Satan in Hell. Satan becomes exactly what he has falsely denounced Messiah to be, a tyrant whose power depends upon his subjects' renunciation of their right, a figurehead who demands the service of elaborate ceremony and who argues that his title derives from "just right and the fixt Laws of Heav'n" (2.18). The key to Satan's transformation from angel to devil is the metamorphosis by envy, and here is the significance of Milton's elaboration on the motive that Protestant theologians had discerned. Theologians had seen that Satan's ardent pursuit of kingship on earth was a direct result of his passionate refusal of Christ's kingship. Milton extends this view, showing us that the tyrant king of books 1 and 2 is a metamorphosed angel, altered to fit exactly the very terms his envy has created to oppose the Son in Heaven. Here is the first and perhaps cruelest transformation, for as he is made in book 10 to resemble the serpent, the agent of his deed, Satan here, as though changed with Aaron's rod, becomes the icon of his envy.

CHAPTER 3

Satan's Rebels: Political
Intrigue in Heaven

Until now we have been considering Milton's interest in showing how evil originates as a creature molded whole and perfect by
a good God conceives envy, grows proud, and deviates from the
soundness of good into error and evil. But although the growth of
evil in the individual is an important aspect of Raphael's narrative
and is delineated to warn Adam and Eve of the potential dangers
from within when rebellious passions rise and lead a creature to
misunderstanding of his God, this caution against inner evil is not
the whole lesson. For Adam and Eve are not to be self-seducers,
as was Satan. Satan, disguising his identity and his intent, will
swell like a wily political orator of Athens as he seduces the
gullible Eve. Part of what is shown to Adam and Eve in the
narrative of the war in Heaven is Satan's ability to form, to shape,
and to carry through master intrigue and to manipulate all-too-
willing hearers and followers into being his tools for the main
business of that intrigue. The war in Heaven as full-scale revolt
cannot exist without the defection of one-third of the heavenly
host; nor can the ruin of Eden occur without Eve and Adam as
perpetrators of the crime Satan initiates. Only part of Satan's
nature will be understood in seeing him merely as the originator of
evil: his role as manipulator and seducer must be fully recognized
by the human couple he will seek to ruin. Further, in books 5 and
6 the shadow of future conspiracies on earth may be discerned,
for in Raphael's narrative Milton speaks not just to Adam and
Eve, but to readers. The master plot, laid down in Heaven, is

archetype not only for the future plot in Eden, but for all plots. The seducer of angels and man is to become the seducer of all the world.

I

For the sixteenth and seventeenth centuries, Satan was the master of political intrigue and the inventor of all the grim engines of war and policy. He was acknowledged not only as the manipulator of individuals, but also as the controlling force in international politics. As in Heaven he had drawn one-third of the angels to him to challenge the empire of God himself, on earth he held the power of the Roman Catholic church (or so said seventeenth-century Englishmen) in order that through the influence and the military force of its supporter nations he might bring the whole earth under his sway. The danger of Satan was that he seldom acted directly or alone; it was through persuading and beguiling others that he gained overwhelming force. Then, through concealment and plotted surprise, the powers he had gained became even more dangerous to those who would oppose him.

To Englishmen of Milton's time, the influence of Satan in the affairs of nations was unarguable fact. How else could one explain the unscrupulous ambition of Catholic Spain or the unutterable wickedness of Catholic France which had not only suppressed but also massacred its dissenting Protestants? Perhaps the greatest fear of seventeenth- century Englishmen was that one of these nations might succeed through force or guile in destroying their Protestant monarchy and placing "Satan" in the form of a Catholic king upon the throne of England. Thus the Gunpowder Plot of 1605 was to Englishmen an instance when this fear proved all too real. Only at the last moment was the gunpowder discovered, laid in the basement of the House of Lords, to be exploded when the king with all his high officials opened Parliament. The conspiracy continued to be a "live" issue throughout the seventeenth century, celebrated by preachers and laymen alike on its anniversary and called to mind whenever a crisis in politics and

87

religion warranted comparison. It engaged the attention of the young Milton when he was a student at Cambridge and inspired not only five epigrams on the subject of conspiratorial folly but also a 226-line "epic" in which Satan as a character makes his first Miltonic appearance. In the decade after Milton's death the conspiracy was still prominent in the minds of Englishmen; the "Popish Plot" of that era was readily believed and compared with the earlier conspiracy so that booksellers, capitalizing upon this, reissued in 1679 the documents concerning the arraignment and trial of the Gunpowder conspirators.[1] Readers of *Paradise Lost* thus will do well to remember that a "Satanic" conspiracy was an event yearly recalled by seventeenth-century Englishmen and that this event had commanded Milton's interest in some of his earliest literary efforts. Moreover, the November fifth conspiracy possesses in its essential outlines many of the same ingredients that recur in the "Satanic" conspiracy of books 5 and 6 of *Paradise Lost:* it begins in conspiratorial secret, it is directed against a newly anointed king, and it uses gunpowder to surprise and overwhelm those plotted against. Thus it is useful to view Satan's intrigue in the light of a political-religious plot of Milton's century, and for this purpose to examine both Milton's early Gunpowder poems and a few of the sermons composed on this subject (some of which Milton himself may have heard or read).

The Gunpowder sermons were sensational tracts; the preachers dramatized the shocking elements of the plot itself to move their audiences. They attempted to show that Satan, the first conspirator and the fabled inventor of gunpowder, was the logical instigator of the English conspirators and the original framer of this "cruelest and severest of plots." William Barlow in his sermon on November 10, 1605, speaks of the "deuelish feritie" of the plot; Cornelius Burges in 1641 calls the plot a

1. *The Gunpowder Treason: With a discourse of the Manner of Its Discovery; And a Perfect Relation of the Proceedings against those horrid Conspirators; Wherein is Contained their Examinations, Tryals, and Condemnations: Likewise King James' Speech to Both Houses of Parliament on that Occasion;* Now Reprinted (London, 1679).

"Master-peece of Hellish invention." Bishop Andrewes names the conspirators the "*primogeniti Satanae,*" and Bishop Ussher calls them the "incendiaries of the world."[2] Barlow suggests that the planting of the gunpowder beneath the House of Lords was Satan's attempt to create a miniature Hell, fiery and dark at the same time. Darkness and fire become metaphors also for the conspirators' Satanic frame of mind. John Howe, writing years after the plot, poses this as a rhetorical question: "For what darkness, but that of hell, could have so much fire in it? so much of destructive rage and fury?"[3] For Lancelot Andrewes the very darkness in which the conspirators delight will ironically predict their doom. "In darkness they delighted, dark vaults, dark cellars, and darkness fell upon them for it. And when they were out of their dark vault, found themselves in a dark prison."[4]

But the conspirators are like their "father" Satan not only in the darkness of their minds, but also in the boldness of their presumption. Much commentary was made upon their presumption, even by Sir Edward Coke, the prosecutor at their trial, who asserted that only those Satanically driven could have made so bold a use of gunpowder, invented by Satan, but brought into the world by a friar, "one of the Romish rabble." The earl of Northampton, in examining Father Garnet, one of the Jesuit priests involved in the conspiracy, says that the conspirators had become even bolder than Satan, when he worked the fall of one-third of the angels. "The Dragons ambition extended no further, than the sweeping away with his tail of the third part of the Stars in the

2. William Barlow, *The Sermon Preached at Paules Crosse, the tenth day of November, being the next Sunday after the Discoverie of this late Horrible Treason* (London, 1606), n.p. Cornelius Burges, *Another Sermon Preached to the Honorable House of Commons now assembled in Parliament, November the fifth, 1641* (London, 1641), p. 1. Lancelot Andrewes, *Ninety-six Sermons* (Oxford, 1841), 4:293. James Ussher, "A Sermon Preached before the Commons House of Parliament, in St. Margaret's Church, at Westminster, the 18th of February, 1620, First Printed in 1621," in *The Whole Works of the Most Rev. James Ussher, D.D.* (Dublin, 1847), 2:454.

3. John Howe, "A Sermon, Preached on the Fifth of November, 1703," in *The Works of the Rev. John Howe* (New York, 1857), 2:957.

4. Andrewes, *Sermons*, 4:311.

Firmament: But now the plot of him and his Disciples was, to sweep away the Sun, the Moon, and the Stars, both out of the Star-Chamber and Parliament, that no light be given in this Kingdom to the best Labourers."[5] Later sermonists would argue that this was the most frightening aspect of the plot: that the total leadership of the nation, king and Parliament alike, would be "swept away." As Archbishop Ussher said in 1620, the plot "exceeded all measure of cruelty; as involving not the king alone, but also his children and the states of the kingdom, and many thousands of innocent people."[6] Had the plot succeeded, the country would have been left prey to those very assassins who had taken devilish devices into their hands and like the devil had destroyed and overthrown the good.

The sermonists not only make the conspirators the agents of the devil, but make the king the true representative of God. Nowhere is the "divine right" of the king more persuasively argued than in the Gunpowder sermons, and no sermonist is more eloquent in his presentation of the king's case than Lancelot Andrewes in sermons preached in the years 1613 and 1614. Citing the royal psalms of David and the proverbs of Solomon to establish the king's prerogative, Andrewes asserts that kingship is a divine and sacred office and that revolt against a king is not merely the revolt of one man against another, but a revolt against the office ordained by God. In appointing a king to reign, says Andrewes, God has designed that the king rule in God's own place: Prov. 8:15, "By me kings reign."

> To think they can set themselves against Kings, and yet never have to do with God at all. But Kings, we said, are in God; so they must go through Him, before they can come at them; they cannot deal with Kings, but they must begin with God first.[7]

One of the offices of Christ on earth is that of king, argues Andrewes; therefore all kings are mere surrogates for Christ. Ac-

5. Earl of Northampton in *The Gunpowder Treason*, pp. 213–214.
6. Ussher, "Sermon," 2:455.
7. Andrewes, *Sermons*, 4:293.

cordingly, the ideal model for the relationship between God and the king becomes the relationship between God and Christ. As God has conferred wisdom on Christ as the second person of the Trinity, he has given wisdom to the king, and it is by virtue of wisdom, not force, that the king possesses true command. The king thus rules in Christ, and the basis for his authority is that, as Christ was granted by God all the kingdoms of the earth ("We see Him, Revelations [*sic*], the nineteenth chapter, 'with many crowns on His head'"), so the king is granted through Christ the lawful right to his throne.[8] Andrewes is thus implying that when the conspirators attempted to alter the established order of the kingdom they were attacking the king as a symbol of Christ the king. In attempting to assassinate James, the conspirators reveal their devilish bias; any royal conspiracy has its root in Satan's rebellion against the royal authority of Christ.

The Gunpowder conspiracy, like its archetype, was designed to subvert the affairs of God. In response, then, God must direct the outcome. Here the sermonists take the opportunity to explicate the purpose and method of God's providence. Even as Satan has acted indirectly in promoting the conspiracy, so God acts indirectly in defeating it. He has allowed the conspirators great license to construct a plot and carry it almost to completion, to believe, in their prejudice, that they can win this affair against men, to ignore the fact that God has vouchsafed divine protection to a truly anointed king. God has allowed evil to flourish, but only so that he might show unmistakably his sure control over it. God, so Bishop Andrewes asserts, has final mastery. "He that sat in Heaven all this while, and from thence looked down and saw all this doing of the devil and his limbs, in that mercy of His which is over all His works . . . He took the matter into His own hand. And if ever God shewed that He had a hook in Leviathan's nose, that the devil can go no farther than his chain, if ever that there is in Him more power to help than in Satan to hurt, in this He did it."[9] Moreover, says Andrewes, as God controls the outcome, he also

8. Ibid. pp. 282–283.
9. Ibid., p. 213.

controls the sequence of events that leads to it. The conspirators were forced, despite their careful planning, to be the source of their own defeat. One of their number, presumably Francis Tresham, having sent an unsigned letter to warn Lord Monteagle of the danger, inadvertently became the cause of the defeat of the entire well-laid plot when Monteagle made the letter public. So God sent Christ to save by turning the plan of the conspiracy against the conspirators. "Christ came to save us; there be manifest steps of His coming. Apparent first, in that He made them they could not contain their own spirits, but brought them out by their own *Dicimus;* made them take pen and paper and tell it out themselves, and so become the instruments of their own destruction, which is worst of all."[10]

The providence of God has two ends in mind: one to show the wicked their impotence, the other to show the faithful their reward for steadfast and unwavering faith. That God could save his people from disaster when all earthly odds seem against it is the very proof of the existence of providence. God could, as Stephen Marshall asserts, prevent evil from raising its head, but that he sometimes permits it almost uncontrolled sway proves more surely his control over it.

> though it is very true that sometimes the Lord crushes them in the egge, and will not let them break out into Serpents; yet very often (as we say in the Gunpowder treason) there wanted nothing, but to put the match to the powder, and the blow had been given; so God lets the plots and contrivances of the enemies of his Church, go on, untill they make account that there be no way in the world to stop them, or to prevent them; so that if Gods people be delivered, *their soules must escape as a bird out of the snare of the Fowler.*[11]

If God's intervention into human affairs occurs in reality only after God has long regarded and weighed events, the actual moment of his intervention comes suddenly. No one but God, after

10. Ibid., p. 259.

11. Stephen Marshall, *Emmanuel: A Thanksgiving-Sermon Preached to the Honourable House of Commons upon their Solemn day of praising God for the victory obtained by the Parliaments Forces in South-wales, May 17, 1648* (London, 1648), p. 21.

all, was apprised of the danger. His salvation comes like a miraculous flash from above, which destroys the evil but guards the good when, as Isaac Barrow comments: "surprisingly, unexpectedly he striketh in with effectual succor."[12] The discovery of the plot is frequently portrayed as though it were a military victory in which God (or Christ) triumphed over Satan. In a sermon on November 5, 1641, before the House of Commons, Cornelius Burges describes Christ as an invincible warrior arriving in a chariot to assure victory and salvation to England: "this is that day where our God came riding to us in his Chariot of Triumph, and made himselfe *fearfull in prayses,* by *doing wonders* and leaving us no more to doe, but *praise* his Name." In this extended military metaphor, Christ is seen to break "*the arrows of the bow, the shield, the sword, and battell,* whereby he is become *more glorious and excellent than the mountaines of prey.*" This victory over the conspirators becomes an occasion for recalling Christ's victory when he shot "his shaft, out of the bowe of his *Crosse,* that *by death, he destroyed him who had the power of death, that is, the devill; and delivered them, who, through fear of death, were all their life time subject unto bondage.*"[13] As Bishop Andrewes also had commented, God so framed Christ's spirit that as he judges, he also delivers. This, perhaps, is the meaning the conspiracy ultimately has for the sermonists. It seemed at the beginning a great occasion for the devil to strike at God through devastating his people, but through the presence and grace of God in Christ it has become at last an occasion for God to show his mercy and strength and to force the devil to acknowledge in the defeat of his conspirators his own defeat.

2

The young Milton in his Gunpowder poems could hardly have failed to react to the vehemence and passion of the sermons.

12. Isaac Barrow, "Sermon XI—On the Gunpowder-Treason," in *The Works of Dr. Isaac Barrow* (New York, 1830), 1:268.
13. Burges, *Another Sermon,* pp. 1–2, 40.

Milton probably did not have Phineas Fletcher's *The Locusts; or, Apollyonists* (1627) as a literary model, if the traditional date of 1626 is to be accepted for the Gunpowder poems. The influence of the sermons is, I think, unquestionable, not only because Milton must have heard such preachers as Lancelot Andrewes, but also because the prime concerns of Milton's Gunpowder poems are the same as the prime concerns of the preachers. In both epigrams and narrative, Milton makes the devil the principal agent in the plot, and he shows us the darkness and fire of Hell as the conceptual forces in the minds of the conspirators. Gunpowder is repeatedly identified as the infernal or Tartarean fire, the hellish perversion of God's heavenly thunderbolt. Like the Gunpowder sermonists, Milton is strongly antipapal; in the epigrams he makes the pope appear as a Tartarean monster, the beast of the seven hills, who wears the triple crown and menaces all with its ten horns: "Frenduit hoc trina monstrum Latiale corona / Movit et horrificum cornua dena minax" (*In Eandem*, lines 3–4). In the narrative poem, Hell is not merely alluded to, it is visually evoked: the fiery streams of Acheron, the wild tempests, the lurid sulfur, the unspeakable and joyless kingdom. The conspiracy is born in a type of antechamber of Hell, the cave of Murder and Treason, a place forever dark, where unburied bodies and bones lie scattered.

The Satan of the narrative poem has come from Hell to stir up trouble and is contrasted with James, who has come from the north to establish peace and prosperity among the English.[14] Envying the blessings of wealth and peace that the English enjoy and angered at their service of the true God, Satan determines to unsettle matters and win England to his domination. His means,

---

14. James is treated with deference by the young Milton in both *In Quintum Novembris* and the Gunpowder epigrams. If not the Christ figure that he is for Andrewes and other of the sermonists, he is the *pius Jacobus*, the father Aeneas of the English people come to bestow the blessings of union upon them (*In Quintum Novembris*, lines 1–6). Or, as in the second epigram, James is the good king lifted to the stars lately (in old age) without the assistance of the blast of infernal powder (*In Eandem*, lines 5–6).

Milton tells us, are to be treachery and guile, for Satan is a master of silent plot and unseen nets, unparalleled in instigating hatred among loyal friends. Satan is called a cruel tyrant, a Caspian tiger that pursues its prey by night, a monster like Typhoeus, who emits sulfurous signs and grinds adamantine teeth. Clearly, Milton is equipping his Satan in this poem with a conventional Plutonian personality; he is a pagan ''god,'' one to whom the pope does service. Milton has pictured the pope himself as an idolator, and the rites of the Roman church, their processions in the streets, and their chants in the temples as analogous to the rites of Bacchus and his followers. But the pope in this poem, in sharp contrast to the figure in the epigrams, is no monster; he is merely profane and wordly, the ruler of kings, the heir of Hell, the secret adulterer. Satan inspires the pope with a detailed suggestion for the plot: to explode nitrous powder under the halls where the king and nobles will assemble. The pope, from then on, becomes principal actor, summoning, when he awakens, Murder and Treason from their dark cave to urge his agents in England to become tools of the plot. Like the Gunpowder sermonists, Milton makes much of the swift action of God, who, discerning the conspiracy, determines to undo it speedily. Fame is dispatched to make the plot known. God has saved the innocent: youths and maidens and old men, all amazed at the abominable plot and joyous at their salvation. Milton concludes that the wicked have been swiftly punished and the people spared from their outrages.

After examining these early poems of Milton, however, we must ask what Milton as the poet of *Paradise Lost* owes to the Gunpowder tradition and to these youthful exercises of his own besides, of course, general assent to the seventeenth-century notion that Satan as a conspirator was acting in the meanest of his roles, as corrupter of men and society.[15] Assuredly, neither the Satan of the sermons nor even the Satan of Milton's own poems is

15. Macon Cheek, ''Milton's 'In Quintum Novembris': An Epic Foreshadowing,'' *SP* 54 (1957): 172–184, considers the figure of Satan an early study of Milton's later epic character.

the Satan of *Paradise Lost;* assuredly, also, a localized conspiracy against an earthly king cannot pretend to vie in significance with a conspiracy against God that threatens the fate of Heaven and earth. But, though the situations of the conspiracies are different, the attitudes evoked by the name *conspiracy* are not. How Milton and the sermonists react to Satan's architecture of evil in the Gunpowder conspiracy is analogous in manner to how the angels react to the discovery of Satan's fully constructed but secret war.

That Milton had changed his mind about "divine" kingship by the time he wrote *Paradise Lost* need not concern us here. There is no evidence that he had changed his mind about political conspiracy or Guy Fawkes. Whatever attitudes he held toward James's son Charles, he still regarded as heinous such acts as Fawkes attempted against the king and Parliament. In that he was not unlike Puritan preachers such as Stephen Marshall, who could with equanimity deplore in their November fifth sermons Fawkes's attempt against the father at the same time as they urged rebellion against the son. In 1650 or 1660, as in the 1620s, Milton condemned conspiracy and treachery.

What had changed in the intervening years, however, was the artistry of Milton as a poet. Hence there is a great difference between the characterization of Milton's early Satan and his later Satan. The Satan of *Paradise Lost,* as he conspires in either Heaven or Hell, is not monstrous or deformed in appearance; physically and intellectually, the later portrait is more subtle. But in many ways the basic concept of Satan as conspirator is the same. When Satan is introduced by Raphael, he is already characterized by one indispensable mannerism of the conspirator: he moves quietly, unseen by all but God. He is dangerous and undiscoverable, as Andrewes had called his plot. As the master of fraud, he tempts even the heart that might appear sealed against sin; he constructs his plots so silently that the nets laid to entangle remain unseen. So Satan appears as he moves Beelzebub to put his plot into action. Interestingly enough, the manner of the conspirator that Milton outlines in the small epic *In Quintum Novembris* has remained largely unchanged, even if his outward demeanor has changed. Milton's later Satan is only inwardly enraged, whereas his earlier Satan had breathed sighs of Tartarean fire and had also flashed fire from his eyes. Hell is literally, not metaphorically, as one might say of the later Satan, present in his person.

Thus in act, if not in person, the early and the later Satan are strongly parallel. Each chooses to approach the person he will persuade to undertake his conspiracy while that person sleeps, disarmed and susceptible. If the early Satan transfers his influence by means of a dream, the later one is yet more subtle. Waking Beelzebub in book 5, he infuses "Bad influence into th' unwary breast / Of his Associate" (5.695–696). Outwardly his rebuke seems one of a friend, who is hurt that his confidant dissents by sleep instead of waking to share thoughts and counsel. Satan in the Gunpowder poem, if he does not appear as a friend, appears as a confessor, a gray-haired Franciscan friar garbed in a hood and trailing robe; he speaks, moreover, to the pope as a father. As in *Paradise Lost,* the rebuke is first gentle, restrained; but Milton's early Satan quickly becomes imperious. He exhorts that the pride and prestige of the pope have been irreparably damaged by the upstart English who challenge him. He urges the pope to remember the devastation of the Armada and the executions of Catholics under Elizabeth and to avenge these injuries to the name of Rome. But at the same time as he presses for revenge against the English, he maintains that it should come not by open and declared war, but by deception and surprise. The military forces should be dispatched only after the king and his nobles have been conquered, their limbs scattered through the air by the explosion of nitrous powder. And the whole conspiracy should be carried out quietly by use of the faithful followers in England, who shall first disarm the land. In *Paradise Lost* the plans for Satan's war in Heaven follow the same order and principle. Satan, in appealing to Beelzebub, insists that secrecy and quiet be maintained. The legions are to be dislodged at night, the faithful led to obey without being told the reason for their obedience. Motives are to be whispered, the cause suggested, but "ambiguous words and jealousies" cast between "to sound / Or taint integrity" (5.702–704). As in the Gunpowder poem, Satan remains aloof, using his second as a tool and luring his followers on. One significant difference exists. in *In Quintum Novembris* Satan employs the terror of his fallen nature to command respect; in *Paradise Lost* he uses the beauty of his unfallen nature to draw allegiance.

> His count'nance, as the Morning Star that guides
> The starry flock, allur'd them, and with lies
> Drew after him the third part of Heav'n's Host.
>
> [5.708–710]

When Satan in *Paradise Lost* does address his angels, it is with the sense of arrogant irony that the earlier Satan used in his address to the pope. As Milton's early Satan suggested that the pope's title and authority were being undermined by the English, the later Satan suggests that the "magnific titles" the angels once possessed are now merely titular, since Messiah has undermined them and engrossed all power to himself. As Milton's early Satan cited examples showing that Elizabeth's reign had caused the Catholics to be abused and undone, his later Satan warns that the reign of the Messiah will exact "knee-tribute" and "prostration vile." As the early Satan asserts that the prestige of Rome must be restored by force, the later Satan pledges that the angels must reassume their native right, become, as their "imperial titles" promise, the governors once more and not the servants.

The manner in which Milton describes God in *Paradise Lost* also owes something to the Gunpowder tradition. When the Gunpowder sermonists portrayed a God who, sitting in his Heaven, looked down and saw the futile rage of the devil his enemy, it is clear that they had in mind the God of Psalm 2 who oversees the tumult of his adversaries and laughs at the presumption of their plottings. Milton in his November fifth epic echoes Psalm 2 as he presents God in triumph, conquering in word and deed, laughing at his enemies.

> Interea longo flectens curvamine caelos
> Despicit aetherea dominus qui fulgurat arce,
> Vanaque perversae ridet conamina turbae,
> Atque sui causam populi volet ipse tueri.
>
> *[In Quintum Novembris,* lines 166–169]

> Meanwhile the Lord, who turns the heavens in their wide revolution and hurls the lightning from his skyey citadel, laughs at the vain undertakings of the degenerate mob and is willing to take upon himself the defence of his people's cause. [Hughes, *Complete Poems and Major Prose,* p. 20]

Milton's God here is imperious, exalted, and amused. For his people he offers an immediate and sure salvation; for his enemies he offers immediate and utter destruction, rendered with impassive laughter. Thus the ironic attitude for which Milton's God in *Paradise Lost* has been known may be traced back to one of his earliest depictions of the deity, a depiction that may well have been influenced by the Gunpowder sermonists, who stressed God's serene, detached scorn for the conspirators. For the Gunpowder sermonists, for the young Milton, and for the later poet of *Paradise Lost,* it is Psalm 2 that is central to this characterization of God.

Thus it may be valuable to look at Milton's own translation of Psalm 2, probably worked out in 1653 when he was producing metrical versions of the psalms. The psalm is framed by Milton as a denunciation not only of rebellion, but of rebellious conspiracy.[16] His translation of the first part of the psalm reads almost like

---

16. Charles Dahlberg, "*Paradise Lost* V, 603, and Milton's Psalm II," *MLN* 67 (1952): 23–24, has remarked that the parenthesis, "though ye rebell," in Milton's translation of Psalm 2, "shows that as early as 1653 Milton associated the idea of rebellion with the idea of elevation to kingship."

a résumé of Raphael's account in book 5 of *Paradise Lost:* "Princes in their Congregations / Lay deep their plots together through each Land, / Against the Lord and his Messiah dear." Chafing against authority, they plan to "break off . . . by strength of hand / Their bonds" (lines 3–7). The central point in Milton's translation becomes the defense by God of the Messiah's place as king.

> he who in Heaven doth dwell
> Shall laugh, the Lord shall scoff them, then severe
> Speak to them in his wrath, and in his fell
> And fierce ire trouble them; but I, saith hee,
> Anointed have my King [though ye rebel]
> On Sion my holi' hill. A firm decree
> I will declare; the Lord to me hath said,
> Thou art my Son, I have begotten thee
> This day. . . .
>
> [*Psalm II*, lines 8–16]

In *Paradise Lost* Milton is to echo this passage of the psalm in two ways: the latter part becomes the council edict by which God announces Messiah's kingship, and the former becomes part of the Son's speech in which he reacts to the Father's announcement of the imminent uprising.

> Mighty Father, thou thy foes
> Justly hast in derision, and secure
> Laugh'st at thir vain designs and tumults vain. . . .
>
> [5.735–737]

The change here is significant. In the psalm, as Milton translates it, we are merely told directly that God laughs at his enemies. This is also, in effect, how Milton presents the scene of God's laughter in *In Quintum Novembris.* But in *Paradise Lost* it is the Son who tells us that God laughs. The Father has been commenting ironically on the aim of those who suppose they are able to erect a throne equal to God's and engage God's power in battle.

He has implied that the conspirators actually expect that God must defend himself and "this our high place, our Sanctuary, our Hill" against their attack. The Son thus is reacting both to the situation the Father has described and to the ironic tone the Father has adopted in face of the conspirators' presumption. The Father's tone has conveyed to the Son the utter folly of the conspirators. The Son responds by saying that no response but laughter would be truly appropriate to a God who is impervious to attack but who is being plotted against by would-be attackers with the pomp and solemnity of secret ceremony. It is not only "just" for God to laugh, as the Son comments; it is unavoidable. Milton has adapted the laughter of God as it occurs in the psalm to a dramatic situation in which the Son responds to and interprets divine laughter.

The conclusion of Psalm 2, as it appears in Milton's 1653 translation, is also relevant to *Paradise Lost*, for it serves as a prediction of the conquering wrath of the Son.

> them shalt thou bring full low
> With Iron Scepter bruis'd, and them disperse
> . . . .
> ye Kings averse,
> Be taught, ye Judges of the earth; with fear
> Jehovah serve, and let your joy converse
> With trembling; kiss the Son lest he appear
> In anger and ye perish in the way. . . .
> [*Psalm II*, lines 19–20, 22–26]

This part of the psalm was not echoed directly by Milton in his 1626 narrative. It does suggest, however, an aspect of his characterization of God even in this early poem: Milton's God is one of swift action. As the Gunpowder sermonists repeatedly portrayed him, he is swift to dispatch his enemies. He has sent Christ not only to save the innocent, but to judge and destroy the wicked. Such is apparent in the closing lines of the brief "epic." In *Paradise Lost,* divine wrath will be manifest with lightning suddenness when the Son appears in the chariot to drive the rebels out of Heaven. However, these lines of Psalm 2 are used by Milton not to portray the scene of the Son's victory but to predict it. At the end of book 5 Abdiel reminds Satan of the danger of tempting "th' insensed Father, and th'insensed Son" (5.847). The Golden Sceptre the rebels have rejected will become "an Iron Rod to bruise and break / [Their] disobedience" (5.887–888). Again, in echoing the psalm Milton has altered the speaker and the situation. It is through the eyes of the humble angel that we see the awesome power of God's anger awakened at insult to Messiah.

Thus *Paradise Lost* marks a genuine advance of technique over the earlier *In Quintum Novembris* in the employment of biblical material. Whereas in the short epic the psalm was echoed only, as it were, to announce on biblical authority that God laughed at his enemies, in *Paradise Lost* the words of the psalm are woven into the dramatic fabric of the situation and the characters themselves. Not only do we hear God's voice from the throne denouncing his enemies, we also hear the Son responding and Abdiel reinforcing the defense of God in the very face of the rebellious. Yet one factor has remained constant; Milton still characterizes God as a deity who holds his enemies in ironic derision.

3

Irony of a different sort is an ingredient in Milton's early Gunpowder epigrams and in the gunpowder sequences of his later epic. If in *In Quintum Novembris* and book 5 of *Paradise Lost* Milton has shown us a God who can laugh at his enemies, in the Gunpowder epigrams and in book 6 he has shown us conspirators who think they can safely laugh at God. The conspirators in both cases assume that their powerful secret weapon accords them a kind of divine control over the fates of others. Arrogating God's power, they also arrogate his ironic manner: secure, they laugh at their enemies. In both the epigrams and *Paradise Lost* Milton tells us that the conspirators think their gunpowder equal to God's thunderbolt. In an epigram on the inventor of gunpowder, Milton says that the inventor seems in effect to have stolen three-forked lightning from Jove. In *Paradise Lost* Satan's rebels boast that they have "disarm'd / The thunderer of his only created bolt" (6.490–491). With elaborate ceremony they compound the powder from the dark and crude elements of Heaven; but, unlike God, they cannot temper their creation with light; thus it can produce only a sulfurous blast that darkens, not a cleansing flash that will illuminate and control.

I believe Milton owes something to the sermon tradition for his depiction of both the Gunpowder conspirators and Satan's rebels.[17] The sermonists had stressed that the original Gunpowder conspirators were haughty and presumptuous yet petty men. They possessed an almost insane confidence in their plot, hoping through the device of their secretly laid powder to win all power to themselves. The young Milton dramatizes the conspirators' presumptuous blasphemy. The conspirators profess with worldly irony that they act piously in laying gunpowder against the king; with its very blast they will "lift" James to Heaven. Likening their exploit to God's own translation of the saintly Elijah in the chariot of flame, they proclaim that they are sending James to the "high courts" above. Milton denounces the conspirators indi-

---

17. To make a specific link between this political conspiracy in England and the portrayal of the archetypal conspiracy in Heaven is not to deny debts Milton may have had to other writers who describe in more general terms the effect of conspiracy on society. For example, Milton certainly would have known Thucydides' celebrated passage on *stasis (The History of the Peloponnesian War,* 3.82–83). There Thucydides, attempting to make a universal application, sums up the disorders in society and language resulting from conspiracy and civil war. He comments on how the conspirators, having overturned the ordinary restraints of society, are carried away by excess, inventing ingenious devices for attack and exacting cruel revenge upon their opponents. Their perversions extend to language also, for, becoming masters of irony, they change the customary meaning of words to suit their own purposes. Those most skilled in cleverness of phrase and in hiding their true purposes are the most admired. Thucydides here provides the paradigm for political manipulation of language to which Milton, specifically illustrating such in the Gunpowder epigrams and in the cannon scenes in *Paradise Lost,* may very well have looked back.

rectly in the first four epigrams by dramatizing their ironic statements and questioning their purposes with his own irony. He thus uncovers their true nature and the nature of their conspiracy. First he attacks the basic hypocrisy of those involved; the perfidious Fawkes, addressed in the first epigram, he upbraids for his attempt to cover up his evil deed with evil "piety." The church of Rome, named in the fourth epigram, he denounces as having first threatened James with passage *below* to Hell, and then attempted with hellish fire to blast him *above* to Heaven. Hypocrisy, Milton shows, is the cloak of those who would play God. But Milton, even while he exposes the high pretensions of the conspirators and their Roman authority, reveals that they with their Tartarean powder have only hellish impotence rather than heavenly power. Like the purgatorial fire they have threatened James with, their power is delusive, a fable. They do not control heavenly fates, and in fact, as Milton scoffs in the second epigram, the only way they and the falsely profane gods of Rome may reach Heaven is to be blasted there physically by their own explosive powder. It is God alone who truly lifts above and judges below, says Milton, who has sent James to Heaven in his own good time, and who by implication has judged and doomed the conspirators.

These dramatic epigrams are interesting exercises in the use of double irony and prefigure its use in the gunpowder sequences of *Paradise Lost*. Their verbal irony is overlaid with dramatic irony. The Gunpowder conspirators jest ironically that they control the situation; they laugh at lifting James to Heaven when they intend to blast him to Hell. But irony for the conspirators proves to be only a verbal subterfuge. Dramatic irony proves that God, not the conspirators, has control. In a similar way, the rebel angels in *Paradise Lost* think themselves masters of the situation: they have constructed the cannon and loaded it with gunpowder, then concealed it in their midst so that only at the last moment will the spark be applied when the cannon is revealed to deliver its destructive blow. Finally, sure of themselves, they approach the loyal angels and, veiling their words in verbal irony, promise to seek peace and composure, propose to receive their enemies with open breast, and hope that they like the overture and "turn not back perverse." Maliciously, the rebel angels pretend peace while with devious intent they promise to "freely" discharge their part, appointing those "in charge" to touch what they "propound" so that all may hear (6.564–567). Of course the opening they propose is not of a conference, but the opening of the flanks of the army to disclose the cannon; and the discharge is not of free will and amity, but the discharge of the gunpowder.

As was true of the Gunpowder conspirators, Satan and his angels propose one thing while they intend another. Their ironic speech is meant to confuse issues, to veil the truth of the situation. There is no doubt, however, that the angels think they are imitating the manner of God, who also speaks ironically, as they have imitated his thunderbolt in constructing the cannon. By ironic words Satan and his angels would assume a type of divine omniscience; that is, they would be omniscient in knowing their true meaning (that the cannon was about to be unveiled) while the loyal angels would remain ignorant and lowly. By ironic control, their superiority would be proved; they could, like God, laugh at their enemies. But, as the cannon was created in parody of God's manner of creation, so Satanic irony is a parody of divine irony. God, in speaking ironically of his enemies, reveals the truth of their situation; that they are creatures rebelling against the source of their being and thus engaged in a process that is basically foolish and vain. Satan, by contrast, in addressing his enemies ironically, is bent on deception; his ironic words lure the loyal angels into what proves a trap.

The guileful irony, used before the discharge of the cannon, degenerates into mocking irony of the aftermath: Belial, "in like gamesome mood" puns that the "terms" offered were too "hard" for the angels to receive and understand. For Satan the overthrow of the loyal angels is an opportunity to ridicule the posture of their surprise. Secure, he ironically questions what strange vagary moved them, for they "flew off . . . As they would dance, yet for a dance they seem'd / Somewhat extravagant and wild, perhaps / For joy of offer'd peace" (6.614–617). As the angels scoff at their enemies, the entire situation turns into a monstrous joke. The destruction of Heaven that the cannon has wrought is not a light matter. The folly and presumption of one's enemies might be a proper target of laughter, but is it appropriate to hold in derision their "foul dissipation" and "forc't rout"? Nor should the devastation of Heaven provoke laughter,

> Immediate in a flame,
> But soon obscur'd with smoke, all Heav'n appear'd,
> From those deep-throated Engines belcht, whose roar
> Embowell'd with outrageous noise the Air,
> And all her entrails tore, disgorging foul
> Thir devilish glut, chain'd Thunderbolts and Hail
> Of Iron Globes. . . .
>
> [6.584–590]

Milton has clearly shown his readers that gunpowder is not God's second thunderbolt, but a foul and pestilential explosive that dirties the atmosphere of Heaven and destroys its concord. How far from scoffing, from gamesome mood and pleasant vein is God's reaction to this disorder. To him war has let loose "disorder'd rage"; it has wrought "wild work in Heav'n, and dangerous to the main" (6.698). The joke the rebels enjoy is as transitory as it is inappropriate. As was true of the Gunpowder conspirators, their end will come swiftly and suddenly. So the loyal angels cover the cannons with the weight of mountains and render them useless; so the blasphemous glee of the conspirators is checked as they must now seek new weapons, deprived instantaneously of the gunpowder they vaunted equal to the lightning of Heaven. That the divine lightning in the hands of the Son will come to amaze and destroy them is only ironically fit, for dramatic irony belongs to the Lord God.

In these gunpowder scenes, with their clear contemporary associations, Milton effectively reduces the stature of Satan and his

conspiracy in Heaven. The emperor of Hell and would-be conqueror of Heaven is linked (through his invention and use of
gunpowder) in the minds of seventeenth-century readers with
petty political activists like Fawkes, who were moved by the
basest of motives and employed the basest of means. The narrator cuts Satan down to size and exposes his pettiness. In describing Satan's plot and his pretensions, his prideful assurance
and gloating irony, Milton permits Raphael to adopt a tone not
unlike that of the Gunpowder sermonists. He, like the preachers,
assures us that God is in control, that all the machinations of the
devil must come to nothing. The Lord God is superior to any of
the vain plots Satan might invent. Readers of *Paradise Lost* may
in fact apply the very words of the sermonists to the Satanic
conspiracy of books 5 and 6. For, as God suddenly showed his
power and exposed the Gunpowder conspiracy, showed that
''there is in Him more power to help than in Satan to hurt,'' so the
God of *Paradise Lost* sends Christ to save: ''surprisingly, unexpectedly he striketh in with effectual succor.'' The description of
the Son's victory in Heaven is not unlike that of his victory on
earth: ''this is that day where our God came riding to us in his
Chariot of Triumph, and made himselfe *fearfull in prayses*, by
doing wonders and leaving us no more to doe, but *praise* his
Name.'' If the Gunpowder conspiracy differs in degree from that
first conspiracy in the courts of Heaven, it differs little in kind. It
too was politically motivated; it too sought to overcome by violence and fraud; and it inspired emotions in the hearts of
seventeenth-century Englishmen not unlike those that Christians
might feel in response to the first archetypal conspiracy in
Heaven. In depicting Satan as a conspirator and in arming him
with gunpowder, Milton clearly reminds his readers that Satan is
still alive and threatening in the political affairs of their own time.

CHAPTER 4

The Warring Saints
and the Dragon

> And there was war in heaven: Michael and his angels
> fought against the dragon; and the dragon fought and his
> angels, And prevailed not; neither was their place found any
> more in heaven.
>
> [Rev. 12:7–8]

If Milton had found in the seventeenth-century political scene
ready demonstration that the old conspirator, Satan, was still at
work, he also found evidence that Satan's adversaries, the warring angels, were alive and striving. For the Christians of the
seventeenth century, life was a battle upon earth; never had the
description of the militant state of faithful believers seemed more
apt. The powers of darkness of which Paul had spoken in Ephesians threatened to overcome church and state, and to withstand
them Christians felt they must put on the whole armor of God.
Many seventeenth-century Christians believed, moreover, that
the fight in which they were engaged was not merely the everlasting fight Christians must expect to wage so long as they lived
upon earth but the last fight of the warring saints that marked the
final age of the Church.[1] With this regard, the whole book of
Revelation was often taken in the seventeenth century to describe
the crisis in the modern world, and the twelfth chapter, which told
of the war in Heaven between Michael and his angels and the

---

1. Barbara K. Lewalski, "*Samson Agonistes* and the 'Tragedy' of the
Apocalypse," *PMLA* 85 (October 1970): 1052–1054, has commented how widespread was the belief among Protestants that they were living in the last ages of
the Church described in Revelation.

dragon and his angels, was held to have contemporary significance. Thus, if we are to understand fully the significance of Milton's having chosen this passage from Revelation as the scriptural basis for his war in book 6, we must explore the contemporary popular and theological interpretation of the text.[2]

Popular tradition, as we shall see in chapter 5, had long connected the war in Heaven of Revelation 12 with the war of Satan's original expulsion. Yet this was by no means the only or even the prevailing tradition among English Protestants of the Seventeenth century. Calvin, who was extremely conservative in his approach to Revelation, did not connect these verses with Satan's expulsion.[3] Luther, however, feeling that the prophecies of Revelation might be of relevance to the Christian, if interpreted cautiously and conservatively, said the verses referred to the early history of the Church, when the angels of Michael (faithful Christians) struggled against the angels of the dragon (reprobate or pagan men) for control of the Church.[4] Indeed, in so interpreting these verses Luther was following tradition set down by patristic commentators as early as the fourth century A.D. Like Luther, the patristic commentators had regarded the war as allegorical rather than literal, a war *propter coelum*, "on account of Heaven," rather than *in coelo*, "in Heaven." The leader of the warring angels, moreover, was held by most interpreters to be Christ himself, for the Hebrew name *Michael* literally signifies "he who

2. Both Michael Fixler, "The Apocalypse with *Paradise Lost*," in *New Essays on "Paradise Lost*," ed. Thomas Kranidas (Berkeley and Los Angeles: University of California Press, 1969), pp. 131–178, and Austin C. Dobbins, *Milton and the Book of Revelation: The Heavenly Cycle* (University: University of Alabama Press, 1975), argue the importance of Revelation to the whole of *Paradise Lost*.

3. For Calvin only 2 Pet. 2:4 and Jude 6 were authoritative commentaries on the fall of the angels, and these texts, he remarks, are "delivered in a brief and rather obscure manner." He felt that curiosity concerning devils was unprofitable for Christians, and information concerning them was "if not passed over in total silence, yet certainly to be touched on but lightly" (John Calvin, *Institutes of the Christian Religion*, bk. 1, chap 14, trans. John Allen [Philadelphia, 1936], 1:193).

4. Martin Luther, "Preface to the Revelation of Saint John," in *Works* (Philadelphia, 1932), 6:481.

is like God."[5] Some interpreters view Michael as the archangel rather than as Christ (this is Milton's view both in *Paradise Lost* and in *De doctrina Christiana*), and one Renaissance interpreter even designates him as the Holy Spirit.[6]

Some commentators assign a strict chronology for the war. David Pareus, a sixteenth-century biblical exegete, and the Cambridge scholars Joseph Mede and Henry More limit the struggle to the first three hundred years of Christianity, designating Constantine's victory in the fourth century as the victory of Michael. Others, however, see the struggle of Christians described in Revelation as continuing into the modern era.[7] Chris-

5. One of the most detailed descriptions of the war in Heaven occurs in a commentary attributed to Ambrose. Michael is said to be Christ, his battle with the dragon his death on the cross; Michael's angels are those disciples of Christ who follow Christ's example by dying in his name; Michael is victorious over the dragon in casting him out of the hearts of the elect (Ambrose, in *Patrologia Latina* [Paris, 1879], 17:959). Luther interprets the word angel to mean bishop and describes the dissension between the angels of Michael and those of the dragon as the struggle that prevailed during the early years of the Church (Luther, *Works* 6:481–483). The commentary to Rev. 12:7 in the Geneva Bible follows a similar vein: the battle alluded to is the attempt made by Satan upon the church ("Revelation," in *The Bible* [London: Robert Barker, 1599], p. 115.

6. John Napier, *A Plaine Discoverie of the Whole Revelation of Saint Iohn* (London, 1594), p. 164.

7. David Pareus, *In divinam apocalypsin S. Apostoli et Evangelistae Johannis commentarius* (Heidelberg, 1618), p. 561. This work is translated into English: David Pareus, *A Commentary upon the Divine Revelation of the Apostle and Evangelist Iohn*, trans. Elias Arnold (Amsterdam, 1644). While making particular applications to the early history of the Church, Pareus allows that Revelation shadows forth not only the time after this first period and the last ages to come, "but the whole period of the Church" (*Commentary*, pp. 21–22). Joseph Mede, *The Works of the Pious and Profoundly-Learned Joseph Mede* (London, 1672), pp. 194–195; Mede comments: "as the War was long, so the Victory was not gotten all at once but by certain degrees, as it were; beginning with *Constantine Anno* 300, and ending in *Theodosius,* about (as I said) the year 390." Henry More, *Apocalypsis Apocalypseos; or, The Revelation of St. John the Divine Unveiled* (London, 1680). Also see *The Revelation Reveled by Two Apocalyptical Treatises* (London, 1654); Samuel Cradock, *A Brief and Plain Exposition of the Whole Book of the Revelation* (London, 1696), pp. 121–123. Thomas Taylor remarks that the early part of the war took place during the Roman era, but that passive war has continued between the Prince of Darkness and Christ and his people (Thomas Taylor, *Christ's Victory over the Dragon: or Satans Downfall: Shewing the Glorious Conquests of our Saviour for his poore Church, against the greatest Persecutors* [London, 1633], pp. 330–334). John Goodwin, reviewing the interpretations of previous commentators, believes that it is not much material to limit the appli-

tians, who then faced the dragonish forces of the Roman Empire, must now face the metamorphosed dragon of the Roman Catholic church. In the years leading up to the Civil War and indeed until the end of the seventeenth-century, English Protestants, as their commentaries on Revelation attest, identified the dragon of Revelation with the Roman church and saw themselves as the angels of Michael resisting its forces.[8]

Milton's own interpretation of Rev. 12:7–9 in *De doctrina Christiana* is remarkably free of either contemporary or historical reference. Rather than placing the war in a specific temporal frame, he seems intent on defining its atemporal character. He terms it a stalemate, interpreting the phrase "prevailed not" to mean that neither side prevailed against the other: "their respective forces were drawn up in battle array and separated after a fairly even fight."[9] Although Michael and his angels resist the dragon, they do not win final victory over him; that victory belongs, as Milton tells us, more properly to Christ and not the archangel. Thus Milton is exact in defining the type of battle, but pointedly inexact in assigning it time or place or even in determin-

---

cation of Rev. 12 too strictly to the past. Rather he would wish to apply the text to the continuing fight against Christ in the world by "*the Dragon and his Angels,* that is, the Devill and his Instruments, ignorant and blood-thirsty-men" who attempt to extirpate and eject "the Doctrine and the way of his Gospel out of the world, by the torments, slaughter and ruine of those who professed them" (John Goodwin, *Theomachia; or, The Grand Impudence of Men Running the Hazard of Fighting against God* [London, 1644], pp. 13–14).

8. Richard Baxter in his preface to the sermons of Dr. Thomas Manton in 1679 commends these works against Catholicism as "most seasonable to the times." Manton, writing earlier in the century, had composed a series of sermons against popery in which he described the modern battle against the Catholic Church as the ever-renewing battle of the angels of Michael against the angels of the Dragon (Thomas Manton, "Eighteen Sermons... containing the Description, Rise, Growth and Fall of Antichrist," in *Works* [London, 1871], 3:70). This is essentially the same view of Revelation as embodying the contemporary struggle of Protestants against Catholics that John Napier took in 1594 when commenting on the meaning of Revelation 12 (Napier, *Plaine Discoverie*, pp. 156–159). For other illustrations, see Christopher Hill, *Antichrist in Seventeenth-Century England* (London, 1971).

9. John Milton, *Complete Prose Works of John Milton* (New Haven, 1973), 6:347.

ing whether it is real or allegorical. In telling us that it is a war of resistance, however, Milton may be making it a type, perhaps the archetype, for that never-ending struggle against evil in which the church militant is engaged.

Certainly, Christians of the seventeenth century would readily have acceded that life was a battle upon earth. Richard Baxter calls the modern world a battlefield where two armies are arrayed "in continual War": the first is made up of the devil and his angels, the second of Christ and his angels and saints.[10] Christians, proclaims Thomas Taylor, will find themselves "beset with . . . enemies so long as [they] liue . . . [never] safe and free, when [they] haue stood out one skirmish or two, seeing [their] enemies are aliue, & euer renewing the assault."[11] In the 1640s and 1650s, however, the military metaphors of Christianity gained a particular pertinence. Puritan sermonists began to suggest that the "maine battell" of the war was about to be fought in England, the line now drawn between "two potent *Armies, under two Generals, Michael* and the *Dragon.*"[12] Those who looked at "naturall and civil affaires" with a "Spirituall eye," as Peter Sterry was to remark in 1650, might discern God and Satan resisting one another and contending for the body of Christ. "Every *Good,* and *Evill* is *Spirituallized* in the midst of us. The *Devill* comes up from *Hell* with his *Invisible Legions. God* comes downe from *Heaven* with His *Invisible Chariots.* While *Men* fight, *Angels* fight: *Michael* and his *Angels,* with the *Dragon,* and his *Angels.*"[13]

10. Richard Baxter, *The Practical Works of the Late Reverend and Pious Mr. Richard Baxter* (London, 1707), 1:83.

11. Thomas Taylor, *Christs Combate and Conquest; or, The Lyon of the Tribe of Iudah, vanquishing the Roaring Lyon, assaulting him in three most fierce and hellish Temptations* (London, 1618), p. 365.

12. Henry Burton, *For God, and the King: The Summe of Two Sermons Preached on the fifth of November last in St. Matthewes Friday-Streete* (London, 1636), pp. 83–84; Thomas Hill, *The Militant Church Triumphant over the Devil and his Angels* (London, 1643), p. 5.

13. Peter Sterry, *The Comings Forth of Christ in the Power of his Death . . . Public Thanksgiving for the Victories obtained by the Parliaments Forces in Ire-*

For the writers and sermonists of the Parliamentary party, the book of Revelation provided the clearest picture of spiritual warfare. The Puritan divines hurled at the Royalists epithets from Revelation, calling them "the Beast and his party," the brats of Babylon and of Antichrist, devils, the angels of the dragon who were destroying the land, while they took to themselves the names of saints, servants of the Lamb, the oppressed of Sion, and the angels of Michael.[14] The vision of the new Sion was theirs. Curiously enough, the Royalists, rather than contesting with them, abandoned Sion to its self-styled saints;[15] they preferred to cling to the Old Testament promise of David and Solomon, kings anointed and upheld by God, or to attack the revolutionaries as new Luciferists attempting to overthrow the throne of God.[16]

Meanwhile, the Puritans ever more insistently described their war as a holy war; a fight for God and not for self and so a battle inherently different from all others. They grounded their scriptural authority in both the Old Testament and the New. Their battle was like that of the Israelites as they advanced out of Egypt toward the promised land or like that of Sion as it struggled

---

land (London, 1650), p. 40. Jerrard Winstanly, in *Fire in the Bush* (London, 1650), makes a similar observation: "These two powers are *Michaell* and the Dragon, and this battaile is fought in Heaven (that is, in mankinde . . .). And this battaile in our age of the world, growes hotter and sharper then formerly; for we are under the dividing of time, which is the last period of the Beasts raigne" (pp. 11–12).

14. See, for example, Robert Baylie, *Satan, the Leader in Chief to all who resist the reparation of Sion* (London, 1643), n. p.; Stephen Marshall, *Emmanuel* (London, 1648) p. 27; John Goodwin, *Anti-Cavalierisme: or, Truth Pleading, as well the Necessity, as the Lawfulnesse of this present War* (London, 1642), p. 2; Joseph Boden, *An Alarme Beat up in Sion, To War Against Babylon* (London 1644), p. 11.

15. Steven Zwicker, *Dryden's Political Poetry* (Providence, R.I.: Brown University Press, 1972), comments that during the Civil War period, the king's party no longer held relevant "the complex of typological associations that looked back to the Edenic state and forward to the New Jerusalem" (p. 39). The Puritan preachers, on the other hand, saw the New Sion in the not-too-distant future of England (p. 41).

16. See the Royalist tract *The Rebells Catechism, composed in an Easy and Familiar way: To let them see, the Heinousness of their Offence, the weakness of their strongest Subterfuges; and to recal them to their duties both to God and Men* (London, 1643).

against Babylon. When they did not look back to the old Sion, they looked forward to the new and identified themselves with the saints who were to war against the beast, the angels of Michael against the angels of the dragon. Identifying themselves with these scriptural types, also faithful to God and attempting to advance his kingdom, the Puritans interchanged (even within a single sermon) names for the faithful; alternately they were Sion, saints, Israel, angels. Collectively, they associated themselves with the people of God throughout the ages who had borne the arms of God, spiritually or physically.

Of course the different terms called to mind different images and associations. When the preachers appeal to the Commonwealth as Sion, they picture the captive nation, long held under the yoke of an all-powerful, oppressive royal power, Egypt or Babylon. Crying upon Sion, they urge the Commonwealth to liberate itself, as the Israelites had long ago. "Deliver [thyself] O Zion; and if thou canst not be delivered without fighting, fight for thy deliverance" (Francis Cheynell, *Sions Memento and Gods Alarum* [London, 1943], p. 12). They assert (see, for example, William Bridge in *Babylons Downfall* [London, 1641]) that the victory is sure because it will come not from their strength, but from God's determination. God will lead them as he led the Israelites, proclaims Robert Jenison, depicting God as the "commander in chief of all the Armies under heaven," "the Lord of hostes" (*The Return of the Sword* [London, 1648], p. 3). Citing Psalms or Ezekiel, Isaiah or Jeremiah, the preachers invoke the Old Testament God who had destroyed his enemies, who had only to appear in battle for the foe to be scattered and driven away. Taking David's maxim against Goliath or quoting the prophets who describe God mustering his men for battle or pouring forth the weapons of his indignation, they declare that the battle is the Lord's. Stephen Marshall, for example, observes that throughout psalm 68, "you may observe such a glorious presence of God, as made the earth shake, the heavens drop, the hills leap, the mountains moved, the Saints rejoyce and sing, Armies to bee routed, kings and Princes to flee'' (*Gods Master-Piece* [London, 1645], p. 14). He applies the psalm, moreover, to Jesus Christ's rescue of his Church, not only from Egypt or Babylon, ''but especially from Satan, death, and Hell, in the spriritual sense'' (p. 15).

Ultimately, therefore, whenever the preachers allude to Old Testament warfare or to old Israel, breaking its chains and freeing itself, it is not the faithful of Sion but the faithful of the New Jerusalem that they look to. The warring Israelites are but types for the warring saints. It is not the battles of the past, but the battle of the future that most concerns the preachers. Evoking past struggles only served to persuade them of the seriousness of the present moment: the struggle of the warring saints. Increasingly, the Puritans described themselves and their struggle in terms of the saints and the final battle. Whether they truly believed that theirs *was* the last age of the Church, the crisis predicted in ''Heaven,'' or whether they merely adopted the struggles of Revelation as analogues for theirs, we cannot say. Yet, whether they cited the battle in Revelation itself or those battles in the Old Testament that they saw as types for it, the preachers made the final battle of the Church the rallying cry for their battle against Charles and the Royalists.

Milton, as a leading pamphleteer of the era, did not hesitate either to call the Parliamentarians saints or to urge them to assume the power promised them in Revelation to destroy the kings of the earth who had too long oppressed the people with the ''burden of thir injustice, disorder, and irreligion.''[17] The army itself he characterizes as a holy army, not only the bravest, but also ''the most sober and devout.'' The soldiers, he says, are sanctified to Christ and devote themselves to the ''search of truth, in careful reading of sacred Scripture.'' They do not deem it ''more glorious to smite the foe, than to instruct [themselves] and others in the knowledge of heavenly things, or think it more noble to practice warlike rather than evangelical combat.'' They are

17. Milton, ''Eikonoklastes,'' in *Complete Prose Works*, 3:598.

defenders of the law, guardians of justice, and champions of the Church, and as such they know that the proper aim of soldiers is "not to sow and reap warfare, but to cultivate peace and safety for the human race."[18]

In so describing the Parliamentarian army, Milton is perfectly consonant with the Puritan descriptions of his own time. This is an army of "saints," whose function it was to establish God's kingdom upon earth. It is the army that will bring peace to the land and end the devastation of "Satanic war." Yet a reader of *Paradise Lost* will also recognize that this army of saints is related to that army sent forth by God in book 6 of *Paradise Lost* to bring peace to heaven and reestablish Messiah's kingdom. Thus it is entirely appropriate in reading Milton's remarks upon the Parliamentarian army to look both backward and forward— backward to those warring saints described by Puritan sermonists as the type of Christian named in Revelation and forward to Milton's warring angels in *Paradise Lost,* who also struggle long and hard against Satan.

The resemblances between Milton's angels and the warring saints of pamphlet literature are more than incidental. Both are engaged in holy wars, attempting to check a tyrant king's usurpation of Messiah's throne. Both look to the Son of God as their ultimate commander, himself absent from the field, but ever encouraging his soldiers to resist Satanic evil. And, finally, both recognize that Satan's attack upon them as followers of Messiah is indirectly an attack upon Messiah himself, whose authority he would subvert.

For embattled Christians and loyal angels alike the war is paradoxical. Theirs is a struggle they cannot win: none but the Son of God possesses the power to crush Satan. But should they for one moment doubt the value of this struggle, Messiah and his cause would be undermined and they themselves undone. Satan must be resisted by the faithful on earth and in Heaven. While

---

18. Milton, "Second Defence" in *Complete Prose Works,* 4, pt. 1:648–649.

Christ neither needs nor will use their strength to effect the victory itself, it is their support that will make the victory glorious. Christ will not act in isolation. In the truest sense, though he effects his victory singly, he has done so as the leader of a great army that rallies to him. Thomas Taylor affirms this principle: "Though our Lord overcommeth the dragon alone in plaine field, and single combate, Mat. 4. yet it is not for the honour of the Captaine to bee without an army to lead and traine."[19] God's army will not lack numbers. So it is in *Paradise Lost* that the angels assemble spontaneously to support God's and Messiah's cause. Though this army cannot and will not win the victory over Satan (as God foreknows in sending them forth), yet their rallying to the cause and their long-held warfare are no meaningless gestures. Not the smallest meaning of discipleship will be the willing assumption of God's war and thereby the blazoning forth of his glory.

The war, of course, as both angelic participants and saints on earth come to realize, is God's war. The Puritan divines repeatedly tell us that the events and the force of the fight are directed by him. He controls the strength of each warrior, directing it as he pleases, and he regulates the violence produced by battle. He strengthens, as it were, his army's arm and "weakens the other parties." "The battel is the Lords," says John Arrowsmith; God "musters the men," "orders the ammunition," and has "*brought forth the weapons of his indignation.*"[20] Stephen Marshall seems to see God almost bodily present in the action, arising and scattering his foes, permitting for a while the rage of the wicked, then appointing whom he will to conclude the battle according to his will.[21] If indeed, as the sermonists insist, God is so minutely ordering the war, it is futile to imagine that

19. Taylor, *Christ's Victory over the Dragon*, p. 343.
20. John Arrowsmith, *The Covenant-Avenging Sword Brandished: In a Sermon before the Honorable House of Commons* (London, 1643), p. 5.
21. Stephen Marshall, *Gods Master-Piece: A Sermon Tending to manifest Gods glorious appearing in the building up of Zion; Preached to the Right Honourable, the House of Peers . . .* (London, 1645), p. 14.

human beings can resist his purpose. And this is precisely what the sermonists say. Those who resist the army and the leaders appointed by Christ, as Stephen Marshall puts it, are warring against Christ: "it is *Emmanuels* cause that you oppose, it is *Emmanuels* people, that you fight against; it is *Emmanuel* who is the Leader, the Generall of that Army, one that will out-wit you, and out-plot you, and out-fight you, one for whom you are too few, and he alone will be too many for you, for it is against Christ."[22]

Certainly Milton, no less than the Puritan sermonist, sees God firmly in control, ordering the events and regulating the strengths of adversaries. He had ordained precisely three days for the war, and he has matched the angels in numbers and in force so that Satan's crew might wage war with strength undiminished by the corruption of sin. Providentially, he has guarded the empyrean against irreparable damage, and finally he has, when the fighting has grown too violent, dispatched the Son to end the war. Yet though in *Paradise Lost* there is no doubt of God's control over events, there is some doubt of his unqualified approval of this "holy" war. Clearly, the zeal some sermonists express for righteous battle is missing in the voice of Milton's narrator and his God. Indeed, God's succinct comment upon sending forth the Son, "War wearied hath perform'd what War can do" (6.495), seems to express a disaffection rather than an enthusiasm for battle. As an instrument of divine purpose, war seems less than perfect.[23]

22. Stephen Marshall, *Emmanuel: A Thanksgiving-Sermon Preached to the Honourable of Commons upon their Solemn day of praising God for the victory obtained by the Parliaments Forces in South-wales. May 17, 1648.* (London, 1648), p. 7.

23. Milton, while admitting that war is permissible according to Old Testament law, is consistent throughout *Paradise Lost* and other works in repudiating heroic warfare that finds the exercise of arms rewarding in itself (see esp. *PR* 3.387–393). I would not agree with Jackie Di Salvo (" 'The Lord's Battells': *Samson Agonistes* and the Puritan Revolution," *MS,* vol. 4 [1972], 39–62) that the spiritual motivation of the loyal angels lent full justification to their use of arms or that Milton would have been wholly in agreement with the Puritan preachers who "used the battle of God and Satan to urge the 'saints' to arm themselves against the demonic royalist armies" (pp. 49–50).

In withholding enthusiastic divine sanction from war, Milton is not alone. Among the Puritan sermonists, some who seem most strongly to support the Civil War, there is reluctance to applaud war-making, however Christian its purpose. John Arrowsmith, for example, insists that a soldier should be a bringer of peace, not a sower of war. True Christian victory may be won not in the fields of battle but in the "fields of faith, prayer, and new obedience."[24] Stephen Marshall goes so far as to suggest that the real strength of the soldier should be in "the preaching of the word."[25] The kingdom should be founded not upon force but upon the zealous preaching of the gospel.[26] Many preachers felt that, when men took up armed force, they were taking up the instrument of the devil. John Goodwin, translating the work of Jacob Acontius, warns Christians that when they "arm themselves against Satan, with the material sword, they do but insure his victory and triumph." The strength of Christians is in the faith revealed to them by God, and in warring against Satan they must cling to that faith and call "more for light, and less for *fire from Heaven.*" Therefore, instead of reaching for the sword, they should "catch hold," he urges, "to the Word of God."[27] In sermon after sermon the preachers urge that Christians fight Satan and his followers through testifying to the truth of the gospel. This, they exhort, it what it truly means to be a soldier of Christ, and in this way they may perform the duty of each Christian to advance the kingdom. In the final sense, as is expressed in the following sermon by Thomas Hill, victory for the Christian is not military triumph but the triumph of the kingdom, achieved

---

24. Arrowsmith, *Covenant-Avenging Sword*, p. 27.
25. Marshall, *Gods Master-Piece*, p. 14.
26. Stephen Marshall, *A Sacred Record to be made of Gods Mercies to Zion: A Thanksgiving Sermon . . . Being the Day of their Publike Thanksgiving to Almighty God for the Great and Glorious Victory obtained by Parliaments army under the Conduct of Sir Thomas Fairfax in Naseby-field* (London, 1645), pp. 19–21.
27. Jacobus Acontius, *Satans Strategems; or, The Devils Cabinet-Counsel Discovered*, trans. John Goodwin (London, 1648), pp. 54–55, 104–106. Also see John Geree, *The Red Horse; or, The Bloodiness of War* (London, 1648), who regards war as the "madnesse of our times, to be bewailed with teares of bloud" (p. 4).

through the ascendance of the word over the sword. "The *cause* of the true *Church* is a *prevailing cause,* and therefore doubtlesse the Church will be *triumphant.* What is the Churches cause, but the advancement of the *Kingdome* of Christ, which was the great designe of the three Glorious Persons in *Trinity* from eternity, wherein they will not suffer themselves to be disappointed."[28]

In describing the war in Heaven in *Paradise Lost* Milton seems always to keep in mind these principles of faithful soldiership, for how his angels behave as witnesses to the truth and how they strive thereby to advance the kingdom is more important to him than their accomplishments in arms. He had demonstrated in books 1 and 2 that it is Satan and his followers who believe in war as a true gauge for right. Moreover, he had already indicated for us with the short scene at the end of book 4 how we ought to approach the question of force as an instrument for righteousness. There Satan has been discovered in the bower of Adam and Eve by the loyal angels Ithuriel and Zephon, who bring him before Gabriel for questioning. Gabriel and Satan, ancient enemies who have already met in battle, are prepared to demonstrate their prowess at arms. Satan flouts Gabriel's authority, and Gabriel is eager to expel Satan forcibly from Eden and drive him back to Hell. The stage is set for an armed confrontation.

> While thus he spake, th'Angelic Squadron bright
> Turn'd fiery red, sharp'ning in mooned horns
> Thir Phalanx, and began to hem him round
> With ported Spears....
>
> . . . .
>   On th'other side *Satan* alarm'd
> Collecting all his might dilated stood,
> Like *Teneriff* or *Atlas* unremov'd:
> His stature reacht the Sky, and on his Crest
> Sat horror Plum'd....
>
> [4.977–980, 985–989]

Yet at the last moment Gabriel, sure though he is of victory in the

28. Hill, *The Militant Church Triumphant,* p. 6.

duel, denies himself the opportunity to win at armed combat. He defers to God the decision to fight or not to fight as he points out to Satan the golden scales of Heaven "hung forth . . . to prevent such horrid fray" (4.996–997). What is seen in Gabriel is the primacy of faith over force; he eschews any pride in his individual strength: "*Satan*, I know thy strength, and thou know'st mine, / Neither our own but giv'n; what folly then / To boast what Arms can do" (4.1006–1008). While he does not exercise his military expertise, he does achieve another kind of victory. Through his rigorous questioning of Satan, he beats Satan in a battle of wits. Challenging Satan's assertion that he has come to Paradise only "to change / Torment with ease, and soonest recompense / Dole with delight," (4.892–894), Gabriel questions why he appears alone.

> wherefore with thee
> Came not all Hell broke loose? is pain to them
> Less pain, less to be fled, or thou than they
> Less hardy to endure?
>
> [4.917–920]

When Satan proposes that in coming alone, he acts the part of the "faithful Leader," Gabriel challenges that he has contradicted himself,

> To say and straight unsay, pretending first
> Wise to fly pain, professing next the Spy,
> Argues no Leader, but a liar trac't. . . .
>
> [4.947–949]

Not content with having unraveled the toils of Satanic logic, Gabriel presses on to object that the "sacred name of faithfulness" should be profaned by Satan whose very "faithfulness" to his "rebellious crew" has been engaged through dissolution of "allegiance to the acknowledg'd Power supreme" (4.956). Gabriel has conquered by comprehending and analyzing first, then by repulsing evil.[29]

29. See Stanley Fish's discussion of this scene, *Surprised by Sin,* pp. 173–176.

This episode in which Gabriel and his angels confront Satan introduces us to our first group of loyal angels, and we remark that the values they hold are strikingly different from those Satan had inculcated as *natively* angelic. Skilled in the same prowess of arms that Satan boasts, Gabriel and his angels are able to subordinate their individualized strengths to the will to serve the higher purpose of God. While they are undoubtedly committed to the good and fully able to act in its defense, they understand that it is by dynamic will, not by outward act, that their loyalty to God will be demonstrated.

In book 6 the angels are involved in learning just how faith may attain primacy over force. In conduct of arms, despite courage and determination, their achievements are equivocal. Not so, however, is their conduct of the word. From the lowly Abdiel to the majestic Michael, the loyal angels testify for truth and advance the kingdom, and as such they exemplify the Puritan ideal of soldiership. Abdiel is clearly the champion of truth when he attacks the false premises upon which Satan has based his war or when he points out the meaninglessness of Satan's splendid array stripped of the splendor of fealty to the God who first so arrayed him. His truth underlies the folly of Satan's contesting with the Omnipotent, who "out of smallest things could without end / Have rais'd incessant Armies to defeat / Thy folly" (6.137–139). And finally his truth contends with Satan's falsehood to reveal how the so-called liberty that Satan advances is in fact servitude, servitude to the unwise in lieu of service to the worthiest. As he testifies to the truth, Abdiel is also laying down the precepts or touchstones for the kingdom. For, showing the falsehood of Satan's kingdom, he thereby, so to speak, unbuilds it stone by stone at the same time that he builds with his affirmations and faith the kingdom of Messiah. Messiah's kingdom is built, as the sermonists earnestly believed, when the faithful joyously affirm themselves a part of it.

Michael in book 6 is not only a loyal spokesman for truth but also a prophet. It is a mistake to limit his role here to his general-

ship over the angels or to his heroic armed duel with Satan.
Michael is more than the strongest of the angels. As the wielder of
the two-handed sword that inflicts the first wound upon Satan, he
is the wielder of truth as well as justice. He is not the conventional battle victor. Clearly, in characterizing the war in Heaven
as a stalemate rather than a clear-cut victory, Milton has changed
our apprehension of Michael's part in the war. Splendid warrior
though he is, all his resource in arms wins him no more than a
temporary repulse of Satan. Yet we should recognize that, if not
in arms, in the wielding of the word Michael is triumphant. Milton
prefigures in book 6 his later assignment to Michael of the role of
prophet, for Michael before he duels against Satan predicts his
defeat and fall and the purging of Heaven. The mighty sword with
which he is to do battle is emblematic of prophetic power as well
as of invincibility.[30] Michael as prophet sees into the deep tragedy
of evil that threatens the society of Heaven. He understands how
misery is the product of evil for good and bad alike. Yet, as he
predicts, the good have hope that their misery will end with the
restoration of peace to Heaven; for the evil their misery is the true
punishment for their crime. Like the Old Testament seer, he
"judges" the wickedness before him and promises alleviation of
misery to the good. The holy rest of Heaven may not be perma-
nently disturbed. Heaven will heal itself and expel spontaneously
those who have destroyed its peace: "Heav'n the seat of bliss /
Brooks not the works of violence and War" (6.273–274). In the
truest sense, in these passages Michael is looking forward to the
coming of the Son. Like Deutero-Isaiah, he cries forth the kingdom; like John the Baptist, he announces the way of the Lord.

The coming of the Son in the chariot is replete with symbolic
significance. Its assignment to the dawn of the third day of battle,
as critics have pointed out, suggests the Resurrection, Yet its

30. The sword emblematic of judgment and prophecy, as well as military destruction, appears in Rev. 19:15 coming from the mouth of Christ. Geree, *Red
Horse*, p. 6, identifies the great sword as "the sword of the Spirit, the Word of
God." See Pareus, *Commentary*, p. 25. Sterry also calls the word of God the
sword of the spirit (*Spirit Convincing of Sinne*, n.p.).

placement at the conclusion of long-drawn-out battle can have no other significance, as many critics have urged, than to prefigure the Second Coming.[31] Certainly what is being predicted allusively is not just the personal victory that occurred on the cross when, to use the military metaphor sermonists so frequently employed in the seventeenth century, Christ single-handedly defeated Satan and stripped him of the spoils of battle. What is also foretold is the end of the great battle with Satan when the Son will come, not alone, but as in *Paradise Lost* "attended with ten thousand thousand Saints" and with twenty thousand "Chariots of God, half on each hand ... seen" (6.767–770). Coming, he will also rescue an embattled army of saints who have long maintained battle against the armies of iniquity. When in *Paradise Lost* Milton chooses to address the loyal angels as saints and to promise them that they might "this day from Battle rest," he is telling us that the struggle he has described of these loyal "saints" in Heaven looks forward to that of the loyal on earth and that their struggle will end, as this one has, with the coming of Christ.

The coming of Christ in a chariot of victory was a popular image in the sermons of the seventeenth century. Employed not only during the Civil War but also at other times of crisis (after the Gunpowder conspiracy), it symbolized the saving grace that Christ had once brought to man and that he continued to offer. Thus this triumphal coming had a double sense: it looked backward to a promise fulfilled with the Incarnation and forward to a promise yet to be fulfilled with the Second Coming. And the military aspect of the chariot itself suggested that Christ was coming not only to rescue the righteous but to judge the wicked. For

31. William B. Hunter, Jr., "Milton on the Exaltation of the Son: The War in Heaven in *Paradise Lost,*" *ELH* 36 (1969): 215–231, argues that throughout his account of the war Milton wishes the reader to remember the Resurrection of the Son. Joseph Summers says that the coming of the Son in the chariot is an anticipation of the Last Judgment (*The Muse's Method* [Cambridge: Harvard University Press, 1962], p. 135). John Knott also discusses the relevance of the Last Judgment to the Son's appearance (*Milton's Pastoral Vision* [Chicago: University of Chicago Press, 1971], pp. 71–74). Also see William Madsen, *From Shadowy Types to Truth*, p. 111; Lawry, *Shadow of Heaven*, pp. 210–212.

some seventeenth-century writers, Christ's future coming was depicted in the prophecies of Ezekiel, specifically in the vision of the chariot; the vision was thought directly parallel to sequences, for example, in chapter 3 of Revelation, that tell of the Second Coming. William Greenhill in his commentary on Ezekiel (1650) states that the chariot foretells "the double coming of Christ ... that coming of his in mercy, when he took our nature upon him" and his coming in judgment.[32] Or, as Peter Sterry tells us, quoting from Ezekiel in his sermon on the victory of the Parliamentarian army in Ireland, Christ's rescue of the Puritan army on earth predicts his future rescue of the saints on earth, when he will come, as depicted in Ezekiel, and reveal himself in his chariot of power. Sterry has closely followed Ezekiel in describing the parts of the chariot, acting "Joynting by *One Spirit*" to make up "*One Appearance* of the *Glory* of God," and quotes from Samuel and from Psalms 18 and 38 to suggest the divine power in battle.

> *Hee rode upon a Cherub, and did fly, yea Hee did fly upon the Wings of the Wind.* The *Angels,* and the *Elements* have marched, and fought in their Course under the Banner of the Almighty. *Angels* have been the *Horses. Winds* the *Wheels* of the *Chariots* of the *Lord of Hosts.* On these Hee did fly over the Heads of our Enemies. . . . *Then the Earth shook, and the Foundations also of the Hills mooved, and were shaken.* . . . While *God* passeth by among us, in the midst of all His Holy *Angels,* by *Glorious,* and *Active Providences*: His *Angels* lay their Hands upon the Eyes of most men, not suffering them to see the *Glory,* the *Face* of that *Divine Presence.*[33]

For Milton, therefore, the image of the chariot had strong con-

32. William Greenhill, *An Exposition of the Prophet Ezekiel, A.D. 1650,* ed. James Sherman (London, 1839), pp. 232–333. Pareus also points out the likenesses between Ezekiel's chariot and John's vision of the four beasts in Revelation. For him, both are visions of the last age (Pareus, *Commentary,* pp. 90–93).

33. Sterry, *Comings Forth of Christ* pp. 27, 28, 41, 42, 45. Also see Marshall, *Gods Master-Piece,* wherein Marshall interprets psalm 68 both as a prophecy of Parlimentarian victories and a description of "Christs ascending to the right hand of God, to take possession of the rule and government of the Church," having "led all the enemies of the Church, as captives at his chariot wheeles" (p. 14).

temporary associations. It may be, as J. H. Adamson has suggested, that Milton also knew the Jewish mystical tradition in which the chariot of Ezekiel was connected with the restoration to come at the end of the world.[34] But I believe it is more likely that Milton looked at the chariot as his contemporaries did, as a symbol of succor for the present world and of final judgment for the world to come.

In responding, however, to the image of the chariot or to the evocation of the warring saints, Milton is not narrow. His chariot transcends in image and meaning those victory chariots in the Puritan sermons, and his warring saints, however much they resemble in some particulars the warriors of the Commonwealth, are not identical with them. The preachers wrote with the fervent hope that the coming of Christ was imminent and with it the establishment of his kingdom on earth. Milton, writing more likely after 1660, had no such expectations, and his views on the efficacy of "holy war" were more somber.

Accordingly, many of the lessons for the saints in book 6 are grim. The zealous Abdiel must learn, as William Madsen has pointed out, that "his reason did not overcome Satan's might, and the first blow struck against evil did not end the war."[35] The loyal angels, who looked forward to demonstrating their faith through the exercise of strength in heroic battle, learn instead to survive despite defeat and frustration at the hands of an enemy whose wickedness they may despise, but whose cunning and force they cannot discount. Even the powerful Michael finds that God, not he, holds the power for Satan's defeat and accepts humbly, when victory is withheld, the reward of participation. No individual may have final victory. It is a particularly "Christian" lesson that he and the angels learn. They are taught patience by adversity, true faith through repeated disappointment. Their

34. J. H. Adamson, "The War in Heaven: Milton's Version of the Merkabah," *JEGP* 57 (1958): 690–703. Reprinted in Hunter, Patrides, and Adamson, *Bright Essence: Studies in Milton's Theology* (Salt Lake City, 1971).

35. Madsen, *From Shadowy Types to Truth*, p. 112.

faithfulness, not their resourcefulness or energy, is the quality the Son praises: "Faithful hath been your Warfare, and of God / Accepted" (6.803–804). The angels, through their rejection of and resistance to Satanic evil, have revitalized their faith. Though they have always loved the Son and been loyal to him, only after they have maintained alone their struggle against Satan do they come to understand their need for him. Out of that darkness comes their realization that he is savior as well as lord.

Thus the arrival of the Son is a dawn of recognition for the loyal angels.[36] "Far off," we are told, "his coming shone"; the scene brightens with growing luminescence: first distant light, then the flashes of the thousands of oncoming chariots, and finally the splendor of the Son on the wings of Cherub riding "sublime / On the Crystalline Sky, in Sapphire Thron'd" (6.771–772).[37] And now the angels achieve their finest moment, as they "stand still in bright array" and accept with joy the salvation of the Lord. To wait upon the Lord, as Milton affirmed in the sonnet on his blindness, is the highest service possible. Renewed by faith and chastened through trial, the loyal angels are saved from the pollution of evil that Satan has spread through Heaven; by faith they are confirmed in the spiritualizing good that is God; by faith they are prepared to enjoy the kingdom of the Son.

If this parable of the loyal angels is to have meaning (beyond providing an example to Adam that evil has been and therefore

36. Peter Sterry in a sermon in 1648 also describes the Puritan saints awaiting the illuminating sun of Christ. For him "the Heaven of our Religion" had been "darkened with the Clouds of Dispute," all truth had been lost in "Doubt, Uncertainty and Spiritual Death," these things "manifestly declar[ing] not only a Negation, but a Privation of some Great Light." He calls upon the light of Christ to appear. "The Watch-men watch for the Morning, so doth my Soule wait for the Rising of the Lord Jesus upon Her, and upon the whole Earth, He is the Image of the Invincible God; the Light, that is Sowne even in this our Darkness. But He shall breake these Chains of Darkness" (Peter Sterry, *The Teachings of Christ in the Soule* [London, 1648], Epistle Dedicatory, n.p.).

37. Echoes in this passage of 2 Samuel (22:11) and of Psalms 18 and 68, used by Marshall, Sterry, and others in their war sermons, are particularly significant, for both old Sion and new Jerusalem and the erstwhile triumphant Commonwealth are invoked therein.

can be resisted), we must recognize that for Milton and for his seventeenth-century readers the "warring angels" of Revelation symbolized Christians engaged in present struggle against evil. For some readers the warring saints might retain particular significance as those faithful of the Commonwealth now deadlocked by the "Satanic" Royalists of the Restoration. But Milton spoke not just to these but to all Christians. As a spokesman for Christians, he could hardly feel that the world had changed for the better with Charles's return; though the last days of the Church might not yet be upon us, still to evil days we are fallen, and the world, "under her own weight groaning," goes on "to good malignant, to bad men benign" (12.538–539). Thus the coming of the Son in book 6 is important, for it is not just a flashback but a prophetic vision, balancing structurally as well as thematically that final vision of Michael in book 12 when the day "of respiration to the just / And vengeance to the wicked" appears and the Son, "Now amplier known thy Savior and thy Lord, / Last in the Clouds from Heav'n to be reveal'd / In glory of the Father" (12.539–546). As Milton asked his readers to identify with the loyal angels in their struggle against evil, so he permitted them to share with the faithful in Heaven their moment of "unexpected" joy. For the faithful on earth, the day of the Lord has not come, but the vision of the chariot that rescues the saints in Heaven is the promise of that day.

CHAPTER 5

"War in Procinct"

all the Plain
Cover'd with thick embattl'd Squadrons bright,
Chariots and flaming Arms, and fiery Steeds
Reflecting blaze on blaze, first met his view:
War he perceiv'd, war in procinct....

[6.15–19]

The war in Heaven is a real war. Although in it Milton has, as
Dr. Johnson complained, confused matter and spirit, made killing
as we know it impossible, controlled by divine decree the
strengths of contending adversaries, and finally preordained the
outcome of battle, the war we see develop upon the plains of
Heaven was not meant to be an unreal struggle.[1] Though involving supernatural opponents, it was meant to resemble and be the
archetype for human war. Were it not so, Milton would never
have employed recognizable earthly trappings of warfare—
chariots, shields, swords, spears, javelins, cannons—or have
made use of traditions for the conduct of war that were as old as
Homer yet still current in the countless battle epics of the Renaissance, some of which also described this very celestial war of
Satan against God.

The use of the war in Heaven as a subject for poetry is of rather
ancient currency; the first references to Satan raising battle in
Heaven appear in hexaemeral poems of the early Christian
period. The detailed delineation of the warfare, however, does
not occur until the Renaissance. Thus, whereas Milton could look
back to early Judeo-Christian tradition for corroboration that
Satan was expelled from Heaven by a war, he could look no

1. Samuel Johnson, "Milton," in *Lives of English Poets* (London, 1906),
1:133.

129

further than the Renaissance for *detailed* descriptions of that war. Therefore, as we examine the way Milton describes Satan's warfare in book 6, it is important to consider how those poets who had only recently preceded him had described it. For the war in Heaven, though glanced at only obliquely by theologians and little described by early poets, had become my Milton's time one of the most popular subjects for poetry.

I

Both popular and poetical opinion in the Renaissance held that Satan had been expelled from Heaven at the hands of the archangel Michael "after a long and doubtfull skirmish." So Reginald Scot describes the "wonderful conflict" that grew up between "*Michaël* and the good angels on the one side, and *Lucifer* and his freends on the other," which resulted in Michael overthrowing Lucifer and turning "him and his fellowes out of the doores" (*The Discoverie of Witchcraft* [London, 1584], p. 504). The authority to describe Satan's revolt as a war and to link it with the war with Michael depicted in Revelation 12 was given ultimately, though reluctantly, by theological tradition. There was general consent among theologians that as Satan was the father of evil, so was he also the father of war. The apocryphal books of the Bible ascribe the development of war to fallen angels who instructed men in the arts of warfare. Gâdreêl, the angel in the Book of Enoch who had corrupted Eve, also gave "the shield and coat of mail, and the sword for battle, and all the weapons of death to the children of men" (En. 69:6–7). Evil spirits are supreme in the arts of warfare, but will in the end lose that supremacy as several apocryphal books relate (Dan 6:3–5; Zeb. 9:8; Jud. 25:3; Asmp. M. 10:1–3). At the end of the world, as both the books of the Apocrypha and Revelation predict, the demons—Beliar or Satan—will be defeated in battle and their supremacy over warfare ended.[2]

2. Myths concerning spiritual warfare are also found in Babylonian mythology. In the Babylonian epic of creation, Marduk, the son of the supreme god,

Seventeenth-century theologians, following these old traditions, regarded warfare—particularly aggressive or civil
warfare—as demonic in origin. "Sin, Satan, and warre have all
one name," proclaimed the Puritan preacher John Arrowsmith,
describing the "evill" and "miserie" of his own time (*The
Covenant-Avenging Sword*, p. 7). Of civil war, the Anglican
Bishop Hall said that there was "nothing under Heaven more
ghastly and dreadful . . . nothing that so nearly resembles hell."[3]
Those who incite others to aggressive war, the Puritan Richard
Baxter condemned as devilish: "O what Devils are those Coun-
sellers and Incendiaries to Princes and States, who stir [soldiers]
up to unlawful Wars!"[4] And, describing civil disturbances in
1641, Milton wrote with equal horror of the *"Viper of Sedition"*
that had been "breeding to eat through the entrals of our
Peace."[5]

Thus, early and seventeenth-century Christians alike agreed

---

battles in Heaven against the seven-headed Dragon Tiâmat and destroys him.
R. H. Charles cites a German authority, Gunkel (*Schöpfung*, 379 sqq.), who
traces the account in Revelation 12 to this Babylonian source, noting the similarity
between the dragon of Revelation and Tiâmat, who also casts down a third of the
stars in the strife. R. H. Charles, *A Critical and Exegetical Commentary on the
Revelation of St. John* (New York, 1920), 1:311. Also see Stephen Langdon,
"Semitic," in *The Mythology of All Races* (Boston, 1913), 5:296–302; "Revelation of St. John the Divine," in *The Interpreter's Bible* (New York, 1957), 12:456.

In the Zoroastrian accounts, Ahriman, the principle of darkness, storms
Heaven in hopes of displacing Ormazd, the principle of light. See *Encyclopaedia
Britannica* (Cambridge, 1911), vol. 28, s.v. "Zoroaster"; *Interpreter's Bible*,
12:456–457; Charles, *Commentary on the Revelation*, 1:324; Hastings, *Encyclo-
pedia of Religion and Ethics* (New York, 1912), vol. 4, s.v. "Demons and Spirits:
Persian."

Charles, *Commentary on Revelation*, 1:323, lists battles in the sky that are
referred to in the Apocrypha: 2 Macc. 5:2; Joseph. B. J. 6:5.3; Sib. Or. 3:796–808.
He also makes mention of the Jewish tradition that Satan was cast down from
Heaven in the beginning of time but still had access to Heaven, not to be cast
down again until the last days.

3. Joseph Hall, "The Balm of Gilead," in *Select Pieces from the Practical and
Devotional Writings* (London, 1846), pp. 47–48.

4. Richard Baxter, *The Practical Works of the Late Reverend and Pious Mr.
Richard Baxter* (London, 1707), 1:758.

5. Milton, "Of Reformation," in *Complete Prose Works* (New Haven: Yale
University Press, 1953), 1:614. Also see "Of War" and "Of Civil War" in Mil-
ton's commonplace book (Ruth Mohl, *John Milton and His Commonplace Book*
[New York, 1969], pp. 261–273).

that Satan was the father of war. But that his authority over war was first established by the armed revolt raised in Heaven was less a matter of agreement. The logical proof text for a war in Heaven seems to be Rev. 12:7–9. The text, however, as we have amply seen in the previous chapter, was connected by both the early patristic writers and the later Protestant ones with Satan's attack upon Christians on earth rather than his rebellion against God in Heaven. In strict theological circles, only a small minority held that it might apply to both. In the seventeenth century, the Protestant exegete David Pareus was one of these. Considering varying interpretations of the twelfth chapter of Revelation, Pareus asserts that it may refer to all three stages of the battle of Satan against God: first, his battle in Heaven against God and the Son, second, his battle against Christ at the time of the Crucifixion, and, lastly, his battle against the members of Christ's body during the three-hundred-year struggle of the Church ending with Constantine's victory.[6] Pareus's very specific discussion of these verses is markedly different from Calvin's silence. For Calvin had opposed both precise interpretation of Revelation and precise inquiry into the manner of Satan's expulsion from Heaven.[7] Yet even from the early Christian period there had been speculation that the war in Heaven described in Revelation 12 might provide information about the nature of the revolt Satan raised against God in the beginning. War, even celestial war, was the most logical form of revolt against a supreme god, as the Greek myths

6. David Pareus, *In divinam apocalypsin S. Apostoli et Evangelistae Johannis commentarius* (Heidelberg, 1618), pp. 560–563.

7. Calvin remarks concerning the fall of Satan: "And what does it concern us to know, respecting devils, either more particulars, or for any purpose? Some persons are displeased that the Scripture does not give us, in various places, a distinct and detailed account of their fall, with its cause, manner, time, and nature. But, these things being nothing to us, it was better for them, if not to be passed over in total silence, yet certainly to be touched on but lightly; because it would ill comport with the dignity of the Holy Spirit to feed curiosity with vain and unprofitable histories; and we perceive it to have been the design of the Lord, to deliver nothing in his sacred oracles which we might not learn to our edification" (John Calvin, *Institutes of the Christian Religion*, bk. 1, chap. 14, trans. John Allen [Philadelphia, 1936], 1:193).

testified in telling of the Titans' revolt against Zeus. The very existence of this myth in the Greek accounts seemed to the early Christian fathers corroboration that Satan and his angels were expelled from Heaven by a war. For figures like the Titans or Phaeton or Ophioneus, who had revolted against Zeus, were taken by the Christian fathers as shadowy types of the original Satan.[8]

Gradually, then, although strict theological opinion held that Rev. 12:7–9 described the struggle of "warfaring" Christians against Satan, popular opinion and some theological opinion began to connect this war with the original war of expulsion. The interpretation of verse 4 of Rev. 12 was influential. The third part of the "stars of Heaven" mentioned in verse 4 of chapter 12 was felt by early fathers to be the "third part of men who believe," men perverted from their faith by Satan. However, theologians as early as Victorinus of Petau and John Cassian and later theologians like Thomas Aquinas believed that the third part of the stars

---

8. Origen, for example, in refuting Celsus's assertion that the story of Satan was only a copy of Greek myth, argues that the Bible, older than Greek writings, is the true authority and Greek myth only the imperfect version of that truth. "Mark now, whether he [Celsus] who charges us with having committed errors of the most impious kind, and with having wandered away from the "true meaning" of the divine enigmas, is not himself clearly in error, from not observing that in the writings of Moses, which are much older not merely than Heraclitus and Phere- cydes, but even than Homer, mention is made of this wicked one, and of his having fallen from heaven. For the serpent—from whom the Ophioneus spoken of by Pherecydes is derived—having become the cause of man's expulsion from the divine Paradise, obscurely shadows forth something similar, having deceived the woman by a promise of divinity and of greater blessings." (Origen, "Origen against Celsus," book 6, ch. 43 in *Ante-Nicene Christian Fathers,* 4:592.)

Davis P. Harding, in *Milton and the Renaissance Ovid* (Urbana, Ill., 1946), pp. 84–89, and in *The Club of Hercules: Studies in the Classical Background of "Paradise Lost"* (Urbana, Ill., 1962), pp. 57–58, has discussed Renaissance views on the "allegorical tradition," which identified the war of the Titans with the war in Heaven. He also calls attention to Merritt Hughes's citation of Walter Raleigh, *History of the World* (1. 6.8) as evidence of the Renaissance notion that "the gentile myths were perversions but also corroborations of the Mosaic records" (*Club of Hercules,* p. 57). See Merritt Y. Hughes, "Milton's Celestial Battle and the Theogonies," in *Studies in Honor of T. W. Baldwin,* ed. Don Cameron Allen (Urbana, Ill., 1958), pp. 246–247. Hughes notes that both Milton and Sandys in the seventeenth century regard "classical myths as fabulous but venerable corrobora- tions of Scripture."

were not fallen men but the angels who first fell with Satan.[9] Following these views, Gregory the Great went so far as to connect the war in Heaven of verses 7–9 with Satan's original war of rebellion, the war in which the archangel Michael expelled him from Heaven, and with the final battle on earth in which he is yet to be overcome.[10]

Although theologians after Gregory continue to resist connecting the war in Revelation 12 with the original war, poets do not. For them, Revelation 12 becomes the authoritative description of Satan's first armed rebellion in Heaven. For one poet-theologian of the twelfth century, Rupert of Deutz, this meant espousing in his prose epic, *De victoria Verbi Dei,* a view that he had denied in his conservative theological treatise on Revelation.[11] For in his epic Rupert makes Revelation 12 the scriptural basis for his description of Satan's war against God. Interpreting Michael not as

---

9. See Victorinus, *Commentary on the Apocalypse,* in *Ante-Nicene Christian Fathers,* 7:355; Cassian, in *Nicene and Post-Nicene Fathers,* 2nd ser., 11:378; Aquinas, *Summa theologica,* (I, 63.8) 3:160–161; also Bandinus, *Sententiarum,* in *Patrologia Latina* (Paris, 1880), 192:1034; Victorinus in the third century feels that Rev. 12:4 can be interpreted in alternate ways: "this may be taken in two ways. For many think that he [the dragon] may be able to seduce the third part of the men who believe. But it should more truly be understood, that of the angels that were subject to him, since he was still a prince when he descended from his estate, he seduced the third part." John Cassian presents only one view: that the third part of the stars are Satan's fallen compatriots. "But Holy Scripture relates that these fell not alone from that summit of their station in bliss, as it tells us that the dragon dragged down together with himself the third part of the stars. One of the Apostles too says still more plainly: 'But the angels who kept not their first estate, but left their own dwelling, He hath reserved in everlasting chains under darkness to the judgment of the great day.'" See Harding, *Club of Hercules,* p. 94. Also see C. A. Patrides, *Milton and the Christian Tradition* (Oxford, 1966), p. 94; Robert H. West, *Milton and the Angels* (Athens: University of Georgia Press, 1955), pp. 48–49.

10. Gregory notes that Satan's first war was provoked because of his pride (he cites Isaiah 14) and that the archangel Michael stood forth as leader of that army who first vanquished Satan and put him out of Heaven. Gregorius Magnus, "XL Homilarum in Evangelia, Lib. II"—homil. 34, *Opera Omnia,* in *Patrologia Latina,* ed. J.-P. Migne (Paris, 1898), 76:1251.

11. R. D. D. Rupertus, *Apocalypsim Joannis Apostoli Commentariorum,* bk. 7, Chap. 12, in *Patrologia Latina,* 169:1047–1055.

the archangel but as the Son, he describes how the Son, the *Verbum Dei*, defeated Satan in battle, wielding his sword of righteousness and testifying against Satanic evil. The warfare is to a large degree metaphoric in Rupert's work, for he tells us that no material arms are used. The armies levied, the swords manipulated are spiritual, for the manifestation of the "Word" alone is force sufficient to defeat the wicked, to whom the fire of righteousness is intolerable.[12]

Rupert's prose epic is an important development in the hexaemeral tradition, begun centuries before, which sought to explain scriptural mysteries through dramatization and commentary. Satan's war of rebellion, little discussed in theological treatises, had come to be one of the suitable subjects for poetry. Its inclusion in the hexaemeral tradition, whose original impulse was to recount and elaborate on the events of the first six days, may at first seem strange. It is true that hexaemera later became works that might include, as did the seventeenth-century Scottish "epic" *Doomes-day,* historical surveys from the beginnings till the Last Judgment. The first hexaemera, however, were more modest in their undertakings and usually were restricted to prose commentary or poetic expatiation on the cycle of terrestrial creation. Neither the Jewish commentator Philo nor the Christian Basil (who set the vogue for hexaemera) nor Basil's imitators, Gregory of Nyssa, Gregory Nazianzen, and Ambrose, include

---

12. R. D. D. Rupertus, "De Victoria Verbi Dei," in *Patrologia Latina,* 169:1232. "Michael namque interpretatur *quis sicut Deus?* Iste et tunc in coelo victor effulsit, et nunc in Ecclesia quae ad coelum tendit. Unde et ipsa coelum dicitur, quia coelestem vitam ducit, eumdem [*sic*] antiquum hostem vincit, mystica Apocalypsis continet Scriptura: 'Et factum est, inquit, praelium magnum in coelo. Michael et angeli ejus pugnabat cum dracone, et draco pugnabat, et angeli ejus (*Apoc.* XII),' etc. Magnus igitur princeps iste est princeps belli divini, Verbum autem Dei belli ejusdem virtus est." Grant McColley ("Milton's Battle in Heaven and Rupert of Saint Heribert," *Speculum* 16 [1941], 230–235) argues that Milton may have known Rupert's work in that he is "strikingly close to the Catholic abbot in a number of episodes connected with Satan's revolt and the battle in Heaven" (p. 230).

accounts of the fall of the angels in their hexaemera.[13] The reason
is simply this: that the early fathers, particularly of the Greek
school, felt this event had occurred before the Creation described
in the first chapter of Genesis.[14] They refused to assent to the
notion that the creation of the angels is implied symbolically in
Genesis with the description of first light, and they denied emphatically that the fall of the angels was denoted either in the
separation of the light from the darkness or the separation of the
waters.[15] By the time of Augustine, however, opinion had shifted
on this matter, and many Nicene fathers were disinclined to say
that there had been a creation before that announced in Genesis
with the phrase, "In the beginning." Therefore, the fall of the
angels became a proper subject to be included in the hexaemera,
for it was felt that the angels had been created during the span of

13. Philo Judaeus did not describe the fall of angels in his hexaemeron, but
elsewhere he connected their fall with the pursuit of women. The evil angels, he
says, were not "acquainted with the daughters of right reason, that is with the
sciences and the virtues," but pursued "the pleasures, which can confer no
genuine beauty" ("On the Giants," in *Works,* trans. C. D. Yonge [London, 1900],
1:333). He anatomizes angels also, saying that they hover in the air, were created
in the air itself, and exist on high near the ethereal region (1:331). Also see Harry
A. Wolfson, *Philo: Foundations of Religious Philosophy in Judaism, Christianity,
and Islam* (Cambridge: Harvard University Press, 1947), pp. 369–385.

14. Laurence Stapleton ("Milton's Conception of Time in the Christian Doctrine," *HTR* 57 [1964]: 9–21) discusses the differing doctrines on the time of the
angelic creation. He notes that when Milton in the argument of book 1 of *Paradise
Lost* contends that the angels were created before the visible universe, he is
perhaps following the opinion of these early fathers. Stapleton remarks also that,
though this view could be found in Spenser and Heywood, it was not the prevailing one for the Renaissance. Thus Milton is again following a less popular tradition. Also see Arnold Williams, "The Motivation of Satan's Rebellion in *Paradise
Lost,*" *SP* 42 (1945): 267. See Grant McColley, *"Paradise Lost": An Account of
Its Growth and Major Origins* (Chicago, 1940), pp. 23–29, for discussion of
theological opinion on the existence of the angels before the Creation.

15. Perhaps the adamancy of the Greek fathers on this point came from their
fear that to identify the evil angels with darkness was to give in to the Manichaean
superstitions of their time. Basil (*Hexaemeron,* in *Nicene and Post-Nicene
Fathers,* 2d ser.) attempts to refute the notion that darkness on the face of the
deep means evil. He argues that "the deep is not a multitide of hostile powers, as
has been imagined; nor 'darkness' an evil sovereign force in enmity with the
good." He urges Christians to reject such opinions as dreams or old wives' tales
(8: 61, 71). Also see Ambrose, *Hexameron, Paradise, and Cain and Abel,* trans.
John J. Savage (New York: Fathers of the Church, 1961), p. 31.

the first six days, most likely with the creation of light, and had
fallen within this same span, probably when the darkness was
separated from the light.[16]

Yet references to Satan and the war of his expulsion, though
very often oblique, do occur in the earliest poetry of the church.
The aim of much Christian poetry was not to present history or
poetry for its own sake, but to praise God and to comment upon
the mystery or magnitude of his powers.[17] Thus, for example, the
figure of Lucifer appears in the *Poemata dogmata* of Gregory
Nazianzen only as illustration that angelic nature is mutable in
contrast to the immutability of God. Gregory comments upon the
irony of Lucifer's straining after the glory of God, only to fall
away ingloriously from the splendor he once possessed to complete darkness. The paradox is presented in a nicely balanced
manner in Greek hexameters, but the characterization proves
more truly theological than dramatic.[18] So too, in *Hamartigenia*,
Prudentius pauses in his commentary upon the first murder to
glance backward at the original beauty of that Satan who insti-

16. Augustine justifies the allegorical reading of Genesis in this way: "To me it
does not seem incongruous with the working of God, if we understand that the
angels were created when the first light was made, and that a separation was made
between the holy and the unclean angels, when, as is said, "God divided the light
from darkness; and God called the light Day, and the darkness He called Night."
For He alone could make this discrimination, who was able also before they fell,
to foreknow that they would fall, and that, being deprived of the light of truth, they
would abide in the darkness of pride" (Augustine, *City of God*, bk. 11, chap. 19, in
Nicene and Post-Nicene Fathers, 1st ser., 2:215).

Frank Egleston Robbins, *The Hexaemeral Literature* (Chicago, 1912), pp. 25,
68–69, notes that it was an apocryphal tradition that the angels were created with
first light. P. E. Dustoor, "Legends of Lucifer in Early English and in Milton,"
Anglia 54 (1930): 213–268, points out that medieval works usually portray the
creation of the angels on the first day, though some follow an alternate Hebrew
tradition that they were created on the fifth day with all other winged creatures.
See pp. 214–219.

17. See F. J. E. Raby, *A History of Christian-Latin Poetry* (Oxford, 1927).
Raby points out that there is no definite trace of Latin Christian poetry before the
middle of the third century, and that the first extant Latin Christian poems we
have are hymns of the fourth century (pp. 3–4).

18. Gregory Nazianzen, *Patrologia Graeca*, ed. J.-P. Migne, 37 (Paris, 1862):
443.

gated evil: "horum de numero quidam pulcherrimus ore." He tells how Satan, growing too confident of his own powers, persuaded some of his fellows that he was self-begotten. Prudentius's intent, however, is not truly to investigate the Satanic character, but to refute the Manichaean heresy that Satan sprang spontaneously out of darkness, uncreated by God.[19] One might expect more from the fifth-century Gallic poet Marius Victor, who after all composed a verse commentary upon Genesis in three books, but Marius's remarks on Satan, the author of evil, are confined to the prefatory hymn to his work. There he contrasts Satan's presumption and ingratitude with the greatness and liberality of God and tells that with his evil allies he was cast from high heaven: "cum scelerum sociis celso deiectus Olympo."[20] There are, however, two things significant in these early poetic descriptions of Satan and his fall. First, they include poetic celebrations of Lucifer's beauty, influenced no doubt by patristic interpretation of Isaiah 14 and Ezekiel 28. Second, they attempt to make Lucifer's expulsion from Heaven vivid. Lucifer is not merely convicted of pride and shut away from the presence of the Almighty; he is *thrown out* (deiectus) from *high Olympus* (celso Olympo). For the Christian poet the *manner* of the expulsion begins to be as interesting as the *matter* had been for the Christian theologians.

The *Carmen de Deo* or *De laudibus Dei* of the fifth-century African poet Dracontius is one of the first poems to describe the war of Satan's expulsion.[21] Dracontius's primary aim in his poem

19. Prudentius, *Hamartigenia*, in *Loeb Classical Library* (Cambridge: Harvard University Press, 1942), 1: 216–217.

20. Claudius Marius Victorius, *Alethia*, in *Corpus Christianorum*, 128 (Turnholti: Typographii Brepols Editores Pontificii, 1960): 127.

21. For commentary upon Dracontius see E. S. Ducket, *Latin Writers of the Fifth Century* (New York, 1930); Sister M. St. Margaret, *Dracontii Satisfactio* (Philadelphia, 1936); James F. Irwin, *Liber I, Dracontii De laudibus Dei* (Philadelphia, 1942). The "De Laudibus Dei" was known to the Middle Ages and Renaissance in an incomplete form; the complete poem was discovered and printed by Faustinus Arevalo in 1791. (See Irwin, p. 17: Sister St. Margaret, pp. 17–21) Milton thus could only have known book 1, lines 118–754, of the *De laudibus*, which was regarded as an independent whole under the title *Hexaemeron*. (See Duckett, pp. 90–92.)

is to praise the wonders of God's love, manifest in his creation, and the power of his grace, manifest in Christ. Only incidentally does he mention the fall of Satan and then not in the first book, which celebrates the six days of creation, but in the second, where he is elaborating on the wickedness of man in order to render thanks to God for his mercy.[22] In the course of indicting man for his crimes, he harshly says that man must not attempt to excuse his own misdoings by citing the sins of the angels. The crime of the angels is none of our concern. Yet even while Dracontius urges that we not involve ourselves with the particulars of angelic iniquity, he provides us with a poetic picture of that race of angels, which the kingdom of Heaven held ("quod purior aer, / Et super astra polus, vel coeli regna tenebant"). Without hesitation, moreover, he recounts their fall, using the text from twelfth chapter of Revelation as the basis for his narration.

> Sideris innumeri cecidit pars tertia coelo,
> Cum duce pulsa suo; superum vindicta coercet
> Agmina coelicolum, pereuntia clade perenni.
> Militiae pars tanta poli districta sine usu
> Debuerat nostros ultro compe cere [compescere] mores:
> Et tamen in nobis nullus timor exstitit unquam.

> A third part of the innumerable stars fell from Heaven,
> Smitten along with their leader; the supernal retribution pressed
>> hard
> The battle-lines of the Heaven-dwellers, wasting with
>> ever-constant disaster.
> So great a part of their troops, excluded from the joy of Heaven,

22. Dracontius is hyperbolic in his praise of God and his denunciation of man. Notice the catalog of compliments for the Almighty:

> Omnipotens aeterne Deus, spes unica mundi,
> Inventor, genitor, nutritor, rector, amator
> Cunctorum, quae mundus habet, quae celsa polorum,
> Quae coeli secreta tegunt....

and the contrasting deprecation of man:

> Est homo grande malum, legis trangressor, et audax,
> Criminis inventor, scelerumque repertor, et auctor,
> Immemor auctoris, mortis dux....

Dracontius, *Carmen de Deo*, in *Patrologia Latina*, 60 (Paris, 1862): 769, 770, 799.

> Should have held in check our morals with full assent.
> Nonetheless, no fear ever arose in us.[23]

Of far more interest than that verbal echo of Rev. 12:4 (the reference to the fall of the third part of the stars in Heaven) is the unabashed use of Rev. 12:7–9 and its military images. Satan is the *leader* of the *armies* of the gods, defeated as upon a battleground and brought to everlasting destruction. After a long passage in which he denies that the details of Satan's sin and punishment are in any way relevant to human knowledge, Dracontius goes on to draw one rather important parallel. God in his mercy sent Christ from Heaven to destroy the acts of the serpent, to be victorious over him through his own strength and by the power of the standard of the cross. This, at first glance, seems clearly an allusion to the triumph of Christ through his sacrificial death; Dracontius seems to be reassuring mankind of ultimate salvation from the wiles of the rebel angel whose history he has referred to. But Dracontius's passage identifies Christ not only as the victor through the cross but as the power who threw down the enemy cohorts from the high palace of heaven.

> pietas tamen alma Parentis
> Indulgere volvens cito, quam punire parata,
> Misit ab arce pium coeli per sidera Christum,
> Qui virtute sua serpentis frangeret artes,
> Per vexilla crucis hostis populando cohortes,
> Praecipiti jactu quas celsa palatia coeli
> Exsilio trusere gravi sub perpete culpa.
>
> [Dracontius, p. 810]

> Yet the cherishing love of the Father,
> Pondering to show us mercy and prepared to punish [that spirit],
> Swiftly sent the good Christ through the stars from the citadel of
> Heaven
> To smash valorously the deceits of the serpent,

---

23. Dracontius, *Carmen de Deo*, pp. 808–809. All translations (unless otherwise indicated) are mine. The Latin in this passage (line 5) is corrupt.

Under the standard of the cross, devastating the enemy's cohorts,
Whom with a precipitous thrust, the high imperial ones of Heaven
Drove forth in painful exile and burdened with everlasting guilt.

Thus Dracontius not only has presented Satan as a leader of warring angels, but has also presented Christ as a victorious general who single-handedly wins an impressive victory against him and casts him out of Heaven.[24]

Yet this description of Christ as the commanding general of the war of expulsion is almost singular in its occurrence; only Rupert of Deutz in his twelfth-century prose epic, as we have noted, sees Christ in this capacity. Indeed, actual references to Satan's war of expulsion in the poetry of the Middle Ages are few. After Dracontius, the most direct accounts of battle are to be found, not surprisingly, in the Old English Caedmonian *Genesis A* and *Genesis B. Genesis A,* the more traditional account, follows Isaiah in its rendering of the preliminaries of the war, citing that pride stirred the angel up against God and made him declare that he would possess a throne in the northern part of the kingdom.[25] The military overtones of the passage (the angel's thirst for battle) imply that the crime he planned against God was a rebellion or armed

---

24. Dracontius, p. 810. These passages, since they are from the second book of *Carmen de Deo,* would not have been known by Milton; thus the portraits of angelic warriors and of a triumphing Christ could not have influenced him directly, but only as they influenced the developing hexaemeral tradition.

25. *The Junius Manuscript,* ed. George Philip Krapp (New York: Columbia University Press, 1931).

	Him þær sar gelamp,
æfst and oferhygd,	and þæs engles mod
þe þone unræd ongan	ærest fremman,
wefan and weccean,	þa he worde cwæð,
niþes ofþyrsted,	þæt he on norðdæle
ham and heahsetl	heofena rices
agan wolde.	

[lines 28–34]

"Then sorrow came upon them, envy and insolence and pride of the angel who first began that deed of folly, to plot and hatch it forth, and, thirsting for battle, boasted that in the northern borders of heaven he would stablish a throne and a kingdom" (*The Caedmon Poems,* trans. Charles W. Kennedy [London: Routledge and Sons, 1916], p. 8).

attack. The author refers to the rebel angels as a faithless host, a hostile army whose vaunting and seeking after glory was brought to nothing. He tells that the strife of war was ended and peace reestablished in Heaven when the rebel warriors had been expelled. Thus, though no battle is described, the poet has established the atmosphere of battle: he has portrayed a rebel army who intend to seize power from God by force and has shown how God in retaliation humbled their battle spirits, depriving them of victory and dominion and glory.[26]

Genesis B is more flexible in its treatment of traditional theological background; the defection of the rebel angel (though also patterned on Isaiah) is modified by the heroic mode of Anglo-Saxon poetry. Lucifer speaks as a treacherous vassal who, despite the gifts his lord has bestowed upon him, determines to stir up strife; he rises against his master and boasts that he will no longer serve him. He says he has strong companions who will support him in battle, and he boasts that he is expert in laying down war strategy.[27] Possessing these two requisites for leader-

26.

mæne wið metode,	Ne mihton hygelease,
ac him se mæra	mægyn bryttigan,
bælc forbigde.	mod getwæfde,
besloh synsceaþan	þa he gebolgen wearð,
dome and dugeðe	sigore and gewealde,

[*Junius Manuscript*, lines 51–56]

"The erring spirits, in their sin, might not prevail against the Lord but God, the Mighty, in His wrath, smote their insolence and broke their pride, bereft these impious souls of victory and power and dominion and glory" (Kennedy, *Caedmon Poems*, p. 8).

27.

Bigstandað me strange geneatas,	þa ne willað me æt þam striðe geswican,
hæleþas heardmode.	Hie habbað me to hearran gecorene,
rofe rincas;	mid swilcum mæg man ræd geþencean,
fon mid swilcum folcgesteallan.	Frynd synd hie mine georne,
holde on hyra hygesceaftum.	Ic mæg hyra hearra wesan,
rædan on þis rice.	

[*Junius Manuscript*, lines 284–289]

"Brave comrades stand about me; stout-hearted heroes who will not fail me in the fray. These valiant souls have chosen me their lord. With such peers one may ponder counsel, and gain a following. Devoted are these friends and faithful-hearted; and I may be their lord and rule this realm" (Kennedy, *Cædmon Poems*, p. 16).

ship, he declares himself a lord in battle and thus, according to the Anglo-Saxon war ethic, a future ruler.

The Anglo-Saxon poet has God respond by asserting his right as Lucifer's lord and master. Lucifer's uprising is particularly heinous in that he has abandoned the vassal's prime obligation to support his master in battle and has turned his vassal expertise in arms against the lord who first gave him arms. To the Anglo-Saxon mind, it is likely that Lucifer's warmongering appeared an even greater fault than his pride. Certainly in *Genesis B* it is integral to that sin.

Explicit use of warfare can also be found in poems of the later Middle Ages, specifically the fourteenth-century *Cursor mundi*. When Lucifer in this poem threatens to ascend God's throne, God swiftly retaliates by summoning the armed saint Michael, whom he orders to levy war: "Rais a-gain him for to fight, / Again him gat a batell grim, / Out of þat hei curt kest him."[28] This military maneuver on the part of the Almighty is rather remarkable, for in the English mystery plays of the same period God requires no armed assistance to effect Satan's expulsion from Heaven. In the plays Satan simply falls precipitously at the very moment he attempts to sit upon God's throne.[29] No army has been enlisted by

---

There is considerable scholarly controversy concerning Milton's acquaintance with the Caedmon "Genesis." Mariana Woodhull in her book *The Epic of "Paradise Lost"* (New York, 1907) makes a comparison of *Paradise Lost* and the "Genesis" but feels that Milton need not have been indebted to it. Junius lived in England from 1620 to 1651 and could have known Milton. David Masson believes they were acquainted. Junius published the Caedmon paraphrase in 1655, however, after returning to Holland. A. W. Verity, in his edition of *Paradise Lost* (Cambridge, 1928), vol. 1, notes that there is no record of Milton's having known the Caedmon paraphrase. Hanford points out in *A Milton Handbook* (New York, 1939) that Milton was not well versed in Anglo-Saxon, for in his *History of Britain* (1670) he described "The Battle of Brunanburgh" as quite unintelligible.

28. *Curson mundi,* lines 469–472 (Cotton Ms. Vesp. A 3), ed. Richard Morris (London: Early English Text Society, 1874–1894), 1:34.

29. In the *York Plays* (ed. Lucy Toulmin Smith [Oxford, 1885], p. 4), Lucifer reaches the throne of God and then feels himself falling: "Owe! what I am derworth and defte. —Owe! dewes! all goes downe!" In the *Towneley Plays* (re-ed. George England [London: Early English Text Society, 1897], p. 5), Lucifer's fall is indicated by a change of scene from Heaven to Hell immediately after Lucifer attempts to assume God's seat. Also see *The Chester Plays,* re-ed. Herman Deimling (London: Early English Text, 1893).

Satan to attack God's throne (although he is accompanied by supporting angels), and God requires no military force to repel him. Similarly, in Jacob Ruff's biblical drama *Adam und Heva* (1550), Lucifer is merely thrown out of Heaven by a group of angels headed by Michael.[30] No arms are referred to or required. Token military action does seem to occur, however, in the French mystery *Le mystère de la passion.* God appoints Michael to chase the disobedient angels from Heaven:

> Michel, mon vaillant champion,
> chasse ces dragons venimeux
> par puissance ou puis ténébreux;
> Il est appointé par sentence.[31]

Thereupon Michael steps forward, declares himself supreme in Heaven, and commands Lucifer to leave.

The Renaissance poems and plays that describe the war in Heaven are for the most part more explicit than their medieval precursors. War is not only alluded to, it is delineated in detail. Undoubtedly many Renaissance writers are merely developing those hints of warfare inherent in the medieval poems. Others, however, seem to be developing a new tradition. They clearly are influenced by the rediscovery and publication of ancient hexaemera in the fifteenth and sixteenth centuries. As Thibaut de Maisières has pointed out, the reappearance of hexaemera in the Renaissance had great impact.[32] Sixteenth- and seventeenth-century poets began to translate and imitate these ancient poems, sometimes closely, sometimes with considerable latitude. In treating the episode of Lucifer's rebellion, they frequently expanded and elaborated. In the hexaemera of the Renaissance, this

---

30. Jacob Ruff, *Adam und Heva,* ed. Hermann Kottinger, in *Band der Bibliothek der Deutschen National-Literatur* (Quedlinburg and Leipzig, 1848), 26:10 ff.

31. D'Arnoul Greban, "Prologue," lines 403–406, in *Le mystère de la passion,* ed. Gaston Paris and Gaston Raynaud (Paris, 1878), p. 8.

32. Maury Thibaut de Maisières, *Les poèmes inspirés du début de la genèse à l'époque de la Renaissance* (Louvain: Librairie Universitaire, 1931), pp. 18–19.

episode assumes a more commanding position than it had hitherto held. First of all, the war begins to have a prominent place in the poems dealing with the Creation. It is true that it receives only cursory treatment in Du Bartas's *La sepmaine* or Tasso's *Sette giornate del mondo creato*. But it is a key event in others: Gasparo Murtola, *Della creatione del mondo* (1608); Alonso de Acevedo, *Del creacion del mundo* (1615); and Mollerus, *De creatione et angelorum lapsu carmen* (1596).[33] Second, full-length poems and later dramas are devoted to the subject of angelic warfare. Antonio Alfano's *La battaglia celeste tra Michele e Lucifero* (1568) is one of the first of these, followed by Erasmo di Valvasone's *Angeleida* (1590) and Giovandomenico Peri's five-act *tragicomedia celeste, La guerra angelica* (before 1612).[34] Italian poets seem particularly to have cultivated the subject of celestial battle, if we may call to attest the three works above and the lost poems of Amico Agnifilo, *Il caso di Lucifero* (15?) and Giacinto Verallo, *La guerra degli angeli* (15?).[35] Moreover, there is the celebrated poem of Odorico Valmarana, *Daemonomachiae* (1623), the first section of which recounts the war.

Yet not only Italian, but also Continental and English writers treat the war in Heaven as an important event. Sir William Alexander in *Doomes-day* (1614) and Edmund Spenser in *An Hymne of Heavenly Love* (1596) describe it vividly, if briefly. And Thomas Heywood devotes an entire section of *The Hierarchie of the blessed Angells* (1635) to it. The German writers Naogeorgus

---

33. Gasparo Murtola, *Della creatione del mondo* (Venice, 1608); Alonso de Acevedo, *De la creacion del mundo* (1615) is reprinted in *Biblioteca de autores Españoles*, 29:2 (Madrid, 1864). Fridericus Mollerus, *De creatione et angelorum lapsu carmen* (Leiden: Thomas Basson, 1596).

34. Erasmo di Valvasone, *Angeleida* (Venice, 1590). Giovandomenico Peri, *La guerra angelica* is found in manuscript in the Biblioteca Nazionale, Florence. Kirkconnell dates this work before 1612. Antonio Alfano, *La battaglia celeste tra Michele e Lucifero* (Palermo, 1568), is to be located in the Biblioteca Nazionale, Naples.

35. These works are listed by Watson Kirkconnell, *The Celestial Cycle* (Toronto, 1952).

(Thomas Kirchmeyer) and Friedrich Taubmann have given us "epics" on the war in Heaven, Naogeorgus's a brief work included among his *Satyrae* (bk. 3, no. 1, 1550), and Taubmann's a longer and more ambitious, although unfinished, poem, *Bellum angelicum* (1597), patently imitative of classical epic.[36] And, finally, in the most impressive treatment before Milton, the Dutch poet J. V. Vondel has written a full-length drama, *Lucifer,* on the subject of the archangel's defection and war.[37]

That the war in Heaven was a significant subject for literature is evidenced not only by those poems that make it their central focus, but also by hosts of other poems in which the war is freely alluded to and described. What is important here is that poets refer without hesitation to a very literal warfare. In the Adam plays of the Renaissance, for example, Lucifer, the defeated general, specifically recalls the details of armed combat. In Andreini's *Adamo* (1613) and Salandra's *Adamo caduto* (1647), for example, he tells how he fought fiercely and how Heaven trembled in fear of his army.[38] In Grotius's *Adamus exul* (1601) it is not Lucifer but the chorus that recalls and describes in detail the battle that was waged.[39] Other works of the period also speak of celestial warfare. Tasso's *Gerusalemme liberata* (1581), Vida's *Christiad* (1535), and Phineas Fletcher's *The Locusts; or, Apollyonists* (1627) depict a Lucifer who makes reference to past military exploits in Heaven. As the Satan in *Gerusalemme liberata* instigates resistance to the crusaders, as the Satan in the *Christiad*

36. Naogeorgus's *Satyra*, in *Delitae poetarum Germanorum huius superioresque aevi*, ed. Janus Gruterus, vol. 4 (Frankfurt, 1612). Friedrich Taubmann, *Bellum angelicum*, in *Epulum musaeum* (Leipzig, 1597); MS, Newberry Library, Chicago; William Alexander's *Doomes-day*, though first appearing in Edinburgh, reappeared in a revised edition in London in 1637.

37. J. V. Vondel, *Lucifer* (Amsterdam, 1654). *Lucifer* has been translated from the Dutch by Leonard Charles Van Noppen (New York, 1898) and by Watson Kirkconnell in *Celestial Cycle*.

38. Giambattista Andreini, *L'Adamo* (act 1, scene 3), *Celestial Cycle*, p. 235. Serafino della Salandra, *Adamo caduto* (act 2, scene 1) in *Celestial Cycle*, p. 309.

39. Hugo Grotius, *Adamus exul* (act 1, lines 281–299) in *Celestial Cycle*, p. 114. Kirkconnell reproduces the original Latin of Grotius from the first edition (1601) in the British Museum and renders a translation.

hardens his heart against Christ, or as the Satan of *The Locusts* prepares to inspire the English intriguers with the Gunpowder Plot, each reflects on past glory won on the battlefield of Heaven.[40] Vida in the *Christiad* also offers other perspectives on the war. Like the Renaissance hexaemeral poets, he includes an account of the generation and fall of the angels as part of the Creation sequence narrated by the apostle John. Yet the fullest evocation of the war comes in book 5, where in an extended passage (imitated briefly by the Englishman Robert Clarke in his *Christiad* [1650])[41] the loyal angels, opposing Christ's foes on earth, arm themselves with sword and shield. Vida not only describes in detail their arming, but also takes this opportunity to paint the tableau of that ancient war in which they had previously assumed arms to defend their native Heaven.[42] In other works as well, the war seems to have offered writers the opportunity to create poetic tableaux. In the allegorical drama of Bernardus Mollerus, *Poemandrosatanomachia* (1597), a wholly extraneous account of the war is put into the mouth of the Genius so as to introduce Michael's first appearance upon the scene.[43] Thus the Renaissance, far from avoiding the subject of heavenly warfare, seems to have deliberately cultivated it. War becomes the business of Renaissance poets—their main business.

Theologians and early Christian poets provided ample information about Lucifer's character and motivation; but they gave little or no account of his warring. The Renaissance poets thus found

---

40. Marcus Hieronymus Vida, *Christiados libri sex* (Cremona, 1535), 1:121–235. *The Christiad*, ed. and trans. Gertrude C. Drake and Clarence A. Forbes (Carbondale and Edwardsville: Southern Illinois University Press, 1978), pp. 7–13. Torquato Tasso, *Godfrey of Bulloigne; or, The Recouerie of Ierusalem*, done into English heroicall verse, by Edward Fairefax (London, 1600), book 4, stanzas 9–17, pp. 57–58. Phineas Fletcher, *The Locusts; or, Apollyonists* (Cambridge, 1627), stanzas 22–34, pp. 38–42.

41. Robert Clarke, *Christiados Libri XVII* (London, 1708), bk. 3, lines 1–30. The work was completed in 1650, first published 1670. See Kirkconnell, p. 627.

42. Vida, *Christiados*, bk. 5, lines 525–624; Drake and Forbes, *Christiad*, pp. 217–221.

43. Bernardus Mollerus, *Poemandrosatanomachia* (Westvalus, 1597), p. 70.

that they had to rely on themselves as the principal strategists, so to speak, of an obliquely acknowledged but undescribed war. From the theologians and poets before them they inherited only a few basic facts and traditions. First was the tradition of following Revelation 12 as authority for the names of the opponents (Michael and his angels and the dragon and his angels); the size of the dragon's army (one-third of the stars), and the outcome of the battle (the dragon and his angels did not prevail). Second was the tradition of the lightning fall at the conclusion of battle, provided, of course, from Jesus' testimony in Luke 10:18 that Satan fell like lightning from Heaven. But, beyond these touchstones from the Bible, theologians and earlier poets gave little further information about the battle itself. And there were many questions. How did Lucifer raise his army? In what way did he plan the attack? How did God retaliate? How extensive was the role of Michael and his angels? What form did the battle take? What weapons were used? How, specifically, was Lucifer defeated?

For answers to these questions the poets turned from the Bible to those poems, both ancient and modern, that had most persuasively and skillfully described human and superhuman warfare: the epics of Homer, Hesiod, and Virgil, the mythological poems of late Greek and Latin writers like Nonnos and Claudian, and the chivalric poems of Ariosto, Tasso, and others. Particularly valuable were Homer and Hesiod, whose works were becoming popular in the printed editions of the sixteenth century, in which the Latin translation faced the original Greek. In the *Iliad*, for example, the poets could find leaders assembling an army and setting it in motion against an enemy. There they could learn how to treat a battle scene, focusing first on large-scale action, then moving to the single opponents, first lesser, then major warriors, as they encountered each other in battle. A superhuman warrior like Achilles or Hector could be used as model for a warring Lucifer or Michael. Or the gods of Homeric epic, as they wielded huge weapons and inflicted devastating harm, could serve as models for warring angels. The Renaissance poets first made Lucifer sound like Agamemnon, as he urged his soldiers into battle, or appear like Achilles in a splendidly adorned war chariot, or fight fiercely like Diomedes as he attacked the "gods," or be defeated like Hector overcome by a stronger warrior.

Not all battle scenes that appear Homeric, however, need have Homer as their immediate source. Imitators of Homer abound, from Virgil in his "little" *Iliad* (books 7 through 12 of the *Aeneid*) to Tasso in his battle scenes in *Gerusalemme liberata*. Italian poets quite reasonably may have found Tasso's version of a battle strategy or device more accessible and easier to imitate than its original in Homer or in Virgil. For example, when Valvasone shows Megara stirring up Lucifer's rebels to battle (2.48–61), he may be modeling his scene on the one in *Gerusalemme liberata* (8.72) where Allecto incites the pagans against the Christians rather than on that scene in the *Aeneid* where Allecto similarly incites Turnus (7.415–460).[44] Likewise, writers who describe Michael armed as a Greek god or hero may be thinking not of Homer's description of Ares or Apollo but of Tasso's Michael (7.80–82) wielding his lance and protected by a diamond shield. Ultimately this picture of a God in battle, protecting human warriors as he fights, is Homeric, but the influence of Homer is indirectly rather than directly conveyed.

Hesiod and his imitators Claudian and Nonnos are important for Renaissance poets, but for different reasons. The *Theogony* of Hesiod or the *Gigantomachia* of Claudian could be the model for a cosmic rather than an earthly battle.[45] They included nonhuman

44. A similar scene also occurs in Claudian (*In Rufinum*); see Mason Hammond, "*Concilia Deorum* from Homer through Milton," *Studies in Philology* 30(1933): 1–16.
45. Hughes, "Milton's Celestial Battle and the Theogonies," pp. 237–253. For Milton's debt to Hesiod, also see William Lauder, *An Essay upon Milton's Imitations of the Ancients in His "Paradise Lost"* (London, 1741), p. 36, and Charles G. Osgood, *The Classical Mythology of Milton's English Poems* (New York, 1900), pp. 37–38, 82–83.
Classical accounts of the wars of Zeus with the Titans or giants are rich in descriptive details but sometimes conflicting in narration. According to Apollodorus (*Bibliotheca*, 1.2.1; 1.6.1; 1.6.3), the war of the immortals occupies three

combatants; their warfare ranged throughout the heavens and devastated Heaven and earth. Milton, as Merritt Y. Hughes has documented, turned quite naturally to the Theogonies when he

---

stages. In the first Zeus fights with the Titans, assisted by his brothers and sisters whom he has forced Cronos (Saturn) to disgorge. He is not able to win this war until he calls to his assistance the Cyclopes and the Giants (the Hundred-Handers). The Cyclopes forge thunderbolts for him to use against the Titans, and the Hundred-Handers fight on his side, hurling mountain boulders at the Titans. The war lasts for ten years, at the end of which the Titans fall for nine days to earth, then for nine days into Tartarus, to be imprisoned there. Hesiod's account in *The Theogony* of this first battle is the most famous of the classical "wars in Heaven" and offers the clearest parallels to Milton's war. After this first war, Earth (mother of the Titans) determines to avenge her children, chained in Tartarus, and she gives birth to a second brood of immortals, the Giants, who proceed to attack Zeus. Arming themselves with mountains and other features of the terrain (Earth's own limbs), they attempt the throne of Zeus but are repulsed and destroyed. Claudian's *Gigantomachia* (fourth century A.D.) gives a full account of this battle. Milton's references in book I to the Earth-born brood that warred on Jove seem to allude to this battle. After the defeat of her second brood of children, Earth gives birth to the most terrible monster of all, Typhon (Typhoeus), serpentlike in form, with a voice that bellows like a bull and roars like a lion. Single-handed, Typhon assaults Zeus in a battle that shakes Heaven and earth. Hesiod describes it in the *Theogony* (lines 820–885); so also does the Greek poet Nonnos (fifth century A.D.) in the first two books of his *Dionysiaca*. Those Renaissance accounts of the war in Heaven that tell how Lucifer, transformed into a dragon, fights with Michael depend heavily for descriptive detail on Hesiod and Nonnos (both available to poets in Renaissance editions). Typhon, like the Giants, tears off mountains and huge trees and hurls them at Zeus; Zeus counters with his thunderbolt and finally buries Typhon beneath Etna. Milton refers in book I both to Typhon (1.199) and to Etna (1.233).

Throughout classical literature there are allusions to these various Theogonies. Aeschylus in *Prometheus Bound* refers both to the battle of Zeus and the Titans (lines 201–221) and to the pinioning of Typhon beneath Etna (lines 351–376), the pinioning of Typhon also described by Pindar (Pythian 1.15–26, line numbers to Oxford Classical Texts). Ovid in *Metamorphoses* (1.151–155) and in *Fasti* (5.33–44) describes the assault of Olympus by the Giants, recounting how they piled Pelion on Ossa in order to reach the gods and were hurled thence by Jove's thunderbolt. Conflating the three battles into one, Horace (*Odes* 3. 4.42–80) creates a battle in which impious ungoverned force (the Titans and their allies, the Giants) meets law and true divinity (the Olympian gods) and is thrown down: "vis consili expers mole ruit sua; vim temperatam di quoque provehunt in maius" (lines 65–67). Clearly, Horace's symbolic approach was to have great influence on poets who made Satan and his cohorts ungoverned force warring against lawful divinity. Virgil several times alludes to the wars of the immortals. Like Ovid and Horace, he describes the piling of Pelion on Ossa (*Georgics*, 1.278–283), and he perhaps furnishes Milton with the model for his description of Satan hurled from the heavens. The sons of Earth are hurled down into the abyss by Jove's thunder-

wished to describe the cosmic repercussions of Satan's war.[46] He may have felt authorized to do so in that these cosmic battles of Zeus and the Titans or giants had been "approved," so to speak, by the early Christian fathers as recognizable parallels to the war in Heaven—pagan versions of Christian truth.[47] But in turning to the classical Theogonies, Milton is also doing what Renaissance poets before him had done. The celestial poems of the Renaissance abound with borrowings from Hesiod, Claudian, and other poets of antiquity, who described Zeus's celestial warfare. Renaissance poets quite enthusiastically made Zeus a model for God and the giants and Titans models for the giant angels of celestial epic. Lucifer in *Angeleida* could appear like Briareus, a hundred-armed monster, for Valvasone had asserted in his poem

---

bolt, to writhe there in torment: "fulmine deiecti fundo volvuntur in imo" (*Aeneid*, 6.580–584). Milton, of course, would have known all these references firsthand, but for less erudite poets Natalis Comes, in *Mythologiae* (Venice, 1567), could furnish a useful summary of the Titan-Giant wars, wherein citation of relevant passages in Homer, Callimachus, Virgil, Apollodorus, Hesiod, and others also were to be found (pp. 24–34).

See Harding, *Club of Hercules,* for a discussion of Milton's use of these various classical accounts of the wars of the Titans and the Giants (pp. 57–94). Also see Albert C. Labriola, "The Titans and the Giants: *Paradise Lost* and the Tradition of the Renaissance Ovid," *Milton Quarterly* 12 (March 1978): 9–16.

46. See chapter 5, footnote 8.

47. Jacobus Masenius in *Sarcotis* (London, 1771), bk. 3, p. 142, alludes to the Titans' fall through aspiring pride, connecting it with the fall of Satan and his rebels. Abraham Cowley in *Davideis* (1656) also freely uses the fall of the Titans in a biblical context (*The Complete Works in Verse and Prose of Abraham Cowley,* 2 vols., ed. Alexander Grosart [Edinburgh: Edinburgh University Press, 1881]). Cowley, rather than interpreting the Gigantomachia as the copy of Satan's battle with God, connects it with the human attempt to scale Babel. His description of the war (as wrought on a warrior's shield) verbally looks forward to Milton's description of the Gigantomachia in books 1 and 6.

> Sweating beneath a *Shield's* unruly Weight,
> On which was wrought the *Gods',* and *Giants'* Fight,
> Rare Work! all fill'd with *Terror* and *Delight.*
> Here a vast *Hill* 'gainst thund'ring *Baal* was thrown,
> Trees and *Beasts* on't fell burnt with *Lightning* down.
> One flings a *Mountain,* and its *River* too
> Torn up with 't; that *rains back* on him that threw.
> Some from the *Main* to pluck whole *Islands* try;
> The *Sea* boils round with Flames shot thick from sky.

[3.374–382]

that he would tell the truth of that warfare of Jove and Briareus that Hesiod had falsely recounted.[48] The cosmic upheaval in Heaven could be patterned on the accounts of the devastation of Olympus and earth. The sea could surge and groan; mountains topple or be thrown through the air; the sky could be ablaze with the fire of thunderbolts; the axis of Heaven could be shaken. With Homer, Hesiod, and their imitators as the principal models for Renaissance poets, the warfare of the angels takes on a definite classical tone.

2

When Milton in *Paradise Lost* set about depicting the actual battle in Heaven, the rich poetic tradition of the immediate past stood him in good stead. Accounts of warfare in the celestial poems of the Renaissance were as vivid as accounts of the Satanic personality had been among the theologians. The poets had made the war in Heaven a real war, and they had depicted in detail its devastating physical and societal effects, drawing freely from classical and contemporary poetry. Milton's debt to these poets is apparent in several ways. First, they provide the model for the type of war he is to depict in book 6: both a war formally epic, which depends strongly on Homeric and Virgilian conventions, and a war cosmic in scale, which freely employs as its paradigm the Hesiodic myth of the Titans' struggle with Zeus. Next, they provide him with a general outline for action. There is a marked similarity between the manner in which the war narrative unfolds in Renaissance poems and in *Paradise Lost*. In most poems, five movements to the action may be discerned: (1) the introduction of Lucifer, wherein his motivation is explored and his followers appear to support his cause; (2) God's discovery of Lucifer's plot (spontaneously, to be sure) and his dispatch of the loyal army, headed by Michael; (3) the clash of the opposing armies: (4) the single combat of Michael (or, in *Paradise Lost*, the

48. Valvasone, *Angeleida*, 1.6 (p. 2).

Son) with Lucifer, God's intervention to effect Lucifer's expulsion from Heaven, or both; (5) the aftermath in Heaven or in Hell, with accompanying celebrations or lamentations. Last, the poets provide Milton with specific incidents or variations on the five-movement narrative; two such variations are, as we shall see, the war council of the rebels, in which they plan strategy, and the scene in the rebel camp where a loyalist denounces the proposed revolt and urges conciliation.

Of course Milton will be indebted to specific poets in many other ways: for images or devices (such as the cannon), or for character portrayal. Wherever the case is strong for such an influence, it shall, of course, be noted. But my aim in this study is to look not at Milton's debt to individual poets of the Renaissance, but at his debt to a whole tradition, wherein the war in Heaven was first depicted in detail, not just as an intellectual revolt but as a "physical" war with all the conventions of warfare. Besides, whereas the influence of these poems collectively is difficult neither to discern nor to prove, it is difficult to prove conclusively Milton's knowledge of particular poets in this tradition. For example, we may be fairly sure that Milton had read poems like Alfano's *La guerra celeste tra Michele e Lucifero* or Valvasone's *Angeleida* or Peri's *La guerra angelica*, with their strong depiction of Michael as the hero of the war in Heaven. Milton's own Michael and his Son, as we shall see in chapter 7, show signs of having been influenced by such portraits. Whether Milton knew *each* of these individual poets is another matter. Watson Kirkconnell in *The Celestial Cycle* makes a strong case for Milton's having known Valvasone's *Angeleida,* as do other critics.[49]

49. Books on Milton's sources usually acknowledge that Milton knew Valvasone's work. See Grant McColley, *"Paradise Lost": An Account of Its Growth and Major Origins, with a Discussion of Milton's Use of Sources and Literary Patterns* (Chicago, 1940); Mariana Woodhull, *The Epic of "Paradise Lost"* (New York, 1907); Thibaut de Maisières, *Les poèmes inspirés du début de la genèse à l'époque de la Renaissance.* Watson Kirkconnell translates a number of passages from Valvasone and argues for their influence on Milton (*Celestial Cycle,* pp. 80–87, 576–578). John M. Steadman ("Milton, Valvasone, and the Schoolmen," *Philological Quarterly* 37 (October 1958): 502–504) cites evidence outside *Paradise Lost* to argue Milton's acquaintance with Valvasone.

Alfano's claim is less sure, although Thibaut de Maisières and others have advanced it.[50] And Peri's is still less certain, since knowledge of his play would depend on Milton's having seen the manuscript while he was in Italy (the play does not appear in printed text) or having been present at one of the court performances of the play given during that period.[51] Grant McColley advances Alonso de Acevedo's case,[52] and Kirkconnell urges that of Grotius.[53] Vondel as an influence on Milton has many adherents.[54] My main efforts therefore shall be concerned with showing the influence on Milton not of individual poets but of the collective tradition. For here we are on stronger ground.

In its general scheme, the war in Heaven in *Paradise Lost* most

50. Thibaut de Maisières takes up the question of the Italian influence on Milton, leaving open the possibility that Milton (as others he cites argue) might have known such works as Alfano's (p. 132). Kirkconnell denies on aesthetic grounds that Milton could have owed very much to such crude works as Valmarana's *Daemonomachia* (p. xxii).

51. Giovandomenico (Jacopo) Peri died in 1638. He had attained some prominence in the 1610s and 1620s at the court of Cosimo II in Tuscany where Cosimo had ordered that some of Peri's dramas be presented. Whether Milton knew of Peri or whether any of his dramas were performed in the late 1630s during Milton's visit has not been ascertained. On Peri, see Francesco Trucchi, *Poesie Italiane inedite de Dugento Autori* (Prato, 1847), 4: 194–199.

52. Grant McColley gives some attention to the alleged influence of Acevedo on Milton (p. 13). Thibaut de Maisières points out that though Acevedo plagiarized many sections of his poem from Tasso's *Sette giornate* and Ferrante Guizone's Italian translation of Du Bartas, no known source has been found for his account of the war in Heaven. Apparently, concludes Thibaut, it is his own work (pp. 70–71).

53. Kirkconnell, *Celestial Cycle,* pp. 96, 583–585.

54. Critics have noted correspondences between Milton and Vondel; John Peter, *A Critique of "Paradise Lost"* (New York, 1960), spends some time comparing individual passages. There are two full-length books on Milton and Vondel that argue influence: George Edmundson, *Milton and Vondel: A Curiosity of Literature* (London, 1885), and Jehangir R. P. Mody, *Vondel and Milton* (Bombay, 1942), as well as a long introduction by Van Noppen, the translator of *Lucifer* (New York, 1898), that cites parallels between the two poets. On the other side, however, A. W. Verity in his edition of Milton argues that although Milton had some knowledge of Dutch, it was not among the languages read to him after 1654, when he had already become blind. Moreover, none of his biographers mention Vondel. Kirkconnell argues that Milton could hardly have failed to be interested in the stir that the appearance and production of Vondel's *Lucifer* created in 1654. Also see Woodhull, *The Epic of Paradise Lost,* pp. 211–234.

closely resembles those wars recounted in Renaissance hexaemera as part of the larger narrative of history. But, because of its
lavish use of detail, and because, though an episode, it is longer,
with its more than 1,250 lines, than some self-contained accounts,
Milton's war must also be compared with those poems that treat
the war as their major subject. Milton seems to recognize that his
war is both an episode in a longer work and a kind of "little epic"
in itself. In Raphael's narrative he treats it as a unit, equipping it
with its own "prologue" and "epilogue" in which the angel directly instructs Adam and Eve in his technique and purposes for
narrative. Milton does not invoke Urania again, in the sense that
he offers a formal proem to the war, but he is aware that poets
before him had invoked celestial patrons: Mollerus the Lord himself, Valvasone the Holy Spirit, and Valmarana and Alfano
Michael. (Only Taubmann in *Bellum angelicum* had retained the
classical Calliope.) Milton's celestial "patron" for this episode is
in some sense Raphael, the angelic narrator himself—the eyewit-
ness to the event, if not, like Valmarana's and Alfano's Michael,
its most important angelic warrior. Like poets before him, Milton
makes much of the difficulties of recounting heavenly affairs for
earthly hearers. How can one relate "the invisible exploits of
warring Spirits"? How unfold "the secrets of another world"?
How narrate that which "surmounts the reach of human sense"?
In writing of a war in Heaven, the poet is not merely writing of a
world different from his own: he is writing of a world impossible
for the human imagination to comprehend fully. Poets, as Alfano
and Valvasone remark, require muses themselves heightened.
The subject also has further inherent difficulties, for human beings are required to come to terms with the phenomenon of God's
wrath or, as Peri puts it, the mystery of the divine revenge. Yet,
as both Valmarana and Mollerus insist, it is the responsibility of
the poet to write of the greatest of happenings. Mollerus urges
Christian poets to turn their attention from subjects like the wars
of Cyrus or Scipio or Alexander and to sing of Christ, of the glory
of God, and of heavenly, not earthly, affairs. Milton in the proems

to books 1, 3, and 9 has dealt at large with this problem; in book 5, it suffices for him to say through the angel Raphael that he has undertaken this narrative to dispense something for human good.

Not a few poets, after their formal invocations and apologies, delay the actual account of Lucifer's rebellion still further. In most of the hexaemera, we must first hear of Lucifer's creation, before his fall may be narrated, and this has the particular value not only of introducing Lucifer in all his prelapsarian splendor, but also of magnifying God the Creator who so framed him. Some poets tell not only the account of the framing of the angels, but the account of the entire six days of Creation, generally following the Augustinian time scheme (Milton himself in *Paradise Lost,* of course, does not) that the angels were made on the first day that God commenced the terrestial creation. In *De creatione et angelorum lapsu carmen,* Mollerus goes so far as to justify the placement of these events on the first day, arguing that it is logical that the angels came forth with the first light. In Acevedo's and Murtola's poems, much is made of concurrence of angelic birth with the creation of light. At the climax of the first day of Creation, as Acevedo tells, there was with the outpouring of physical light the spontaneous creation of the angels (p. 249). The angels came forth from God, says Murtola, as the rays of light come forth from the sun (1.53). They were exceedingly brilliant in their creation, remarks Valmarana, and the most brilliant of all was Lucifer (p. 10). So, emphasizing the light of the Creation, the poets look forward, as they begin their accounts of Lucifer's rebellion, to its speedy extinction in the fall.

Yet the poets have one more purpose in mind in recounting or alluding to the Creation. The Creation vividly sets before us the beauty of the universe. Vondel in act 1 of his play *Lucifer* includes an extended account of the glories of Eden (pristine yet); this is the handiwork of God that Lucifer will destroy. Similarly, Valvasone describes for us in *Angeleida* how peaceful things were before Lucifer broke concord. No warring winds strove, on earth only Zephyr blew; the seas were calm and the mountains serene. Hell had not yet been created, and Astraea held all in perfect order. After he has described this beautiful and joyous state, Valvasone need only remark how Lucifer, the worthiest angel in Heaven, will destroy it all, turning brother against brother in civil war (1.14–23). The tragedy of Lucifer's rebellion is thus the more pointedly felt.

Milton also uses the Creation as a touchstone, yet in a different way; for his account of Creation follows rather than precedes the account of the war in Heaven, and as such it turns the mind of the reader from the tragedy of devastation and fall to the consolation of new creation. True, in *Paradise Lost* Satan destroys the beauty of heavenly creation, of that happy heavenly day that begins with harping and singing at God's throne. But the Son's first act in conquering is to restore Heaven, and after Satan's expulsion he sets forth in his chariot to create the terrestrial universe. The emphasis is not upon destruction but upon re-creation. In so doing he focuses his account not on the splendor lost of those first created spirits, but on the splendor yet to be spent as God makes the new world and man in all glory. Thus Milton achieves a stunning effect and reinforces his theme ("So Heav'nly love shall outdo Hellish hate") by transposing the order in which the events of Heaven's first history are usually recounted. And in so doing he tells us that the Son, as he completes the task of creation and reascends to God's throne, is

> greater now in thy return
> Than from the Giant Angels; thee that day
> Thy Thunders magnifi'd; but to create
> Is greater than created to destroy.
>
> [7.604–607]

Milton begins his account of the war in Heaven with a formal tableau that shows us two things: first, the majesty of God surrounded by the sanctities of Heaven and, second, the angels assembled in order.

Under thir Hierarchs in order bright;
Ten thousand thousand Ensigns high advanc'd,
Standards and Gonfalons, twixt Van and Rear
Stream in the Air, and for distinction serve
Of Hierarchies, of Orders, and Degrees.

[5.587–591]

Whether the order here described is a military order will be considered later. Before commencement of the war, Milton ordains only rank, order, degree. Like other Renaissance poets, he makes Satan the leader of "legions," which he dislodges to the North, thus disrupting for the first time the peace of Heaven. In *Lucifer,* Vondel has made Lucifer the leader of certain legions and has designated Michael *veltheer* or field marshal, commander-in-chief of the armies of Heaven, whom he admonishes to fight strongly. Valvasone, after he has just finished praising the perfect peace of Heaven, shows us the faithful angels rallied to arms by God's ministress, Justice. Heywood ranks the angels in military order, though in the strictest sense the Dionysian system of the nine orders of angels that Heywood follows in the *Hierarchie* is not a military ordering. The higher orders of angels, as Heywood himself points out, are not military. They are devoted exclusively to the contemplation of God. But the lower orders have among their functions specific military duties: these "in greater pow'r and eminence shine: / Having vnnumber'd Armies in their sway, / Vnto whose Hests the less degreed obay" (p. 411). Lucifer himself is named a "prime Captaine and King," and he, determined on rebellion, selects the angels for his army out of all nine ranks (p. 412). Correspondingly, God's army seems to come from all ranks and is arrayed under one of the highest angels, Michael.

In the Renaissance poems and dramas on the war in Heaven, a militarily structured society advances before our eyes and is consistently portrayed by countless small details of plot and description, drawn of course for the most part from formal epic. For example, in Taubmann's *Bellum angelicum,* Lucifer's challenge to God is given through the device of the messenger, a typical convention in epic. Lucifer is portrayed by Taubmann as a powerful prince, and when he determines to levy war against God he must, like the princes of epic, deliver a formal announcement of war to his adversary. So he dispatches a messenger to the court of God. In a long formal oration the messenger states his purposes: first recounting Lucifer's reasons for conflict, then describing his military preparedness, and finally setting forth conditions for either settlement or battle. God, having heard Lucifer's embassy, plays the part of the outraged epic opponent and sends the messenger back to Lucifer to counsel peace. Lucifer, still the more perfect epic character, refuses God's peace offer. As Taubmann tells us, he sickens with the cure, the Latin phrase *aegrescitque medendo* being lifted directly from Taubmann's model for epic manners, Virgil.

Both the setting for Lucifer's speeches and the speeches themselves (to be examined in chap. 6) are typically epic. Lucifer is made a general who first confides in his closest lieutenants and then, like the grand imperator, rises before the masses of angels to urge them into battle. With small details the poets make us aware of Lucifer's epic audience. In *La guerra angelica,* for example, Peri takes care to depict in military costume the allegorical vices who accompany and encourage Lucifer. The first two, Invidia and Superbia, are his *fidei consorti,* to whom he confides his plans in the beginning: others—Discordia, Ingratitudine, Guerra, and so forth—join them as lieutenants, to whom Lucifer addresses his battle speeches and to whom he hands the standards of battle as he is about to commence the war. Vondel also surrounds his Lucifer with military comrades—Beelzebub, Belial, and Apollyon—who share his initial plotting and serve as his emissaries and spies to stir up the other angels.

Whereas the main focus in both *Paradise Lost* and its Renaissance predecessors is on the leader Lucifer rather than on his followers (he moves the plot both in speech and in action), yet the followers play a not unimportant role. And this indeed is perfectly traditional in epic. What would the *Iliad* be without the myriads who die victims of Agamemnon's and Achilles' quarrel? And what indeed the battle in Heaven without the third of the stars who fall with Lucifer, victims of his pride and ambition? Besides, if he commands no army and draws no followers, Lucifer's revolt is no more than private sedition. The war is made possible by the supportive force. And thus, though sometimes with only a few descriptive phrases, the poets tell of those angels who committed themselves to Lucifer. First of all, their motives for rebellion are closely connected with his. If he is infected firsthand with pride and madness, they swiftly catch the infection. Both Murtola and Acevedo characterize the angels' desertion of God in favor of Lucifer as a spreading madness or plague. In Acevedo's poem the madness is portrayed allegorically. There, the horrible monster Discordia fills the hearts of Lucifer's angels with hatred and provokes them to their proud assault. In *La guerra angelica*, Superbia and Invidia, having first overcome Lucifer, now move among the angels to pervert them to his cause. They serve both as allegorical figures for the vices of pride and envy and as faithful lieutenants, like those angels in Vondel's *Lucifer* who do Lucifer's work for him. Naogeorgus's *Satyra* provides one of the most realistic depictions of the perversion of the rebel angels. We watch them as they listen to Lucifer's first speech, and Naogeorgus shows us how they are already prime for rebellion. Lucifer, as he points out, merely pours oil upon the fire. They eagerly accept him as king, and just as eagerly they take to arms. Scornful of delay, they press for immediate battle, breathing threats of destruction against God and vaunting that the victory is already theirs. Naogeorgus has portrayed them as full partners in the conspiracy and willing participants in the war that follows. Just as in books 1 and 2 of *Paradise Lost* the vices of Satan may be discerned in those individuals who follow him, so in the *Satyra* the vices of Lucifer are collectively portrayed in his angels. Vondel in *Lucifer* takes another way with the rebel angels. Those closest to Lucifer—Beelzebub, Belial, and Apollyon—are portrayed as accomplices who need only the first suggestion from

Lucifer in order to become fully active movers of his plot. The masses of the angels, however, Vondel portrays as dupes. Ignorant of Lucifer's true plans, they are led to support him, having been fed half-truths by Belial, Beelzebub, and Apollyon.

Milton in book 5 of *Paradise Lost* has only glanced at the masses of angels. We see they all willingly "obey" the wonted signal when Beelzebub commands that they withdraw to the North. How they react to the "ambiguous words and jealousies" cast between "to sound or taint integrity" we can only guess, for Milton does not tell us specifically. He does tell us how they were "allur'd" by the superior voice, the name and countenance of their great potentate, and so they follow him, "heretic," as it were, in their accustomed obedience. The masses of Milton's angels, then, like Vondel's are duped. So too, as they come before Satan, as he takes his throne in the North, they are as a mass deceived. For Satan pretends they have been assembled to consult about the reception of Messiah, and he holds their ears "with calumnious Art / Of counterfeited truth" (5.770–771). Yet, even after they have heard the debate of Satan with Abdiel, none is able or willing to penetrate Satan's guile. Abdiel's zeal none seconded, "as out of season judg'd, / Or singular and rash" (5.850–851). At this moment they change from the dupes of Satan's policy to its willing converts, adhering in their "faith" to him, faithless, as Milton is shortly to brand them, to their God. We hear no words from them, however—only the hoarse murmur of applause, so out of tune in Heaven, where eager hosannas or impromptu hymns have hitherto voiced approval.

> as the sound of waters deep
> Hoarse murmur echo'd to his words applause
> Through the infinite Host.
>
> [5.872–874]

It is an eerie moment, and one would like to think it looks forward to that hoarse hiss that is to greet Satan in book 10 as the last sign of approval. The angels have now turned from passive into active participants, as they second Satan's rejection of Abdiel and heap on the loyal angel hostile scorn, as he slowly makes his long way through their numbers.

No single voice represents the rebel angels in Milton's book 5. As the revolt moves from inception to outbreak, not even Beelzebub is heard, who is the confidant to Satan's plans and his chief tool. And this perhaps is remarkable in that Milton has shown us a Beelzebub in book 1, capable at least of reflecting differently from Satan on the efficacy of eternal war through force or guile. Earlier poets differ in this. In the poems that precede *Paradise Lost,* Lucifer does not appear so alone in the pursuit of rebellion. Valvasone in *Angeleida* provides him with his personal fury Megara to second his plans. She acts both as a lieutenant for Lucifer and as a kind of collective conscience for the rebel angels. The camp of Lucifer before the commencement of battle has turned into a miniature hell, and those splendid angels we first saw in canto 1, shining in arms adorned with jewels, gold, and silver and raising bright banners in the air, have now been metamorphosed into satyrs, hydras, harpies, gorgons, geryons, and other monsters. The snaky-haired fury Megara thus is merely a prototype for the transformed host. After Lucifer has delivered a long speech in which he encourages the entire crew to move on to armed conflict with God, Megara rises to answer. She is, as Valvasone tells us, the most cruel and unhappy of the monsters in livid Acheron, her heart groaning with sorrow and anger. Lucifer has entrusted her with the responsibility of drawing his rebels to the point of battle. Thus she, following her master, attempts to raise the enthusiasm for battle to a yet higher pitch. She urges the rebels not to be content merely with the war in Heaven, but to extend the war to earth. There, should they lose the skies, they may gain supremacy by perverting mankind. With these words she bids the horns of battle sound.

Taubmann and Valmarana also use seconds among the rebels to support and encourage Lucifer in his rebellion. In *Daemonomachiae* the rebel Typhoeus is introduced at a crucial

point in the action. Lucifer has gathered his allies and is preparing
for war. God, having perceived his preparations, denounces him
and warns him sharply of the consequences of war. Lightning
flashes throughout Heaven, and Lucifer is apprehensive. Now
Typhoeus, stepping forward from the midst of a cohort of soldiers, begins to speak. Greatest prince, he says deferentially, do
not let your merit be slighted by those decrees of God that have
upset the traditional order of Heaven and thus have displeased
you. Typhoeus continues by promising that he and his allies are
wholly on Lucifer's side and will follow whatever the consequences. Lucifer can and will equal God's thunder and become
divine. Fortune presses all onward to victory, and the highest
honor is to be won by pursuing this fortune. Lucifer's response to
Typhoeus's speech is significant. He swells with confidence and,
now casting aside any vestige of reverence for God, turns to the
full company of angels and urges them into battle. Perhaps
Typhoeus is here no more than the allegorical Pride we have seen
characterized in plays like *La guerra angelica*. Certainly allegorical figures abound in Renaissance poetry. Moreover Pride, Discord, and War as they appear in poems and plays on the war in
Heaven serve double functions as both abstract representations
of the emotions that control leading characters like Lucifer and
actual participants or soldiers who act to forward the plot of the
poems. In *Bellum angelicum* the soldier who springs up to encourage Lucifer seems, however, a figure out of pure epic, with
little or no allegorical coloring. As he advances, the horsehair
plumes on his helmet shake in typical epic fashion, and before he
speaks he brandishes his spear. Like Valmarana's Typhoeus,
Taubmann's Miastor is deferential, addressing Lucifer as
"greatest ruler." He asks rhetorically how faith toward their
leader can be lacking while the blood flows vigorously, and while
their souls are eager and their lances ready in their hands. He
dismisses, as Typhoeus had done, those laws of Heaven that bind
them to God. For he believes firmly in the ethic of power and
affirms the desirability of acquiring a kingdom through conquest.

So, with the rhetorical flourish of Homeric speaker of words and doer of deeds, he promises to be dauntless in battle. Wherever you order me, he says, I shall go—through Heaven, through earth. Whatever you order me to do, I shall do—to strike at my brothers and at Jehovah himself with my sword. Taubmann also pauses to catalog the angels who spring to Lucifer's defense, naming each and giving a few words of description to individualize them. First is Satanas, a shrewd conspirator, skilled in all wiles and able to entangle the enemy with his frauds; then Psycholetrus, the scoffer at the gods; next Brotoloegus, terrible in his helmet adorned with quivering plumes; and, following, the brothers Scaetes and Phoneus, one skilled with the sling, the other with arrows. These angels, intent on war and eager in their support of Lucifer, serve to supply not only numbers but authority to his plot.

Milton, in book 5 at least, lets Satan stand alone. No angelic supporter, in response to his speech from the magnific throne, urges him on. Perhaps Milton, having presented one diabolic council in book 2, hesitated to write another. More likely, he has chosen to make the war in Heaven the product of solitary rather than collective plotting. Satan needs none to plot with him, none to spur him on. In lonely ambition and pride he forges the rebellion, using the numbers of supporters to carry out what he alone has conceived, needing only silent approval and supportive strength.

In this context the Abdiel scene is all the more remarkable. Here for the first time (except for the brief scene of God and the Son) our attention is drawn away from the central figure of Satan. And our attention is drawn from Satan, not as in *Bellum angelicum* and *Daemonomachiae* in order to hear seconds support his revolt, but to hear that revolt challenged. Among Renaissance poems, only two that I know of provide scenes within the rebel camp where Satan's authority as leader is challenged: Vondel's *Lucifer* and Peri's *La guerra angelica*. In *La guerra angelica*, the allegorical Pace tries to dissuade Lucifer from his plans. Like Abdiel, she urges that it is both morally wrong and effectually futile for Lucifer to oppose God. She protests that he has shattered the "peace" of Heaven. In *Lucifer* as well, the angel Raphael arrives as a last-minute messenger who, olive branch in hand, attempts to heal rebellion with the balm of mercy. He urges Lucifer both to submit himself to God as duty to his post of governor requires and to avoid the awful doom that awaits him and his angels should he not. Like Pace in Peri's play, he is a mediator. While on the surface there is much resemblance between Abdiel and these loyal emissaries of Vondel's and Peri's plays, there are important differences. Abdiel, after all, is not dispatched to "save" Lucifer or to offer him the olive branch; he does not plead with him but denounces him outright. Abdiel's presence, of course, his forceful arguing of God's right, does technically give Satan a chance to reconsider. But Milton gives us no indication that Satan does so. Vondel's Lucifer is moved by Raphael's pleas. Milton's Satan becomes more hardened and imperious as he listens to Abdiel. His dismissal of Abdiel serves to persuade us that conflict is unavoidable. Satan is not to be shaken by the most upright of opponents and will move steadfastly and fearlessly on to battle. On the other hand, with Abdiel Milton has also presented the loyalist case against Satan in a most attractive way. We naturally have sympathy for Abdiel as he stands single against Satan.

In other Renaissance poems it is not the humble Abdiel, surrounded by adversaries who is the one to denounce Satan, but most often the mighty Michael in the midst of God's camp. This, of course, produces a completely different effect. For, though we may still admire the defense, its circumstances provoke far less awe. For example, it is face to face with the Almighty that Peri's or Valvasone's Michael advances the defense, challenging and denouncing Lucifer and swearing to avenge God. Heywood's Michael dismisses Lucifer from God's presence, and Mollerus's and Valmarana's Michael (likewise in full company of Heaven) repudiate Lucifer's words and attempt to dissuade him from revolt. But all is done in the safety of God's presence, so that none of these Michaels become the striking figure that Abdiel does in *Paradise Lost,* standing alone against Satan.

Yet it is with a good deal of care that poets before Milton insist, as Milton himself is to do, that the loyal angels are as spontaneous in their defense of God as the rebels are in their dissent. In Acevedo's poem, the loyal angels respond with horror as they hear that the rebels have defected from God. And in *Angeleida* the loyalists are grieved that they must fight their erstwhile brothers. They assemble about their leader Michael, who carries as his symbol the holy cross, and after he as leader has dedicated himself to the cause of God they echo his words in paeans of praise to the Almighty: "Tu facesti, diceano, tu matieni / Signor, il mondo" (1.127). Similarly, in Alfano's *La battaglia celeste tra Michele e Lucifero* the loyal angels, hearing rumors in Heaven of Lucifer's revolt, eagerly assemble before God's throne and pledge themselves as humble servants to his glory. They express horror at Lucifer's pride and protest their own faith (p. 26). In Peri's play it is the virtues—Prudenza, Vigilanza, Fortezza—who spontaneously spring to God's defense against those vices Lucifer's sin has given birth to. Prudenza, for example, denounces Iniquità's encouragement of the angels to rebellion; she deplores the tumult in the native land and asks how the "children" of God can league themselves against him and take the part of an infidel tyrant. Finally, she and the other virtues gather the army under Michael, and, arming the leader himself with the defenses of the good soldier, they serve as standard-bearers and lieutenants in the cause. Taubmann in *Bellum angelicum,* as he has shown the rebels assemble eagerly to march to battle, also so depicts the loyal army. With epic decorum he treats the reader to a second catalog, where now the loyal angels and their virtues are individualized. Gabriel, Raphael, Uriel, Hierameel all appear and are praised not only for zealous devotion to God, but also for their battle skills. Collectively, Milton's loyal angels are neither described nor treated before we see them assembled in arms at

God's throne in book 6. What their first reactions were to hearing of Satan's defection we do not know. We do know that they—in the battle itself—will be perplexed, as Valvasone's angels were in facing their brothers in war. Milton skips over the preliminaries. Not to the angels, but to the Son alone, will God announce the rebellion of Satan. Angelic loyalty will be presented de facto in book 6, when we see the multitudes of righteous angels already prepared to face Satan's angels in war.

The depiction of God, however, is another matter. Milton has taken care to show us in book 5, as soon as Satan has in fact voiced his intentions to Beelzebub, that God is fully aware of his plans. But Milton's God, in his reactions to the Satanic conspiracy, differs markedly from his predecessors. Renaissance poets most often depicted God bursting forth in anger at the news of Lucifer's rebellion. Taubmann's God, for example, in mixed outrage and disbelief, declares:

> Siccine ais? Dominum patriis expellere regnis
> Decretum est famulo? vix sit mihi credere tantum!
> O audax facinus! ô caeci & lucis egenteis
> Luce sati! Quis vos vobis malus abstulit error?
> Tam citò quae vestras cepit vecordia mentes?
> Ut spretâ ausitis pietate indicere vestro
> Bella Creatori.
>
> [p. 82]

> Just so do you speak? Has it become law for the servant to expel
> The master from the native kingdom? I can scarcely believe so
>   much!
> O presumptuous deed! O blind ones, needful of light,
> Though sewn with light! What evil deception has misled you?
> What madness took away your reason so quickly?
> How could you have spurned his love to proclaim
> War against your creator?

The God of Peri's play is similarly outraged that Lucifer vaunts in his pride and, pretending to give law to Heaven, has raised himself above God and the Son. In a long scene that ends with his

167

sending Michael forth to battle, God explains to his commander-in-chief Michael just why he finds Lucifer's act so appalling. He as God has created Lucifer and all his company, endowing them with singular favor; as Creator he cannot suffer these creatures made by him to flout his majesty and rebel against him. Valmarana's God is outraged at Lucifer's rebellion both because it disregards his authority as God and because it attempts to alter those divine prophecies he has just uttered concerning the Son. God, in the hearing of the full company of Heaven, has proclaimed the Son's lordship over all as the *Verbum Dei*. Lucifer in resistance has planned his revolt. Now God speaks further prophecies to the angels: the revolt of Lucifer, he assures them, will fail and the *Verbum Dei* will indeed, as predicted, prevail and extend his yoke over all Heaven and earth, in time taking on human form.

God in *Angeleida* also takes the announcement of Lucifer's revolt as occasion to expatiate on future history. "Nature," the mother of all things, has approached the throne of God and, fearful that the proposed rebellion will bring destruction to both Heaven and earth, has asked God for reassurance. God tells her that Lucifer's revolt will indeed take place and will cause great discord in Heaven. Further, Lucifer will incite revolt on earth and cause man, like himself, to sin against his Creator with ingratitude. Unleashing primal evil, Lucifer will spoil God's creation, ruining not only himself, but man also and the terrestial universe man inhabits. Heaven will easily expel Lucifer and his sin; but earth, disproportioned by sin, its beauty spoiled, will only with difficulty be restored. Justice, God explains, demands that the polluted be destroyed. Mercy, however, pleads that man and his world be spared. God, resolving the conflict, declares that man shall find grace, Lucifer none. Although debates between Justice and Mercy are commonplace in Renaissance literature, this particular debate strongly calls to mind that scene in book 3 of *Paradise Lost* where Father and Son voice the alternate demands of Justice and Mercy, the Son resolving the conflict, as Valvasone's God had, by affirming that man shall find grace. Milton has used book 3, of course, as a kind of prologue to the action. Like Valvasone, he shows God preparing a remedy for ills that have not eventuated. In *Paradise Lost* the dramatic occasion is God's sighting of Satan on his way to Eden about to tempt man; in *Angeleida* it is God's announcement of Lucifer's future rebellion. In an absolute time scheme, God's comments concerning sin and free will in *Paradise Lost* should look forward only to man's rebellion, but in the relative scheme they also look forward to Satan's rebellion, the events of which are yet to be narrated. The sin anatomized by Milton's God is Satan's as well as Adam's; the grace extended to man shall be denied at the end of book 6 to Satan. As Valvasone has provided in God's long narrative speech a kind of theological prologue to the action, Milton has also done so. Full justification of God's actions is presented in each. And Milton in book 5 of *Paradise Lost* first has the opportunity to apply these justifications as Satan fails, when he might freely have stood. There is no need for God to interrupt the rising action of the war with extended commentary. The reader has only to glance backward at book 3 to understand fully what is taking place. Only the briefest parenthesis is needed, in which God's ironic laughter is apt response to Satan's folly.

God's appearance in book 6, where with full pomp and ceremony he dispatches the faithful angels to war, serves another purpose. There he appears neither to discuss theology nor to predict history nor even in any way (but a perfunctory one) to react to the outrage of Satan's rebellion. What we see instead is the Deity on his throne formally declaring the beginning of the war. Albeit a stock scene, it is a magnificent one. For in the ancient, medieval, and Renaissance literature Milton found ample precedents. As hexaemeral writers had delighted in portraying Lucifer at the very moment he contemplates rebellion, so they had delighted in portraying God sending his armed saints to combat. From *Cursor mundi* to Vondel's *Lucifer,* the words of God are reported to us. "Go," says God to his saints, and the word rings down the centuries whether in Taubmann's Latin or Valvasone's Italian or Milton's English. The actual commission God delivers to Michael and his angels is in all works basically the same. In *Paradise Lost* God commands Michael and Gabriel to lead forth the "armed Saints / By Thousands and by Millions rang'd for fight," to pursue "the Godless crew . . . with Fire and hostile Arms," and to "drive them out from God and bliss, / Into thir place of punishment" (6.46–53). Peri's God had commanded that Michael drive from Heaven "questa perversa peste," and Taubmann's God, no less explicitly, had told his angels to shatter the battle line and overcome the dragon. Although Milton's God reassures the faithful that they will be equal in number of that godless crew, he offers neither commendation nor advice. In other poems, however, God is lavish in praise of his angels even before they have proved themselves in action. Valvasone's God calls them his *diletto stuolo* and promises they will win great honor and glory in this enterprise. Taubmann's God tells of the paeans of praise that future ages will sing to Michael and his angels. Alfano's God liberally lauds their love, their faith, and their service, Milton's God, however, who has been liberal in his praise of Abdiel's "better fight," is silent concerning the "glory" of battle the loyal angels will win. For he alone (among those Gods portrayed by Renaissance poets) is sending forth an army to carry out a commission he knows perfectly well they cannot complete. Other Renaissance poets portray a God of straightforward and simple intention. He sends armies forth to conquer and they do conquer; he tells them they will win glory and honor in the fight and they do. But Milton's God dispatches his saints to learn a humbling lesson. Glories of battle they will not win; conventional honor and renown will not be theirs; no spoils of the enemies will they exultingly hang up in triumph. Therefore it is highly significant that Milton's God promises them none of these. The saints will glean a different reward from "heroic" battle. All this, however, is perceived only in retrospect. On the surface this ceremonial scene seems to announce in *Paradise Lost* what it does in most other poems of the Renaissance: that the formal beginning of the war in Heaven occurs with fit pomp as God himself speaks and the "loud / Ethereal Trumpet from on high" begins to blow.

Epic color abounds in the scenes that follow: the armies are contrasted in the traditional Homeric way as they march toward one another and form their battle lines, catalogs of warriors are produced, and formal flyting occurs between the major warriors. As Homer had signaled a difference between his Trojans and Greeks in describing how the first advanced with clamor like birds and the second marched in silent step, breathing deliberate valor, so the Renaissance poets contrast the advancing rebels and loyalists. For example, in *La guerra angelica* Lucifer rushes forward with disorderly throngs of angels about him, led by the monstrous trio Discordia, Rabbia, and Ingratitudine. Michael, in contrast, is serene and splendid as his captains Potenza, Concordia, and the invincible Fortezza march before him bearing banners. Vondel in *Lucifer* similarly distinguishes the two armies by describing the formation each takes. Michael's army assumes the shape of a triangle (clearly symbolizing the Trinity); angels are posted at each angle, and the marshal at the center angle bears the banner of God. In opposition, Lucifer has ordered his angels to assume the form of a crescent moon; he himself guards the center, Beelzebub and Belial secure the horns, and Apollyon the standard-bearer goes before, lifting aloft the banner of the morning star. Acevedo, Murtola, and Valvasone also describe the armies marching in close order. Acevedo and Valvasone tell us that Michael's army goes forth under Christ's banner, inscribed, as Acevedo depicts it, with the blood of the Lamb. Murtola contrasts the brilliant equipage of the loyal angels with the dullness of the rebels. God's angels, shining splendidly and gracefully winged with feathers, bear immortal arms of fire and shimmering gold; they wear transparent helmets, cuirasses of light, and adamantine breastplates. The rebels, however, are girt with cloudy and dark armor, and their banners are dull in color. For Murtola their appearance also suggests the contrasting emotions that inspire them. The loyal army is moved by love and piety and just anger against the rebels; the opposing army, arrogant and proud, is spurred on by envy, impiety, and scorn. In words not too dissimilar, Valvasone also sums up this contrast: "Da l'un lato humiltà, valor, & fede / Et da l'altro superbia, ira & despitto" (On the one side humility, valor, and faith; on the other pride, anger, and despite; (2.83). Valmarana chooses to catalog the loyal angels at the moment they advance into battle. Gabriel and Raphael appear first; then Iesonias, who listens always to the Lord; Iahiel, who awaits a favorable sign; Uriel and Iedial, both lit with eager spirits; Iasiel, who divides the host; and the three Eleazars, brothers. It is the most epic of flourishes.

Milton's treatment of the loyal and rebel angels is markedly different. As his loyalists assemble "in mighty Quadrate join'd," we are irresistibly reminded of the scenes where Satan's army assembled in Hell. Marching out in silence like Homer's Greeks, stepping "to the sound of instrumental Harmony," the loyalists recall the rebel troops who, risen from the burning lake, in perfect phalanx "move on in silence to soft pipes." Not in outer appearance alone do they resemble them, moreover, but in their stalwart commitment to heroic ideals. In Heaven, God's bright legions pledge their "Heroic Ardor to advent'rous deeds/ Under thir God-like leaders, in the Cause/ Of God and his Messiah" (6.64–68). In Hell the devils had been no less devoted to their cause, however bad, and "instead of rage/ Deliberate valor breath'd" (1.545–554). Milton has not drawn a simple contrast between his rebel and loyal angels. He has shown both as devoted to and exercised in the classical values and trappings of warfare. In this first description of the armies he is perhaps even more deliberately Homeric than his Renaissance followers, for he adapts one of the most common Homeric similes, the comparison of the assembled army to birds in flight, for his description of his loyalists.[55] The simile, moreover, comes as a surprise, for it is the

55. Merritt Y. Hughes, *Complete Poems and Major Prose*, p. 325 (note 74), identifies the Homeric and Virgilian originals: *Iliad*, 2.459–463 and *Aeneid*, 7.699–701.

first, though not the last, to be used to describe a scene in Heaven. (Hell, of course, had abounded in similes.) Milton's description of the rebels' fiery approach from the North not only brings with it a touch of Hell, but also, as with the bird simile, suggests a Homeric original: book 2 of the *Iliad* (lines 455–458, 780–782) where Homer twice compares the blaze in arms to the progress of a fire across the land. The approach of the rebels, of course, as this fiery comparison denotes, is fearful. In the distance, the horizon bristles with "rigid Spears and Helmets throng'd, and Shields/ Various, with boastful Argument portray'd" (6.82–84). In their furious expedition, Milton may be alluding to the fury of their cause; the boastful arguments on their shields portray their boastful purpose: to win the mount of God by surprise and place there "the envier of his State." But Milton is far less concerned than his Renaissance predecessors to paint the holy on one side and the blasphemous on the other. In what they say and do far more than in how they look will Milton's rebels be revealed.

The preliminaries to warfare are not complete, however, with the description of the dispatch and the advance of the respective armies. For, in *Paradise Lost* and in other poems as well, the armies pause before beginning battle. This is the last of the epic formalities. Advancing upon one another, the armies leave a little space between—"a dreadful interval," as Milton calls it, "Front to Front/ Presented stood in terrible array/ Of hideous length" (6.105–107). Vondel too honors this convention, showing the angels standing in ranks, squadron by squadron, each at his post along the battle line awaiting the command of the drum and trumpet to begin battle. In *Bellum Angelicum* the armies not only draw up ranks before the commencement of the battle but also dispatch leaders from each side to engage in formal flyting. For Taubmann this is Michael's and Lucifer's principal exchange in words before (presumably) they exchange blows in battle. It resembles (as we shall see as we examine it more closely in chap. 6) the flyting in *Paradise Lost* between Satan and Abdiel, though in the former general meets general, and in the latter the mighty general meets the humble private. With the flyting finished (and in *Paradise Lost,* the exchange of blows between Satan and Abdiel), the battle begins. In *Paradise Lost,* as in the epics and dramas of the Renaissance, it begins with a last epic formality. Michael bids the trumpet sound.

3

Two schools of opinion are apparent in the Renaissance concerning the battle proper: one that it was a "real" contest of arms, the other that, though armies were drawn up, no battle as we think of it occurred. Spenser and Sir William Alexander, the poet of *Doomes-Day,* are the most striking proponents of the second view. Alexander succinctly announces: "God would judge, not fight" (First Houre, stanza 52). Michael has assembled his squadrons to oppose Lucifer, but God, to humiliate the rebels' pride, disdains to let them fall, graced, as it were, with a blow. He matches their guilty weakness against his pure might, and "looking" lightning, he "thunders" forth the command that they leave Heaven. Spenser likewise has God act directly; he "seeing their so bold assay,/ Kindled the flame of his consuming yre,/ And with his onely breath them blew away / From heauens hight" (*An Hymne of Heavenly Love,* lines 85–88). This obviously is the medieval way, for in both medieval poems and mystery plays Lucifer falls by God's express order. Actual "physical" battle is avoided.

But while Renaissance poets like Spenser and Alexander avoid physical battle, they do not opt for psychic battle. The twelfth-century hexaemeral writer Rupert of Deutz had suggested that the war in Heaven was a *psychomachia.* Few follow his suggestion. Heywood is the only one who squarely faces this issue. In The *Hierarchie of the blessed Angels,* he insists that heavenly warfare was totally unlike earthly warfare. Angels did not bear earthly arms:

> No Lances, Swords, nor Bombards they had then,
> Or other Weapons now in vse with men;

None of the least materiall substance made,
Spirits by such giue no offence or aid.
Onely spirituall Armes to them were lent,
And these were call'd *Affection* and *Consent*.

[p. 341]

The pictures in the 1635 edition of the *Hierarchie* show the angels in armor with swords in hand. But, says Heywood, not sword to sword did Michael combat Lucifer. He won mastery over him when the force of his humility and reverence defeated Lucifer's insolence and spleen. Heywood, however, does not describe the conflict. Peri in *La guerra angelica* gives us something of a mixed *psychomachia*. The masses of angels who oppose one another are arrayed in conventional arms, but each group is led by its own set of allegorical Virtues or Vices. Peri seems to indicate thereby that the war in Heaven was both a conventional war and a *psychomachia*. Valvasone and Murtola solve the problem in a different way. They suggest that the angels, since they are spirits, must have employed spiritual arms. But what these spiritual arms were they do not say. (By definition, spiritual arms cannot be physically described.) Murtola implies (it is a fanciful notion) that spiritual arms were simply lighter and more transparent than earthly arms. By and large, other poets, sometimes with an apology, sometimes without it, follow this convention. Raphael's apology in *Paradise Lost* that he is likening heavenly to earthly forms takes care of the question of arms and armor, as well as a multitude of other things. Thus it is that the angels of the various epics and dramas bear swords, lances, and spears; hurl darts and fire at one another; and protect themselves from injury with cuirasses, breastplates, helmets, and shields. Had Dr. Johnson read any of the celestial epics of the sixteenth and seventeenth centuries, he would hardly have been surprised at the ease with which Milton's spiritual angels adopt material arms. They were doing what their fellows in previous epics had also effortlessly done.

In depicting the opening encounters of the war itself, therefore, most poets labor to present convincing "physical" battle. Ar-

175

rows, darts, and lances fly through the air; angels on foot or on the wing struggle against one another, helmet to helmet, shield to shield,[56] Acevedo's angels stand in the black air hurling balls of fire or charge fiercely at one another. The angels in Vondel's drama (their warfare described by a messenger) meet in hand-to-hand engagements, fighting with mace and halberd, sword, spear, and dagger (5.1). Vondel also describes the ensuing devastation as pearled hoods, tresses of hair, feathers, gold, diamonds, and broken arrows flutter through the air. Taubmann gives the most detailed account of physical warfare. His soldiers stand brandishing their spears or hang in mid-air. Eager for combat, they shout assurances to their leader that they are ready to follow. As the armies fall upon one another, the field bristles with drawn swords; dust rises; the horns of battle sound. Soldiers meet helmet-to-helmet, shield-to-shield. Missiles are thrown through the air, flaming pine and javelins, hissing with nitrous salts and sulfur. So thick are the missiles that the sky, sown with weapons, grows dark and night hangs over the field. As Peri also described it in *La guerra angelica,* the sky seems to rain weapons.

The rain of weapons is one of the most conventional of descriptions in the battle epic. We need only turn to *Gerusalemme liberata* to find a tableau similar to the ones described.

> So thick flew stones and darts, that no man sees
> The azure heavens, the sun his brightness lost,
> The clouds of weapons, like two swarms of bees,
> Met in the air, and there each other cross'd.
>
> [11, stanza 48]

56. This description of close combat—helmet to helmet, shield to shield—that recurs in so many of the Renaissance poems probably goes back to such passages as *Iliad,* 13.131–133 or 16.215–217. There Homer seems to be describing, however, the close formation of soldiers advancing on a single side, not the clash of two sides as in the hoplite style of fighting. Later writers in the Greek tradition, such as Tyrtaeus (seventh century B.C.) use the phrase—helmet to helmet, shield to shield—to describe the hoplite style of fighting, and later writers (including those of the Renaissance with whom we are dealing) also seem to understand it this way. (See "Notes on Tyrtaeus," in *Greek Lyric Poetry,* ed. David Campbell [London: Macmillan, 1967], pp. 175–176.)

In *Paradise Lost* a storm of weapons also fills the sky, and the "dismal hiss of fiery darts" produces above a "fiery Cope" under which the armies rush at one another with "ruinous assault / And inextinguishable rage" (6.212–217). In this first combat of the war Milton insists on the fierceness of hand-to-hand combat. "Arms on Armor clashing bray'd" and the "madding Wheels / Of brazen Chariots rag'd" (6.209–211). Clearly, in depicting the violence of battle in Heaven, he is following a well-established tradition. Perhaps the earliest poem to employ vivid battle descriptions and to suggest that the war in Heaven was conducted with the full spectrum of classical weaponry was Vida's *Christiad*. In book 5 the angels, hearing of Christ's imminent crucifixion, rush forward to defend him. One angel seizes a spear, another a javelin, some take their arrows, others their slings and fiery arms. Once more arms clash and the ether rings with loud alarms. And at this point Vida recollects for us the first use of arms in Heaven, when the loyal angels took up their weapons (now long disused) to expel Lucifer and his rebels. Indeed, this battle may have served the sixteenth and seventeenth centuries (since Vida's poem was widely popular) as the "father" or prototype for the battles in Heaven that follow. The war in Heaven, Vida tells us, was depicted by a heavenly artist all in gold. In this depiction the armies may be seen fighting in mid-air. Now here, now there they fight in close combat, some with darts, some grasping the enemy by the hair. All Heaven is obscured with missiles. Though only a brief scene, Vida's war is remarkable for its graphic military detail.

Although the poets indulge in conventional battle description, they do not lose sight of the fact that Heaven is an incongruous location for fierce hosting. Both Valvasone and Vondel comment on the tragic loss of brotherhood among the angels, and Milton's Raphael echoes the sentiment: "strange to us it seem'd / At first, that Angel should with Angel war, / And in fierce hosting meet, who wont to meet / So oft in Festivals of joy and love" (6.91–94). Yet it is not the angels alone who react to the tragic violence. Heaven itself shudders, perceiving the imminence of battle. "The lights of heaven look'd pale," recounts Alexander in *Doomesday,* "clouds (thundring) shed, / Winds (roaring trumpets) bellow'd loud alarmes" (first houre, stanza 49). In Vondel's *Lucifer,* Gabriel, looking at the sky, interprets the disorder in the elements as a sign of impending war: "a wild, disorder'd noise / Of thundering roars fast, above, below. / It lightens, storms, and rages, in such pain / As almost shakes the pillars of our Court" (p. 399). Further omens of war are recorded by other poets: the axis of the universe shakes in anticipation; the concave of Heaven groans; stars are eclipsed; the sun stands still in the sky. When the war itself begins, the cosmic storm that has been brewing strikes with full violence. Heaven, Acevedo tells us, is alternately obscured by darkness and seared by flashes of lightning. At the signal for battle the thundercloud, which Gabriel had described in *Lucifer,* breaks, and lightning flashes bolt on bolt with flaming hail. The storm is so fierce that it shakes God's court, bewildering the spheres and the stars in their orbits: "Lightning alone is seen, and thunder heard / Nothing can stand. The highest is struck down" (p. 411). The storm of battle in Grotius's *Adam exul* seems to occur in the elements alone; there is no actual description of armies upon the battlefield. Instead the discord in nature is minutely described.

> The Sphere perceived the rebel throng;
> All aether shudder'd at the sin;
> The Poles with trembling fear did spin;
> Nor did the Axis steadfast hold;
> The pole-star seeing manifold
> The change in nature, fear'd the Ocean
> . . . .
> The Sun had gone to rule the dark
> Leaving the day to Luna's spark,
> Had Michael not, at God's command,
> Made fearless war on Satan's band.
>
> [1.281–286, 291–295][57]

57. Kirkconnell, *Celestial Cycle,* pp. 114–115. The original Latin is as follows:
   Sensit turbas Sphaera rebelles,
   Totusque nefas horruit aether,

With these other poets, Milton also records the horrid shock of battle. Heaven trembles to its very foundations: "all Heav'n / Resounded, and had Earth been then, all Earth / Had to her Centre shook" (6.217–219). This succinct comment is in marked contrast with other poets' longer accounts of cosmic disturbances. As earth felt the wound at the moment of Adam's and Eve's fall, so Heaven is not insensitive to the wound of cosmic war. But as in book 9, Milton defers until later his descriptions of this shock. Nor does he at this point suggest with simile how the cosmos is going to wrack. From Homer on, similes depicting the violence in nature of earthquake, fire, volcanic eruption, or hurricane were used to evoke the violence of contending armies. For Valvasone the armies' clashing is like the colliding of Alpine mountains or like the opposition of the winds Aquilon and Notus in midsky—contending with equal power and not yielding, but with unswerving restraint holding the sea, the clouds, the earth, the sky at the mercy of their cruel violence.

Not until book 10, when he is describing the violence unleashed on earth by man's sin, will Milton employ a wind simile to delineate a universe gone to ruin.

> As when two Polar Winds blowing adverse
> Upon the Conian Sea, together drive

> Geminique Poli tremuere malis,
> Nec bene firmus substitit axis,
> Et Naturae facie versa
> Metuit tingi Cynosura salo,
> Metuere graves Aras aquilones,
> Heliceque Notos.
> Ipse inciperet mox Aegoceros
> Laxare diem, Cancerque breves
> Ducere noctes, Solque in tenebras
> Capiens regnum tradere lucis
> Jura sorori, nisi magna Dei
> Jussa capessens sumpserat audax
> Arma Michaël. Ille rebelles
> Domuit turmas: Ille tenaci
> Compede vinctas jussit superis
> Migrare locis, et praecipites
> In Tartareas depulit umbras.

[1.281–299]

> Mountains of Ice, that stop th' imagin'd way
> Beyond *Petsora* Eastward, to the rich
> *Cathaian* Coast.
>
> [10.289–293]

The Renaissance poets anticipate him, however, with their frequent use of wind similes to suggest the intangible but highly destructive force of angelic warfare. So it is, even from the very beginning of the revolt. The roar that the rebel armies raise in response to Lucifer's speech urging them to battle is likened by Taubmann to the clash of winds swollen with thunder. Lucifer's own speech rousing his army is for Valmarana like the impact of diverse winds coming from the distant parts of the earth to spread plague. And for Acevedo Lucifer's entry into battle is like the north wind challenging Notus in anger. These similes are particularly reminiscent of special ones in the *Iliad.* As Lucifer's words affect his soldiers with the force of winds, so Agamemnon's had been compared in impetus to winds upon the sea that drive the waves crashing upon the shore (2.143–151). Similarly, the assault of rebels upon loyal soldiers likened by Valvasone to the assault of winds finds its precedent in book 13 of the *Iliad,* where the attack of Trojans upon Achaeans is like an attack of winds stirred up by Zeus's thunderbolt (13.795–800; also 13.334–338). Not in Homer only, however, but in *Gerusalemme liberata,* where Tasso describes the assault of Christians upon the pagans, are wind similes effectively employed.

> With equal rage as when the southern wind
> Meeteth in battle strong the northern blast,
> The sea and air to neither is resign'd,
> But cloud 'gainst cloud, and wave 'gainst wave they cast.
> So from this skirmish neither part declin'd,
> But fought it out, and kept their footings fast,
> And oft with furious shock together rush,
> And shield 'gainst shield, and helm 'gainst helm they crush.
>
> [9, stanza 52]

The wind simile, so frequently used by the Renaissance poets in their delineations of angelic warfare, thus has a long and honorable history.

For Milton, the primary emphasis on the first day of battle is on the violence of soldiers at war, not on the violence unleashed either directly or metaphorically upon the universe. Until the meeting of Michael and Lucifer in single combat, the battle is depicted in terms of soldier pitted against soldier, not wind against wind or mountain colliding with mountain. Milton's opening battle scenes, though violent, are well-disciplined epic contests. We see angels fighting on the ground or soaring into the air. Raphael praises the "professionalism" of each warrior: "single as in Chief, expert / When to advance, or stand, or turn the sway / Of Battle, open when, and when to close / The ridges of grim War" (6.233–236); he tells that there was "no thought of flight, / None of retreat, no unbecoming deed / That argu'd fear" (6.236–238). The day of battle closes with a series of single episodes, which recount the rout of the rebels: the flight of Moloch, the victory of Uriel and Raphael over their foes, and the overthrow by Abdiel of Ariel, Arioch, and Ramiel.[58]

Only with sidelong glances does Milton acknowledge on this first day of battle that the war he is depicting is anything other than typical "earthly" epic battle. First of all, he does tell us that the violence of the angels has been carefully controlled by God, who has limited their strength. Second, he does say that, unless limited, the warring angels could have done dreadful damage to the cosmos.

> What wonder? when
> Millions of fierce encount'ring Angels fought
> On either side, the least of whom could wield

58. George de Forest Lord, in *Heroic Mockery: Variations on Epic Themes from Homer to Joyce* (Newark, 1977), has demonstrated that many of the hand-to-hand contests of book 6 go back to Homer, especially books 5 and 6 of the *Iliad,* where Diomedes fights not only with the Olympian gods but also with human epic opponents (see esp. pp. 67–73).

These Elements, and arm him with the force
Of all thir Regions. . . .

[6.219–223]

As the warfare on this first day becomes intense, moreover, Milton does suggest that all the air seemed "conflicting fire." And with the duel of Michael and Lucifer, he finally breaks forth with an epic simile, which, like those of his predecessors, depicts the cosmic force unleashed by angelic warfare.

                                such as, to set forth
Great things by small, if Nature's concord broke,
Among the Constellations war were sprung,
Two Planets rushing from aspect malign
Of fiercest opposition in mid Sky,
Should combat, and thir jarring Spheres confound.

[6.310–315]

But even this magnificent simile is only a glance ahead; the duel of Michael and Lucifer is a duel of weapons; cosmic violence is not yet to become ruinous.

Milton is distinct among the poets of the Renaissance in that he carefully divides the warfare into three stages, three consecutive days, and carefully assigns a "kind" of warfare to each day. Most poets move the warfare swiftly from beginning to end; all is concluded in one day with one battle proper. Or, if there is any kind of division, it is usually the division between the general warfare and the conclusive duel of Michael and Lucifer. In many ways, what in some Renaissance poems is the course of the whole war involves in *Paradise Lost* merely the action of the first day. The armies strike fiercely at one another and for some time the battle remains even; then the rebels weaken before the sinless superiority of the loyal angels; finally Michael, in single combat with Lucifer, wins the day. What follows in the typical Renaissance poem is the rebels' expulsion from Heaven; what follows in *Paradise Lost,* however, is the realignment of the rebel's forces.

This first day of battle provides many clear resemblances in detail between Milton and his predecessors. In point after point Milton follows traditions that seem to have become Renaissance commonplaces for describing the celestial battle. Where the Renaissance poets are consciously epic in showing the armies lined up against one another, Milton is the same. Where they elect to describe physical weapons and physical techniques of battle, he does so too. And when they assign the rebel weakening to their sinful disposition, Milton also tells us that sin makes the Satanists liable to fear and flight and pain. He may actually have had Valvasone directly in mind here, for Valvasone tells how the loyal angels fight with fresh spirits and secure hearts, invulnerable to pain or wound, whereas the rebels suffer weariness, are wounded, and writhe in pain, becoming weaker and weaker (2.86–87).

Angels in other poems also suffer psychologically. In Acevedo's and Murtola's poems, the rebels are overcome at the very sight of the splendidly arrayed loyal angels and flee helplessly as the loyal angels pursue them hurling "darts of glory." In *Angeleida, La guerra angelica,* and *Lucifer,* the loyalists' spiritual preeminence is depicted symbolically. In the last attack they appear before the rebels, their ranks arranged in a symbolic formation that attests their loyalty and their virtue. In Valvasone's and Peri's poems, Michael has arranged the army in the form of the cross and so strikes at the rebels, crushing them. In Vondel's play, Michael and his forces mount into the air and, formed in a symbolic triangle, smite and break the rebels' opposing half-moon formation. Milton's loyal troops are comparable to the angels in *Angeleida, La guerra angelica,* and *Lucifer* only in that they too win (though only temporarily) a stunning first-day victory over the rebels and win it by a combination of military and spiritual force. The victory is, however, a series of single routs, with Gabriel, then Uriel and Raphael, and finally Abdiel repulsing their enemies, after Michael has put down Satan. No collective stroke routs the rebels. Although the loyal angels advance "in

Cubic Phalanx firm . . . entire. / Invulnerable'' (6.399–400), their victory is temporary. Hence Milton does not invest it either with the overwhelming confidence or the decisive force the Son's victory is to have. Instead of dramatizing the loyalists' exultation, he attends to the rebels' dismay, describing the deformed rout and foul disorder of the army that at the beginning of battle had marched with confidence, order, and spirit.

In ordering the events of this first day of battle Milton has placed Michael's duel with Satan before rather than after the beginning of the rout of the rebels. Therefore, although it remains an important event in the first day's battle, it is neither the decisive nor the climactic event it had been in the Renaissance poems preceding *Paradise Lost*. Milton has used, of course, as model for the duel between Michael and Satan (and to a lesser degree also the encounter between the Son and Satan, as we shall see in chap. 7) the duel between Michael and Lucifer that many Renaissance poems describe. Perhaps the encounter that is closest to the Michael-Satan duel of *Paradise Lost* occurs, as Watson Kirkconnell has pointed out, in *Angeleida*. There Valvasone's Michael sights Lucifer working havoc in the field and determines to end the war with his defeat. (The reverse takes place in *Paradise Lost,* for Satan first seeks out Michael.) Valvasone's duel, like Milton's, is closely patterned on the traditional duel of epic, even though Valvasone's Lucifer (already transformed into a hundred-armed giant) little resembles the traditional epic adversary. Like the heroes of the *Iliad* or the *Aeneid,* Michael first prays for victory and then hurls his lance, shattering and piercing the gold of Lucifer's shield. Now pursuing Lucifer, he delivers a two-stanza speech that strongly calls to mind the speech Milton's Michael utters. Like Milton's Michael, Valvasone's Michael denounces Lucifer as a traitor and orders him to leave Heaven, taking with him every form of terror and anger. He predicts his fall, saying that he is unworthy of a heavenly dwelling. Here in Heaven, says Michael, dwell those who wish to serve God.

Traditor, mostro diuerso...
Di quante sceleragini cosperso
Hai d'ognintorno l'infelice busto,
Di tanti busti ti raddoppia, & gira
Teco ogni forma di spauento, & d'ira.

Tu sei giunto all' occaso, & questa spada
Nel tuo giusto supplicio hoggi s'affina,
Perche ne l'Alba tua vinto tu cada,
Non degno più della magion diuina:
Questa albergo è di Dio, questa contrada
E di popul, ch'a lui serue, & s'inchina:
Vattene tu co' tuoi seguaci rei,
Che fattura esser sua non ti credei.

Traitor, strange monster...
With however many evils you have sprinkled about
Your unhappy body in every part,
With just so many bodies every form
Of terror and of anger redoubles you and turns about
        you.

At dusk you are cheated, and this sword
Grounds you down today in your just punishment,
Because at your dawning, conquered, you fall,
No longer worthy of this divine dwelling:
This habitation is God's, this country belongs
To people who serve him and bow to him;
Go hence with your wicked followers,
Because I do not believe you that the work was
        yours.[59]

After this speech Michael lifts his sword and cuts through
Lucifer's wing and arm into his body. The blood pours forth.
Lucifer is defeated and driven from Heaven by the victorious
archangel. Comparable scenes occur in other Renaissance
poems; Acevedo, Murtola, and Alfano all credit Lucifer's defeat

59. Valvasone, *Angeleida,* 2, stanzas 119–120.

to a single decisive blow by Michael. Milton has closely imitated this scene up to and including the wounding blow at the hands of the archangel. But Michael's duel in *Paradise Lost* proves indecisive.

The indecisiveness of this duel and of the loyalists' victory of the first day is, of course, crucial for *Paradise Lost*. And it is here we remark that Milton begins to differ sharply from his predecessors. Like them, Milton does show the rebels in inglorious rout and does grant the loyalists glory. Unlike them, he shows that the loyal angels, though able to win a victory, are unable to root the rebels out of Heaven. Moreover, he not only discredits the rebels in battle, he discredits the heroic ethic of the battle they were waging. For it is not only they who were defeated, but their reliance on bright arms. We see the "shiver'd armor strown" and "on a heap / Chariot and Charioteer... overturn'd / And fiery foaming Steeds" (6.389–391). We see the confidence and deliberate valor they had in approaching now turned to fear and flight and pain. Their boast of skill and heroic expertise, their reliance on courage and might as the highest values, are now exposed as specious. Indeed, those very qualities that loomed so large in book 1 and by which Satan maintained the loyalty of his angels and attracted the admiration of the readers now seem vain. Neither might nor heroic enterprise gains the day, but innocence and obedience.

The second day of battle is Milton's most independent contribution to the war. Whereas his first day follows closely the plan—at least in narrative and use of detail—of the Renaissance celestial poems, his second day does not. In two ways only is the narrative of the second day linked to Renaissance epic: in that it describes Satan's rebels planning strategy for the war, and in that it narrates the invention and first use of gunpowder. Renaissance poems in general show Satan as a conspirator planning strategy in close conclave with his intimates. So he appears in *Gerusalemme liberata, The Locusts,* Vida's *Christiad,* the Adam plays, and hosts of others. But only one poem I know of has a Satanic

council in which surprise strategy for the heavenly war is medi-
tated. In Taubmann's *Bellum angelicum,* Lucifer sets up a council before the actual commencement of battle, and this council
evolves a plan to ambush the loyal angels. The plan comes not
from Lucifer, but from two stripling angels, Mocus and Thes-
celus, who suggest that Lucifer divide the army, set a party to lie
in wait for Michael's troops in the rocks above a level plain and to
rush down upon them, taking them by surprise, when the signal is
given. Lucifer's delight at the plan is like the delight Satan's
rebels express at Satan's own strategem in *Paradise Lost.*
Lucifer bestows helmets and breastplates on the rebel "Nisus"
and "Euryalus" and receives their praises in turn. He then dispatches his lieutenant Satanas to put the strategem into operation.
Yet here *Bellum angelicum* differs markedly from *Paradise Lost.*
Lucifer's angels do not surprise God's company; Satanas's plan is
well known in advance. Michael not only easily eludes them, but
takes Satanas himself by surprise. The sentry Satanas has posted
has time only to call out a last-minute warning. Satanas, trembling
with fear, wonders both how he can resist Michael's numbers and
how he can get word of his plight to Draco (Lucifer). Instead of
ambushing Michael's army, he finds his own escape cut off and
has no choice but to stand and hope for reinforcements. There is
no strong evidence that Milton was influenced by this incident in
Taubmann's epic, but it is an interesting parallel, being the only
other episode in a poem on celestial war that shows the rebels
organizing and carrying out a strategy against the loyalists.
Taubmann, however, is more conservative than Milton in that he
permits his rebels only to frame their strategy and put it into
execution; he does not permit them success. But Milton's rebels,
unlike Taubmann's, do surprise their foes. Milton's God, at this
point at least—unlike the traditional overseeing God of the Renaissance— has not interfered. He even permits the rebels some
degree of success, a success checked not by divine intervention,
but because their opponents themselves reply strategically and
bury the cannons. Milton is, of course, reading his audience a

lesson concerning gunpowder's future use. Therefore Raphael predicts how men in time to come may discover gunpowder and, like the rebels, use it to gain advantage over their enemies. Even in Heaven, Milton shows, the good are not impervious to indecent overthrow when force combines with guile to work against them.

In the gunpowder episode itself, Milton is deeply indebted to his Renaissance forebears, for both Spenser and Ariosto had described gunpowder as a Satanic invention, though crediting it with hellish rather than heavenly origin.[60] Ariosto has given in *Orlando Furioso,* moreover, a detailed description of the operation of the cannon, telling further how when flame was applied to powder this strange new invention caused an iron ball to fly forth with thunder and lightning (*Orlando Furioso,* 9.28–29). Milton may be looking back to Ariosto for his description in book 6 of the firing of the cannon. Watson Kirkconnell and others have claimed that his source was Valvasone's *Angeleida,* however, for Valvasone, like Milton, shows that the cannon was a device invented by Satan in Heaven for pursuit of heavenly war.[61] Placing Milton's description side by side with Valvasone's, moreover, we can note many resemblances. Both poets describe the cannon in close detail, treating it as a realistic implement of war and recounting how it is loaded with powder and fired.

> Sulphurous and Nitrous Foam
> They found, they mingl'd, and with subtle Art,

---

60. See *Orlando Furioso* 9.91, ed. Walter Binni (Florence, 1938–1940), p. 66; *Faerie Queene* 1., 7.13, 1–4 (*The Complete Works of Spenser* [Cambridge, 1908], pp. 186–187). See Hughes's note in *Complete Poems and Major Prose* (p. 335); Hughes places Milton's indebtedness to these poets in the context of Renaissance commonplace.

61. Kirkconnell, *Celestial Cycle,* pp. 81, 577. In *Milton and the Book of Revelation* (University, Ala., 1975), Austin C. Dobbins suggests that Milton's use of gunpowder in this sequence of the war in Heaven was influenced by the common belief in the Renaissance that Rev. 9:17–18 prophesied the use of gunpowder by the Turkish army. He cites the Protestant theologian, Thomas Brightman, as one of the leading proponents of this view (pp. 39–45).

Concocted and adusted they reduc'd
To blackest grain. . . .

Which into hollow Engines long and round
Thick ramm'd, at th' other bore with touch of fire
Dilated and infuriate shall send forth
From far with thund'ring noise among our foes
Such implements of mischief as shall dash
To pieces, and o'erwhelm whatever stands
Adverse, that they shall fear we have disarm'd
The Thunderer of his only dreaded bolt.

[*Paradise Lost*, 6.512–515, 484–491]

Di salnitro, & di Zolfo oscura polue
Chiude altri in ferro cauo, & poi la toccä
Dietro col foco, e in foco la risolue,
Onde fragoso tuon subito scocca:
Scocca, & lampeggia, & una palla volue,
Al cui scontro ogni duro arde, & trabocca:
Crudel Saetta, ch' imitar s'attenta
L'arme, che' l sommo Dio dal Cielo auenta.

[Valvasone, 2.20]

Another placed a nitrous sulfurous dust,
Inside an iron tube, and then with fire
Touched it within and caused it to combust
And burst abroad with crashing din more dire;
And as it flashed, a bullet forth was thrust
That sped at any mark with burning ire,
A cruel shaft that sought to imitate
The sky-hurl'd thunderbolt of God most Great.

[Kirkconnell, p. 81]

Both Milton's and Valvasone's descriptions are set pieces, abounding in commonplaces: the compounding of the nitrous-sulfurous dust, the fire and noise of the cannon's explosion, and the likening of the cannon to God's thunderbolt. Both demonstrate the hellishness of Satan's conduct of heavenly war. Valvasone makes no use of the cannon beyond this set description, however. We do not see it employed by the rebels in their warfare, nor does it function to surprise or overthrow the loyalists. He describes the cannon merely to show what monstrous weapons the rebels, themselves metamorphosed into monsters, have at their disposal. Milton, on the other hand, not only has given us a set description in which the monstrousness of the cannon is illustrated, but has also created an episode in which the cannon serves as the centerpiece for Satanic strategy.

With the use of this cannon episode on the second day of battle, Milton has the opportunity to make some rather independent comments about the nature of the war in Heaven. At the end of the first day it was clear that he held back from according complete victory to the loyal angels. But, like his Renaissance predecessors, he still treated the loyalists as noble victors. Heroic battle had not failed them as it had failed the rebels. But on the second day he shows how vain heroic arms may be to the noblest of heroes. As fair morn reappears in Heaven and the trumpet sounds, the loyal angels, singing matins, gird on their adamantine coats, fit well their helms, and grip fast their orbed shields. But these very arms prove their undoing. With the assault of the cannon, they fall down: "By thousands, Angel on Arch-angel roll'd; / The sooner for thir Arms" (6.594–595). "Unarm'd," as Raphael remarks, "they might / Have easily as Spirits evaded" overthrow; but so encumbered they are prey not only to discomfiture and defeat, but to the laughter of their enemies. It is astonishing that Milton has permitted his splendid loyal warriors to experience such humiliation—and humiliation it is, comparable to that the rebels experienced on the first day. Likewise astonishing is it that Milton permits the rebels such success, for no band of rebels in the Renaissance poems we have been looking at achieves so decided a victory. Of course, it is not the loyal angels that Milton is criticizing, nor the rebels he is praising for their clever invention. As I commented in the previous chapter, the loyal angels must learn how vain is their trust in material arms and the glory of material warfare. They are not permitted the glory of sword or spear. They throw down their arms, and in this combat they never resume them. Not through arms will Satan and his crew be routed. By the end of the second day it will become clear that the army assembled to defeat Satan will not and cannot do so. Milton has invented the episode of the cannon not merely to show the devilishness of the schemes Satan and his company can hatch (Taubmann and Valvasone show that with their episodes). Milton has Satan invent the cannon to demonstrate the ineffectuality as well as the perversity of wars of "weaponry." Ironically enough, Satan, along with the good angels, learns the lesson, while Moloch with his compeers still longs in Hell for "more valid Arms, / Weapons more violent" (6.438–439), yearning to turn Tartarean sulfur into horrid arms (2.60–64).

It is sometimes asked whether Milton's marshaling the machinery of conventional epic battle for the first two days of the war in Heaven does not express a purpose at variance with the scorn he states in book 9 for the way epic glorifies such machinery. The Renaissance celestial epic clearly equips its loyal angels with shining armor and swords and shields to glorify their achievement in arms. This is pointedly so because most of the epics end with some kind of display of arms. Either Michael singly or the angels joining with him achieve victory by the sword. In Peri's and Vondel's plays, in Acevedo's and Murtola's poems, Michael's blow drives Lucifer, followed by his terrified company, from Heaven. In Valvasone's poem, after Michael wounds Lucifer, Michael's army joins to rout the rebel angels. Raising their weapons and praising God, they strike the fleeing soldiers, while God, watching, hurls thunder with his right hand. But Milton's loyal angels are spectators to rather than participants in Satan's rout. Their war of weapons ends on the second day when arms are thrown down and Satan's cannons are buried beneath the volley of hills. It is almost a gesture of distaste on Milton's part for what the Son of God in *Paradise Regained* will call the cumbrous luggage of war.

The final episode of the second day makes still more forceful Milton's critique not merely of heroic warfare, but of war in general. The loyal angels throw away their arms but, plucking up the hills and hurling them, find still more deadly "arms" with which to oppose the mischief of the cannon. In what could only be an ironic comment, Milton permits Raphael to commend the excellence of their invention. Of course, from the merely tactical view, it is brilliant to render the cannons useless by burying them beneath heavenly hills. But in the light of the wholesale ravage of Heaven's landscape that occurs, it is hardly so. Milton is not unindebted to Renaissance traditions for this violent climax to the second day of battle. From the first premonitory tremblings of the cosmos, Renaissance poets had warned that Heaven was threatened by the war. At the climax of his war, Peri had shown how Lucifer as a fiery dragon devastated Heaven. Milton, who on the first day recorded that Heaven resounded with the shock of battle and the sky flamed, holds back until the climax of the second day from evoking a serious picture of cosmic discord. Then, as the hills fly, darkening the heavenly landscape, he gives us a Heaven going to wrack. His picture of heavenly disorder is interesting in that he adheres rather more closely than most of his predecessors to the classical model that portrayed the devastation of a war of the gods. Hesiod had shown how the Titans in their attempt upon Zeus caused all kinds of disturbances in nature: the infinite great sea moaned, the earth crashed, and the wide sky resounded, Olympus rocked at its very bases, the winds rushed wildly, and Tartarus shuddered in its depths. Claudian and Nonnos also had depicted cosmic devastation in their epics. The Renaissance poets, as we have seen, record like effects but make no clear allusion to the giants' warfare. Milton, however, does not adopt so general a picture of cosmic discord. He gives us instead a specific scene that cannot fail to suggest its original in classical literature. The loyal angels who bury the cannons with their volley of hills distinctly recall the giants who in service to Zeus overwhelm the Titans with volleys of rock and literally bury them.

Kottos and Briareus and Gyes,
Insatiable in war among the foremost,
Waged sharp battle. They hurled from their
Strong hands three hundred rocks,
One after another, overshadowed
The Titans with their missiles,
Sent them beneath the wide-wayed earth,
And bound them with cruel chains. . . .

[*Theogony,* lines 713–718][62]

The scene in book 6 seems clearly to echo Hesiod. Milton's giant angels are poised one against the other as Hesiod's giants and Titans are in the *Theogony*. First the loyal angels run and loosen the foundations of the mountains: "They pluckt the seated Hills with all thir load, / Rocks, Waters, Woods, and by the shaggy tops / Uplifting bore them in thir hands" (6.644–646). The mountains bury the rebels at first underground, as the mountain rocks bury the Titans; then working their way "out of such prison," the rebels "in imitation to like Arms / Betook them, and neighboring Hills uptore" (6.662–663). The ensuing tableau depicts a scene of mass disturbance such as Hesiod portrays. Like the warring giants and Titans, Milton's angels are overshadowed by this massive missile warfare.

So Hills amid the Air encounter'd Hills
Hurl'd to and fro with jaculation dire,
That under ground they fought in dismal shade:
Infernal noise. . . .

[6.664–667]

The echo of Hesiod is reinforced, moreover, by the fact that this is not the first time Milton has alluded to the Titans, the giants, and their warfare. In book 1 Satan is compared in bulk to those "whom the Fables name of monstrous size, *Titanian,* or *Earth-*

---

62. Hesiod, "Theogony," in *Homeric Hymns and Homerica,* ed. H. G. Evelyn-White (London: William Heinemann, 1926), p. 130 (my translation).

born, that warr'd on *Jove,* / *Briareos* or *Typhon,* whom the Den / By ancient *Tarsus* held'' (1.197–200). Satan's flight in book 1 over the burning lake, compared to the flight of a mountain torn "from *Pelorus,* or the shatter'd side / Of thund'ring *Aetna*'' (1.232–233) also had suggested the Titans' volleying or the rage of Typhon or Typhoeus, the last monstrous opponent of Zeus, whom the poets described imprisoned under Etna.[63]

That Milton concludes the warfare of the second day with an episode that has classical echoes has two effects. It aptly predicts the doom of the rebel angels as it permits them to adopt the demeanor of the enemies of Zeus whom he overcame and imprisoned in Tartarus; Heaven overshadowed becomes for them rightly that Hell they will soon inhabit. But the scene also reduces the stature of the loyal angels as they war against their "pagan" opponents. Now identified with the opponents of the fallen Titans, they wage a monstrous war, themselves almost metamorphosed into those giants of mythology. Milton's well-meaning angels, lit at the beginning of the war with spiritual enthusiasm and love of God, have taken on one incongruous role after another: first epic warriors with material swords and spears, then medieval knights whose armor crushed them as they engage against modern artillery, and finally mythic figures who act out the most primitive yet most deadly of struggles. How ironic it is that these loyal angels sent forth to save Heaven and purge it of pestilence should join with the rebels to produce the Hell-in-Heaven that we see at the climax of the second day, the place of dismal shade and dolorous groan and confusion heaped on confusion.[64] How far removed

63. The description of the mountains in flight probably goes back to poets like Claudian and Nonnos, as well as to Hesiod, who both included accounts in their Gigantomachiae of the hills uprooted, along with rocks, waters, and woods. See, for example, Claudian, *Gigantomachia,* 63–71, in the Aldine edition (Venice, 1523), pp. 171–174.

64. Isabel G. MacCaffrey has described the process by which Milton shows us, through repeated images of fire and darkness, Heaven being transformed to Hell (*"Paradise Lost"* as *"Myth"* [Cambridge, Mass., 1959], pp. 162–165).

they are from their fellows in Renaissance epic who effect a speedy victory over the foe.

As we shall see in chapter 7 when we examine the role of the Son, Milton's substitution of the Son of God for Michael as victor in the heavenly combat is almost unique in hexaemeral literature. Renaissance poets had two basic ways of bringing the war in Heaven to its conclusion. The first was through a single combat of Michael with Lucifer (in chapter 7 we shall also look at the depiction of the hero Michael in the Renaissance poem). The second was the traditional way, with God himself hurling Lucifer from Heaven. This had been the method of the medieval mysteries. Spenser and Sir William Alexander, who shun descriptions of heavenly war, depict God expelling Lucifer. Naogeorgus in his *Satyra* has God, perceiving the armies deadlocked in battle, step forward and, seizing Lucifer, amid thunder and lightning hurl him from Heaven. Mollerus's God acts similarly. And Valmarana, having had the *Verbum Dei* join with Michael's army to effect the rout of Lucifer's rebels, has God himself, hurling lightning and stripping him of his beauty and angelic honors, put Lucifer out of Heaven. But whether it is Michael or God who effects his expulsion, Lucifer is in effect defeated before this last blow. (Only Naogeorgus shows God breaking a deadlock.) Satan's rebels have already been repulsed by Michael or by his army; the war is all but won. But in *Paradise Lost,* before the arrival of the Son, the war is not only hopelessly stalemated, but hopelessly degenerate. It is not only that the angels have no hope of winning without the Son (Valmarana had also shown this), but that without him they would have wasted eternity in futile combat.

As in most Renaissance poems, Milton's war in Heaven begins as a glorious expedition of arms and ends with a decisive rout of Satan and his army. But, during the time intervening, not only is Milton's war different structurally from its Renaissance predecessors, it is different in its attitudes toward the participants and in its manipulation of events. It does not move upward in an unbroken curve, recording loyalists' successes. Involving not only struggle for the loyal angels, but major setbacks, the war can hardly be described as an uncritical triumph. Only with the coming of the Son do the tone and the nature of the war alter.

War, as I noted at the beginning of this chapter, was frequently regarded in the seventeenth century as the offspring of Satan and Hell. Milton differs from this view in book 6 only to show that the "Hell" of war was first created in Heaven. Though many Renaissance poets show their distaste for war, particularly as glorious angel first meets angel in combat or as the heavenly atmosphere is upset by the discord of battle, their praise of the loyal angels' war making is enthusiastic and uncritical. And, as we shall see in chapter 7, the celebrations they stage for Michael's returning army rival the roman triumphs. In taking over the details of war making from classical and contemporary epic traditions, the poets also take over many of the attitudes. As Virgil glorified Aeneas's war because it was designed to found the Roman empire, as Tasso has God and the angel Michael sanction Godfrey's efforts to capture Jerusalem, so Renaissance poets glorify Michael and his angels. Milton's apology, put into the mouth of Raphael on the first day, reveals a different attitude. For Milton has made his narrator refrain from recounting glorious acts of war. The elect are content with fame in Heaven, the others

> In might though wondrous and in Acts of War,
> Nor of Renown less eager, yet by doom
> Cancell'd from Heav'n and sacred memory,
> Nameless in dark oblivion let them dwell.
> For strength from Truth divided and from Just,
> Illaudable, naught merits but dispraise
> And ignominy, yet to glory aspires
> Vain-glorious, and through infamy seeks fame;
> Therefore Eternal silence be thir doom.
>
> [6.377–385]

The war waged before us in *Paradise Lost* is Satanic in essence. Rebel and loyal angel alike—even though the loyal are upheld by truth and justice—subscribe to the classical ethic of war making wherein skill and strength determine victory. No wonder the war ends in a deadlock. Milton makes his angels take on the demeanor of classical warriors in order to discredit the ethic of heroic battle. Whereas his predecessors built their wars in Heaven with the bricks of Homer and Virgil, Ariosto and Tasso, sure that in so doing they were giving literary quality to their celestial poems, Milton is not so uncritical. He makes Satan into an epic hero not because Taubmann or Valvasone or Vondel before him had done so, but to show what was wrong with the conventional epic hero. He allows the angels to raise heroic battle in Heaven not so that he may have the opportunity to create a splendid tableau of arms and armor, but to demonstrate what is essentially perverse in the ethic of typical heroic poems. On the last day he totally departs from the conventional celestial poem in making the Son his hero; and so, as we shall see in the final chapter, he creates for us a new idea of the heroic.

CHAPTER 6

Satan as Epic Hero

On the rough edge of battle ere it join'd
Satan with vast and haughty strides advanc'd,
Came tow'ring, arm'd in Adamant and Gold....

[6.108–110]

Satan, proud but magnificent, unyieldingly resolute in battle, emerges in the Renaissance poems wearing the full splendor of epic trappings. To these poems we owe in large measure the hero Satan as he is developed in *Paradise Lost*. Renaissance poets drew on two traditions to depict Satan or Lucifer: the hexaemeral and the epic. Hexaemera described Lucifer as a prince, glorious and unsurpassed, whose ambition caused him to strive above his sphere; epics described their heroes as superhuman in battle and accorded them, whatever their arrogance or mistakes in judgment, "grace" to offend, even as they are called to account for their offenses. The Lucifer of the Renaissance thus combines Isaiah's Lucifer with Homer's Agamemnon, Virgil's Turnus, and Tasso's Rinaldo. Milton's Satan, in turn, follows the Renaissance Lucifer and is both the prince depicted in hexaemera and the classical battle hero.

As he had been in hexaemera, the Renaissance Lucifer is the first and most beautiful of the angels. So he is described by Taubmann, Acevedo, Valvasone, Alfano, and Vondel. Heywood calls him the first in creation and the first in virtue.[1] Murtola

---

1. Taubmann, *Bellum angelicum*: "ante alios Genius pulcherrimus omneis" (p. 78); Acevedo, "Dia Primero," in *De la creacion del mundo:* "Del olimpo crió la inmortal gente, / Resplandeciendo con ardor glorioso, / Y entre ellas la mas bella criatura / Se deslumbró de ver su hermosura" (p. 249); Valvasone, *Angeleida*: "Di questi il più diletto, il più gagliardo, / Et di tutte le gratie il più splendente, / Ne

198

remarks that Lucifer outshone all the angels in beauty as the sun outshines everything else in the sky.

Fra quanti furo in Cielo Angeli Amori
Semplici, luminosi, e fiammeggianti,
Lucifero più chiari almi splendori
Più bello aprì fra tanti spiriti, e tanti,
E come il Sol più viui aurei folgori
Spande, e più vaga è l'Alba al Sole auanti.[2]

[Stanza 56]

Among so many angels as were in Heaven, Loves,
Pure, shining, and blazing,
The most clear splendid souls,
Lucifer appeared most beautiful among so many spirits, and by so
    much,
As the Sun scatters the most brilliant golden splendors,
Even so the Dawn seems most beautiful when the Sun has
    advanced.

Lucifer's power, moreover, is celebrated along with his beauty. Medieval poets had related that Lucifer held high position in Heaven; Renaissance poets, however, assign him specific political powers. For them his position in Heaven is not merely orna-

---

la bellezza sua rivolse il guardo, / E s'alzò ne la sua superba mente'' (1.26); Alfano, *La battaglia celeste tra Michele e Lucifero*: ''L'Angel piu bel che ne le sedie eccelse / Si godea, egli altri di beltade adorni / A l'ira hai persuaso, astringer l'else, / Onde la pace lor turbi, e i soggiorni'' (p. 25); Vondel, *Lucifer:* ''*Belz.* Daer hoor ick Lucifer, en zie hem, die den nacht / Van's hemels aengezicht verdrijven kan, en jaegen. / Waer hy vershijnt, begint het heerlijck op te daegen. / Zijn wassend licht, het eerste en allernaeste aen Godt, / Vermindert nemmermeer'' (pp. 13–14). (''There I hear Lucifer, and see the star /That drives away the night from Heaven's face! / For where he shines, day gloriously begins. / His crescent radiance, brightest next to God, / Shall never wane'' [(Kirkconnell, *Celestial Cycle,* p. 373].) Thomas Heywood, *The Hierarchie of the blessed Angells* (London, 1635): ''Amongst which *Lucifer* was chiefe; and hee, / As he might challenge a prioritie / In his Creation, so aboue the rest / A supereminence, as first and best: / For he was chiefe of all the Principalities, / And had in him the stupendious qualities / Of the most holy Trinitie, which include / First, Greatnesse, Wisedome, next, then Pulchritude'' (p. 336).

2. Gasparo Murtola, *Della creatione del mondo* (Venice, 1608), canto primo, stanza 56.

mental or ceremonial, a complement, so to speak, to the splendor
he possessed as the loveliest of the angels. Lucifer is a regent or
viceroy or governor. Valmarana tells us that as he is the angel
closest to God and partakes of the fountain of light; he is the
"magister" in Heaven.[3] Vondel makes him viceroy and allows
his readers to infer from the manner in which he is treated by
Gabriel and Raphael that he was principal governor of Heaven.
Valvasone and Taubmann and Alfano make him a great prince
with angels to administer. Heywood makes him head of all the
principalities of Heaven.

Milton, like his Renaissance predecessors, places strong emphasis on Satan's position in Heaven before his fall: "Great in
Power, / In favor and preeminence" (5.660–661). Unlike them, he
glances only obliquely at his prelapsarian beauty. Only after his
fall does Raphael accord him his former name *Lucifer* or describe
him as "brighter once amidst the Host / Of Angels, than that Star
the Stars among" (7.132–133). Only in Hell do we see a beauty
now eclipsed or in Eden a splendor vaunted but no longer recognizable to others (1.591–600; 4.835–840). In Heaven Milton first
and foremost shows us Satan not as the most beautiful, but as the
most powerful of the angels. He describes him as a potentate with
great name and high degree, whose angels obey his superior voice
without demur. He is the one whose power easily conveys one-
third of God's angels away from their God. It is not unlikely that
he has taken his cue for this portrait of power from his Renaissance
predecessors. For in their poems Lucifer is designated, as was the
great king Agamemnon in the *Iliad,* as the leader of multitudes,
the *anax andrōn* (lord of men). Lucifer as general and epic leader
is a creation of the Renaissance.

We may discern this clearly as we study his genesis and development in the Renaissance poems. In them pride and ambition, long identified as Lucifer's sins, acquire specific political

3. Odoricus Valmarana, *Daemonomachiae*, "Liber Primus" (1623), pp.
10–11.

ramifications. They are more than the personal or private sins medieval tradition had sometimes made them. Medieval poets tended to look at Lucifer's ambition simply. Lucifer yearned to aggrandize himself personally and to be worshiped like God. In the mysteries, his pride takes the form of an absurd and blasphemous desire to sit in God's seat. In the Lucifer play from the Coventry cycle, for example, Lucifer, hearing the angels sing a song of praise to God, decides that he is worthy to sit in God's seat and be so praised.

> To whos wurchipe synge ʒe þis songe
> to wurchip god or reverens me?
> but ʒe me wurchipe ʒe do me wronge
> ffor I am þe wurthyest þat evyr may be.[4]

Intoxicated by his own vaunted excellence, he attempts to sit in God's seat when God's absence affords him the occasion. In the York and Towneley cycles, he feels himself falling the moment he ascends to God's place; in the Coventry and Chester cycles, God returns and, finding Lucifer in his place, orders him to Hell.[5] What the mysteries have done, of course, is to take quite literally Isaiah's account of Lucifer's vaunt: "I will exalt my throne above the stars of God: I will sit also upon the mount of the congregation" (Isa. 14:13). In so doing they succeed in dramatizing his personal ambition to be like God, but they sometimes create

4. *Ludus Coventriae,* ed. K. S. Block (London: Early English Text Society, 1922), p. 17.

5. See *York Plays,* ed. Lucy Toulmin Smith, p. 4; *Towneley Plays,* re-ed. George England, p. 5; *Ludus Coventriae,* p. 18; *The Chester Plays,* re-ed. Herman Deimling, p. 17.

Several poems of the thirteenth and fourteenth centuries treat Lucifer's rebellion in a similar manner. They tell how Lucifer boasted that he would ascend the throne of God, exactly quoting Lucifer's words from Isaiah. They do not, however, picture the event. Lucifer falls immediately after his boast is made. See *The Story of Genesis and Exodus,* ed. Richard Morris (London, 1865), and "Clannesse," in *Early English Alliterative Poems,* ed. Richard Morris (London, 1864). For a full account of the fall of Lucifer in medieval literature, see P. E. Dustoor, "Legends of Lucifer in Early English and in Milton," *Anglia 54* (1930); 213–268.

grotesque and comic effects. Lucifer becomes a strutting braggart who attempts to take his master's seat and falls from it.

Of course, some biblical dramas treat Lucifer's rebellion simply and seriously. In *Adam und Heva,* performed in Zurich in 1550, Jacob Ruff creates a Lucifer whose ambitions can be easily presented and easily controlled. His Lucifer has wished to be like God. God, recognizing this wish, has dispatched Michael with a group of angels to throw Lucifer from Heaven. Michael, confronting the apostate angel, accuses him of having thought in his heart to place his seat above the stars and be like the most high. For this sin—and clearly it is a mental sin or transgression—Lucifer must be punished with pains of Hell. And so the angels literally carry out their commission.[6]

For the Renaissance, however, Lucifer's pride is not portrayed merely as a forbidden wish or a breaking of a taboo (sitting in God's seat). Wish is rendered not only into action, but into military action. So it is that the Lucifer of Mollerus's poem, *De creatione et angelorum lapsu carmen,* may begin with longings not unlike those of the Lucifers in the English mysteries or in Ruff's play. He longs—Mollerus permits us to eavesdrop—for praise comparable to that God receives. He wishes that his state not be inferior to God's. But as he reflects upon honors of higher estate, he becomes not so much the blaspheming angel as the epic opponent. He declares that as leader of legions of angels he deserves greater recognition. Thus he determines to seek the counsel of his allies and, gaining that, to challenge God's empire.[7] For most of the Renaissance poets Lucifer's vaunt to sit in God's seat and be like the most high is no empty blasphemy. It is a challenge to war. Like the medieval poets before them, many render Isaiah's words exactly, translating them into the language of the poem. But they restore them to their metaphorical rather than their literal sense. Their Lucifer is no simple egoist admiring his

6. Jacob Ruff, *Adam und Heva,* in *Band der Bibliothek der Deutschen National-Literatur* (Quedlinburg and Leipzig, 1848).
7. Fridericus Mollerus, *De creatione et angelorum lapsu carmen,* n. p.

own beauty and desiring praise. Nor is his projected act so baldly absurd that its attempt can only move us to laughter. The poets not only treat Lucifer's attempt seriously; they glamorize it by according it the trappings of an epic enterprise. They permit Lucifer, like Achilles, to dream of glory or, like Tamerlane or Alexander, to attempt to realize it through conquest. If the sheer fact of his ambition is unattractive (and the poets do deplore his ingratitude to God and his greediness for power), its expression as military ambition places it in a human category that epic poets had long rendered acceptable and understandable.

But besides rationalizing Lucifer's ambition, many poets provide him with yet stronger motives for his revolt. As it was not merely rivalry with Agamemnon that stirred Achilles in his quarrel, but a loss of place, a sense of honor forfeited or merit injured, so is it with the epic Lucifer. He is first moved not because he desires a higher place, but because he feels the place he already occupies is dishonored. New Honors given to the Son or to man make Lucifer feel he lacks sufficient honor. Of course Valmarana and Taubmann, who record Lucifer's resentment of the Son, and Peri and Vondel, who tell how he felt threatened by man's creation and exaltation, do not invent these motives for their Lucifers. The tradition that Lucifer was rival to the Son, though little used in literary works, goes as far back as the church father Lactantius. More popular in literature, however, was the tradition of Lucifer's rivalry with man; dating back to the church father Irenaeus and passed down by the Books of Adam and Eve, it had found place in medieval poems.[8] Both the Auchinleck and the Trinity manuscripts contain poems, for example, that recount how Satan refused to bow down and worship man as God's image and for his sin was excluded from Heaven.[9] The Renaissance poets take these motives and reshape them. They make Lucifer's

---

8. See chapter 2, notes 2, 3, and 4.

9. "Canticum de Creatione," MS Trinity College, Oxford, and MS Auchinleck, Edinburgh, in *Sammlung Altengischer Legenden,* ed. C. Horstmann (Heilbronn, 1878), pp. 124–138, pp. 139 ff.

resentment of the Son or of man the occasion for his rising in arms against God and attempting to rival the Almighty in power.

Thus both motives, as interpreted by Renaissance poets, gain a certain political thrust. In *Bellum angelicum,* it is not just that Lucifer resents the splendor and majesty of the Son (this was often, as we saw in chapter 2, the theologian's emphasis), but that he resented the power the Son wielded. Lucifer begins, as Taubmann tells us, with the euphoria of pure pride. He reflects that since he is the highest and the most beautiful of the angels, he is able as prince of Heaven to sway the kingdom alone. Full of himself, so to speak, and swelling with pride, he sends a messenger to God proclaiming that he will no longer abide beneath the yoke of God and the Son. The Son, he observes, rules earth like a demigod and men and angels are required to bow the knee to him. He, declares Lucifer, and not the Son is better qualified to rule.

> Huic ego sim supplex? ego? quo praestantior alter
> Non agit in superis, mihi jus dabit ille, suumque
> Dat caput alterius sub jus & vincula legum?
>
> [p. 79]

> To him should I be subordinate? I? Than whom no other
> holds sway more illustriously in the upper world? To me
> will he give law? Does he put another's rights under
> authority and the bonds of law?

Lucifer in *Daemonomachiae* has like ambitions. He asks God to place the world under his authority and is indignant at God's reply that the world belongs to the Son to rule. He is further incensed when God goes on to explain that all things are to be placed under the yoke of the Son and all must bow before him. Displeased that he is to be second in Heaven and oppressed by the yoke of the *Verbum Dei,* Lucifer utters his famous vaunt that he will place his seat in the North and be like the most high.

Valmarana in this sequence makes Lucifer's revolt the direct result of the thwarting of his political ambitions.

Lucifer in Peri's and Vondel's plays is likewise thwarted by circumstances and placed in a position of being second in God's favor. Man, however, and not the Son supersedes him. As Heywood's use of this story in his *Hierarchie of the blessed Angells* testifies, it had attained some currency in the Renaissance to supplement the accounts of pride—which Heywood also quotes—that Isaiah and Ezekiel narrated. At man's creation, so Heywood says, God intended some singular honor for him, either because man was made in God's own image or because in future time Christ was to be incarnated as man. Thus God ordains that the angels bow before man or serve him. Heywood offers the following rationalization: the angels were superior to man in all but one respect, that being:

> God from all eternitie decreed,
> That his owne Sonne, the euerlasting *Word*
> (Who to all Creatures *Being* doth afford,
> By which they first were made) should Heav'n forsake,
> And in his Mercy, humane Nature take.
>
> [p. 339]

Lucifer, hearing God's decree, swells with pride and envy, resenting that man, "being but Terrene" should receive such favors and not he and the angels, by nature "much more excellent." Drawing his angels to his side, he determines to raise seditious war in order to "hinder this irrevocable Deed" (pp. 338–340).[10]

Like Heywood, Peri and Vondel make the war in Heaven

---

10. The popularity of this motif is further attested by the Adam plays of the seventeenth century. In *Adamo caduto* (2.1), for example, Lucifer recounts that he was hurled to Hell because he refused to worship man. Similarly, in *L'Adamo* Lucifer tells him he prevented the angels from bowing down before man as the Word incarnate and thus provoked war with God (Kirkconnell, *Celestial Cycle*, pp. 307, 237–238).

spring directly from Lucifer's resentment of man's elevation. Peri devotes two scenes to the dramatization of this motive. The first is a political council in which Lucifer's allegorical advisors, Invidia and Superbia, spur him to action. Lucifer first explains to them that God has so blessed man in his creation that he has given him angel servitors. That he who was created first by the divine mind should be required to serve man seems insupportable. He contrasts his own incorruptible and immortal essence, his beauty and presence sublime, with man's vile substance and low origin. His high estate as head of angelic squadrons further supports his conviction that he should not bow before man. Superbia assures him of the justice of his case, reiterating the very arguments Lucifer had first introduced. She calls Lucifer the highest hero in Heaven and urges that it is man who should serve him, not he man. Lucifer now orders his two *fidei consorti* to gather his brothers to him while he himself erects his throne in the North. In act 2 Lucifer is permitted once more to argue the justice of his revolt. In the intervening time, still more faithful cohorts have risen to support Lucifer, among them his daughters Discordia and Ingratitudine, who, like Sin in *Paradise Lost,* are born spontaneously of his revolt. They endeavor to persuade the angels to Lucifer's cause. A strong opposition led by the angel Michael likewise has arisen. Therefore Lucifer must now argue the justice of his revolt not to Superbia and Invidia, the shadows of his desire, but to Pace, who is disturbed that war has sprung up in Heaven. What is interesting in this second justification is that Peri permits Lucifer even greater latitude in his arguments. Did not God deceive him, asks Lucifer, for he created him noble and beautiful but ordained that his nobility and beauty be obscured by vileness. What vileness could God do, questions Pace. Do you not think it vile to create from earth a man and make me serve him, counters Lucifer. Pace of course, tries to reason with Lucifer, arguing that God intended the angels as custodians rather than servants of man. Besides, she says, it is foolish and vain to oppose God the Creator, who after all was the one who created all things—not Lucifer. Lucifer, however, will not be moved, and as the scene mounts to a climax he vows that man will not boast that he had him as a servant.[11]

The Lucifer of Vondel's play is likewise eloquent in arguing his prerogatives to higher station than man. Act I compellingly lays the foundation. The angel Apollyon returns from Eden, having been dispatched there by Lucifer himself, to report on the pleasures Adam and Eve enjoy as lords of Paradise. Lucifer's closest angels—Belial and Beelzebub—express their wonder and also their envy at man's blessings. At this moment Gabriel arrives to announce that man's state is to be raised still higher. God has ordained that the everlasting Word is to become man, and in recognition of this future honor to man the angels are bidden to serve Adam and bow before him. A chorus of angels glorify this decree and pledge their obedience. As this chorus dies away, Lucifer enters for the first time and announces to Beelzebub that the "morning star" is past its zenith.

> Embroider no more crowns upon my robes!
> Gild not my forehead with the light of dawn's
> Bright star to which Archangels bow the head!
> Another radiance now rises, lit
> With glory from the Deity Himself

---

11. Giouandomenico Peri, *La guerra angelica* (MS Florence), 1.1; 2.2. Lucifer in Alfano's *La battaglia celeste tra Michele e Lucifero* is also angered at the announcement of the Son's coming Incarnation.

> Lucifero piu d'altri il cor trafitto,
> Di quel parlar, di quella spoglia hauea,
> E d'ira & d'odio, e di superbia abbonda,
> Qual mar che per gran vento gonfia l'onda.
>
> Non potea senza orgoglio, e senza affanni
> Di cor, veder quell' honorata spoglia.
> Era tutto di frodi pieno e 'nganni.
> Di peruersa, maluaggia, e fiera voglia;
> Dona principio à suoi, e d' all' altrui danni
> Mentre s'attrista dentro l'alma, e addoglia.
> Mentre pensa di far quel tanto ond' egli
> Sia à Dio nemico, egli altri al male suegli.

[p. 23]

That dulls our light. . . . Go hence, rejoice and serve
And honour this new race in mean subjection.
Man has been made for God, but we for man;
And now his feet shall tread on Angels' necks,
Yea, we must guard him, draw him by the hand,
Or bear him on our wings to thrones on high.
Our birthright goes to him, the favorite son,
Who violates our primogeniture.
The youngest son, in face so like the Father,
Obtains the crown; and there is given him
The sceptre before which the first-born bow
And tremble greatly.

                                              [2.2, p. 372]

Borduurt geen kroonen meer in Lucifers geweat;
Vergult zijn voorhooft niet met eenen dageraet
Van morgenstarre en strael, waer voor d'Aertsenglen nijgen;
Een andre klaerheit komt in't licht der Godtheit stijgen,
En schijnt ons glanses doot;

· · · · · · · · · · · · · · · · ·
                    gaet heene, viert, en dient,
En eert dit nieuw geslacht, als onderdane knapen:
De menschen zijn om Godt, en wy om hen geschapen.
't Is tijt dat's Engles neck hun voeten onderschraegh',
Dat ieder op hun passe, en op de handen draegh',
Of op de vleugels voere, in d'allerhooghste troonen:
Onze erfnis komt hun, als uitverkore zoonen.
Onze eerstgeboorte leit nu achter, in dit Rijck.
De zoon des zesten daghs, den Vader zoo gelijck
Gaschapen, strijckt de kroon.[12]

Like Superbia and Invidia in Peri's play, Beelzebub seconds his lord's dissatisfaction. (He had himself registered distress at Gabriel's decree: "That man will be exalted, we abased? / That we are born to serve, and man to rule?") But it is Lucifer who first plans revolt and "seduces" Beelzebub to his plans. Now, Vondel shows that there is pride in Lucifer's plans for revolt. He is hun-

---

12. Vondel, *Lucifer*, p. 12. (Kirkconnell, *Celestial Cycle*, pp. 371–372).

gry for first place in Heaven, and Vondel puts sentiments in his mouth not too unlike the Satanic boast of *Paradise Lost* 1.263: "Better to reign in Hell, than serve in Heav'n."

> Better it were by far
> To be the first Prince in a lower Court
> Than second, or still less, in heaven's light.[13]

[p. 374]

> En liever d'eerste Vorst in eenigh laeger hof,
> Dan in 't gezalight licht de tweede, of noch een minder.

[p. 14]

But there are other emotions and motives that Vondel also exploits. There is anger at alleged power or tyranny used to crush him: "Submit who will: I shall not yield a foot" (p. 374). There is the anxious desire to preserve his own: "I am a Son of Light, a ruler too, / In realms of Light, and shall defend my own" (p. 373). The crux of the matter is the same reluctance that Lucifer in Peri's play evinced: the reluctance of the angel as a superior creature to bow before an inferior. Lucifer openly admits to Gabriel how distasteful it is for him who has never bowed except before God now to bow to man. God's own honor, he argues, is abased when the angelic nature, until now closest to God's own, is abased. Gabriel in response does no more than advise obedience and caution Lucifer about the results of disobedience.

It is hardly surprising that dramatists like Peri and Vondel or

---

13. Milton echoes a traditional sentiment in his lines in book 1. Not only Vondel, but also Salandra in *Adamo caduto* had made his Lucifer express preference for kingship in Hell over mere princehood in Heaven (Kirkconnell, *Celestial Cycle,* p. 309). The phrasing for the line "Better to reign in Heaven" Milton probably owes to Phineas Fletcher. In the *Apollyonists,* 1.18, Fletcher had exclaimed, "O, let him serve in hell, who scorns in heaven to reign"; in the *Purple Island,* 7.10, he had stated, "In heav'n they scorn'd to serve, so now in hell they reigne" (Kirkconnell, *Celestial Cycle,* pp. 275, 282). Milton has achieved his stunning success with Fletcher's line by transposing the "reign" and "serve" of the *Apollyonists* line and by placing it (as in Vondel and Salandra) not in the mouth of the poet, but in Satan's own mouth.

epic poets like Valmarana and Vondel felt the need for motivation stronger than spontaneous pride. Lucifer does not wake up one morning and decide to displace the Father. Only when his own place is threatened does he move to usurp God's. Pride clearly impels him, true, but fear first stirs him—fear that he might lose his own vicegerent power. As a motive, this fear of lost power, this sense of injured merit, is more dramatically and psychologically complex than the spontaneous pride patristic writers had ascribed to Lucifer. C. S. Lewis, even as he berated the absurdity of Satan's claim to "injured" merit, recognized its force.[14] It is a motive that makes Satan as a character more humanly understandable. We can sympathize with his fear; we can understand his disappointments; we can even feel his sense of injured merit. These emotions, of course, do not excuse his actions, but they show how his actions have come about. Dame Helen Gardner was certainly right in recognizing that the villain-hero of Jacobean drama with his "reasonable" motives for action was an ancestor of Milton's Satan.[15] But the Lucifer of the Renaissance poem with his deep sense of humiliation at the Son's or Adam's advancement is an ancestor as well. The force that chagrin or political disappointment exerts upon him is not to be minimized. Dramatically, a villain with a motive makes better sense than a motiveless malignancy (which patristic tradition gives us) or a strutting egotist (which the medieval mysteries pose). And Milton's Satan is that: a character with a motive. Of the two motives available to him, Milton chose the one less current in the Renaissance. He chose to make Satan rebellious at the advancement of a superior rather than an inferior. Accordingly, he strikes a kind of mean. Milton's Satan evokes less sympathy from the reader with his refusal to bow the knee to *the Son* (newly appointed king) than does Peri's or Vondel's with the parallel refusal to bow to

14. See C. S. Lewis, *A Preface to "Paradise Lost"* (London: Oxford University Press, 1942), pp. 93–95.
15. Helen Gardner, *A Reading of "Paradise Lost"* (Oxford: Clarendon Press, 1965), pp. 99–120.

Adam. (Adam's advancement—whatever its reasons—had at least the advantage of "appearing" arbitrary.) Clearly, in providing Satan a motive Milton wants that motive to be one both reasonably understood and also reasonably answered. The answer, moreover, that Abdiel voices in book 5 is more incisive than the answer Pace or Gabriel had provided to Lucifer in the plays. Abdiel, like them, on the one hand argues that God may do as he likes, but on the other hand points out with superb logic that the Son was, even before his appointment as king, Satan's superior. No such case can Pace or Gabriel make for Adam; they can merely urge Lucifer to find a benevolent purpose in God's designs. Milton thus shows Satan suffering from deep chagrin at the disappointment of his political ambitions, but he denies him a fully acceptable motive for that chagrin.

If Renaissance poets work hard to show that Lucifer's motives for rebellion were compelling, if not excusable, they work even harder to accord him a kind of magnificence as he plans and carries out his revolt. There is the princely flourish with which Lucifer dispatches the messenger to God in *Bellum angelicum* and the impetuous anger with which he hears God's negative reply. His eyes flash fire, and he proudly asks himself if he should desist and withdraw his words. Then imperiously he declares that God's threats are vain and urges his angels to take up their weapons and raise their battle standards. Like an epic adversary, he dispatches the messenger back to the tyrant God to report his reaction. Or there is Lucifer in *Daemonomachiae,* who passionately resists God's decree of the Son's supremacy:

> O superans pia vota, Dei largissima dextra,
> Quid dignum tanto referam pro munere patri?
> Ergo mihi (neque enim mundi praeclarius ullum
> Exemplar statuisse reor) coniugia Verbi
> Decernis?
>
> [p. 15]

> Prevailing over holy vows, over the most bountiful pledges of
>   God,

Why should I exchange my honors for such great duty to the
    Father?
Wherefore (since I do not believe a more splendid model to have
    been set up for the world)
Do you determine for me the yoke of the Word?

Not in words only but in appearance the poets describe Lucifer
as an imperious epic figure. Acevedo shows him at the head of his
army, envious and proud: "angel superbio y invidioso, / Ver-
tiendo por los ojos abrasados / Y por la boca fuego impetuoso"
(p. 249). In two similes, moreover, Acevedo gives Lucifer the
appearance of an epic hero, comparing him first to a bull in majestic anger pawing the earth and then to a falcon swooping down on
his prey.[16] Homer had, of course, compared Agamemnon to a
bull who stood conspicuous in the herd (2.480–483) and had compared Achilles as he pursued Hector to the falcon (22.139–142).
Lucifer is treated in simile analogously to these classical warriors.
Also, as Agamemnon is described as kingly in appearance, with
eyes and head like those of Zeus who delights in thunder, girth
like Ares', and chest like Poseidon's, so Lucifer is kingly. Taubmann compares him, striding among his soldiers, to Orion plung-
ing into the ocean waves, then arising head and shoulders above
the ocean. Moreover, the kind of princely anger Lucifer indulges
in is both like the classical anger of Agamemnon or Achilles and
like the anger of Tasso's Soliman or Ariosto's pagan kings. In
book 10 of *Gerusalemme liberata,* for example, Soliman strides
forth from the mist to repudiate the pagans for suggesting com-

16. Acevedo, *Angeleida,* pp. 249–250. The pagan Argantes in book 6 of
Gerusalemme Liberata is also compared to a bull, as he readies himself for battle.
    Like as a bull, when prick'd with jealousy
      He spies the rival of his hot desire,
    Through all the fields doth bellow, roar, and cry,
      And with his thund'ring voice augments his ire,
    And threat'ning battle to the empty sky,
      Tears with his horn each tree, plant, bush and briar,
    And with his foot casts up the sand on height,
    Defying his strong foe to deadly fight:
        [Godfrey of Bulloigne (trans. Edward Fairfax), 7.55]

promise; or in canto 38 of *Orlando Furioso* the pagan kings contend whether to advance a new assault on the Christians. Accordingly, when Taubmann and Valmarana show Lucifer passionately denouncing his adversaries, they have models in both classical and chivalric literature.

For the Renaissance poets who write wars in Heaven, Lucifer is primarily a kind of "pagan" general or prince. To give him proper ceremony, many poets create "council" scenes before the war in which he can demonstrate his princely qualities. These council scenes are peculiar to Renaissance literature, which found its precedents for them in the classical tradition. Medieval literature rarely showed Lucifer in consult with his angels before the war. It is also interesting that these prelapsarian councils often have as direct analogues or sources "hellish" councils, which some poets of the Renaissance had granted to the fallen Lucifer. A very definite correspondence exists between the behavior of the princely Lucifer who calls together his allies in Heaven and urges them to revolt against God and the prince of Hell who calls together his allies and urges them to a new enterprise. Poets writing councils in Heaven could model their Lucifers not only on King Agamemnon or King Agramant in consult, but also on Vida's Prince Satan or Tasso's kingly devil. The Renaissance permitted its pagan kings and its Satans to be imposing figures who speak with persuasive logic. Assuredly, of course, Vida and Tasso first make Satan in Hell a monster attended, as we have seen in Valvasone's *Angeleida,* with harpies, chimeras, and so forth. The moment he begins to speak, however, his grotesqueness is forgotten. Like an epic hero, he speaks passionately and persuasively. First, Vida's Lucifer pricks the resentment of his followers by reminding them how God hurled them from Heaven and imprisoned them in Hell. At the same time he compliments their valiant resistance to God's tyranny. On the one hand he insinuates that God intends to impose new chains on them in Hell, and on the other he appeals to their courage and resourcefulness to prevent further enslavement to God by swiftly arming against him.[17] Tasso's Satan (some fifty years later) similarly plays on the vanity and fear of his auditors. He praises their angelic origins, reminding them of their glory in Heaven and the boldness of their war against God. He pricks resentment by recalling at the same time how God usurped their rights in Heaven and committed outrage against them. And, to persuade them to a new cause, he threatens that God will encroach upon their rights in Hell if they do not rouse themselves and once more fight courageously (*GL* 4.1.-19).

These two council scenes, which present a Lucifer exhorting his followers, influence *Paradise Lost* in that they provide, directly or indirectly, the models for Satan's speeches from the throne both in Hell and in Heaven. In Hell Satan glances at lost glory, guilefully encouraging his angels to think of regaining their seats in Heaven, while in truth encouraging them to new enterprises on earth. In Heaven he attempts to prick the angels' resentment of the yoke imposed upon them by the kingship of the Son and make them fear that still heavier yokes will be imposed. In both these scenes Milton looks back to Vida and Tasso themselves and to later poems influenced by them.

Council scenes (in Heaven, rather than in Hell) come to dominate the poems that describe the war in Heaven. Renaissance poets, after they have shown Lucifer himself moved to revolt, are eager to show how he moved others. They frequently demonstrate how Lucifer appeals, as he did in Vida's *Christiad,* to the twin emotions of vanity and fear. Mollerus's Lucifer invokes pride of place to urge the angels that they deserve greater rights and recognition than they have been given. Then he uses the spurs of virtue, honor, and praise to stir them.

> Ingens consilium latitat sub mente repostum,
> Vnde manet virtus, laus, honor, unde decus.

---

17. For discussion of Vida's council in Hell, see Olin H. Moore, "The Infernal Council," *Modern Philology* 16 (1918): 169–193. Also see Gertrude C. Drake, "Satan's Councils in the *Christiad, Paradise Lost,* and *Paradise Regained*" in the Third *Acta Conventus Neo-Latini Turonensis,* forthcoming.

Scitis ut in nostra sit magna potentia gente,
Quòd nullus nostros aequet honore gradus.

[n.p.]

Mighty counsel lies hidden, remote in the mind,
Whence abides virtue, praise, honor, hence glory.
You know that there is in our race great power,
Because no one compares with us in degree of honor.

Taubmann's Lucifer also intimates that the angels have been badly treated by God, who puts servile yokes upon them; he appeals to them that in the name of liberty they cast off these yokes. Honor also he invokes, telling them to be heroes and fight for fame without shrinking.[18] Naogeorgus's Lucifer, in like vein, tells the angels that they suffer an unworthy servitude. He has discerned in them willing hearts, faith, and virtue, and in obedience to these qualities they should throw off the yoke they bear and aspire to a rank equal to God's. Valvasone's Lucifer becomes rhapsodic when he speaks of glory. He too has pled the cause of lost honor and place, and he now presents his angels with the grim necessity of war. Invoking justice, reverence, faith, he promises that they will conquer gloriously:

Che dirò de la gloria? O quanta pompa,
O che trionfo conduremo in Cielo:
O frati, o frati, homai nulla interrompa
Lenta dimora il vostro innato zelo:

[Valvasone, 1.99]

What should I say of glory? Of such pomp?
Oh, what a triumph I shall lead in Heaven!
Oh, brothers, brothers, let no slow delay
Impede your inborn fervor.

---

18. In *Daemonomachiae,* as well, Lucifer heaps praises on his angels, naming them eternal spirits, lit by light and virtue, eager for the good. Considering their excellence, he next demands, should they suffer the *Verbum Dei* to impose his yoke on them and permit man to appear superior? Finally, he exhorts them to hinder this imminent evil, strengthened by the very power God gave them (pp. 15–16).

In light, then, not only of Vida and Tasso but of Mollerus, Taubmann, Valmarana, Naogeorgus, and Valvasone, it seems apparent that Milton was following a well-established tradition when he had his Satan appeal to the angels' pride of title: "If these magnific Titles yet remain / Not merely titular" (5.773–774). Lucifers before Milton's had inveighed against the "knee-tribute," "prostration vile," and the yoke imposed in Heaven. Of angelic virtues, Milton's Satan chooses to extol liberty and in its name to suggest that the angels band together to "govern, not to serve" (5.802). Thus in book 5, when Satan rises before the multitude, readers familiar with the traditions knew what to expect. English readers could look back to the Satan of Phineas Fletcher, who had called upon the name of honor that the fallen angels throw off their yokes in Hell, or the Satan in Cowley's *Davideis,* who had likewise argued.[19] Milton in *Paradise Lost* does not disappoint his readers. But the effects he produces as Satan prepares to speak are necessarily different. For in book 5 it is not the first time we have seen Satan address a council like an epic hero. We have the experience of books 1 and 2 behind us. We have already heard Satan speak of equality and liberty, honor and degree (cf. 2.18–36). We will not be startled at the epic nobility of this figure. In book 5, however, Satan's epic speech, noble though it is, has lost something of its eloquence. The fact is, almost everything we hear him speak in book 5 we have heard before. And the echoes are hollow. For example, in book 1 Satan provokes his followers' resentment by suggesting that God had "tempted our attempt, and wrought our fall" (1.642); in book 5 he provokes resentment by suggesting that God has selfishly engrossed all power to himself and eclipsed the angels. In Hell he asks, "who can think subjection?" (1.661); in Heaven, "Will ye submit your necks, and choose to bend / The supple knee?" (5.787–788); and still further he states that God demands from them "Knee-tribute, yet unpaid, prostration vile" (5.782). In Hell he encourages aspiring

19. See Kirkconnell, *Celestial Cycle,* pp. 276, 421–422.

minds to "reascend / Self-rais'd" (1.633–634); in Heaven he described the angels as "self-begot, self-rais'd / By [their] own
quick'ning power" (5.860–861). The effect of these words is curious. Sounding the first time in Hell, they possess a vigorous
heroic ring. They grant to Satan, as they had to the Lucifers in the
Renaissance poems, the status of an epic hero. But repeated in
book 5 they are tired and empty. They are clearly the words of a
figure who only sounds heroic, whose assurances we have heard
before and now no longer believe. In rendering the heroic Satan in
book 5, Milton has reduced him.

In Renaissance literature, Lucifer the epic hero and Lucifer the
general are one. Not only soldier and hero is he—an Achilles or a
Hector—but also a leader of multitudes—an Agamemnon, a Soliman. So, early in the Renaissance epics and dramas, he stands
out to issue a call to arms. His supreme trust is in the ethic of
force. In assembling his army, therefore, he urges that all he and
his angels require to cast off the yoke of the tyrant is unfailing
courage in the exercise of arms. Mollerus's Lucifer proposes giving God a choice; either he abdicate in their favor or they chase
him from his seat by force. Naogeorgus's Lucifer is likewise direct. If God refuses to divide his empire and concede equal honor
to the angels (and Lucifer admits such concession is unlikely),
then force must be prepared and used. An encomium on arms
follows. Lucifer urges that the enterprise is in itself worth the
peril it entails. If the angels will join their might with his and
accept him as their leader, they will conquer. But if they refuse
such an opportunity, they can only repent in vain. Following this
tradition, in book 5 Milton glances, if only briefly, at Satan the
general. (He had given us a full-length portrait in books 1 and 2.)
Near the end of book 5 Satan the general flexes his muscles and
threatens military reprisal against the single angel Abdiel, who
has risen as an opponent.

> Our puissance is our own, our own right hand
> Shall teach us highest deeds, by proof to try

Who is our equal; then thou shalt behold
Whether by supplication we intend
Address, and to begirt th' Almighty Throne
Beseeching or besieging.

[5.864–869]

The scene is necessarily quite different, however, from what we
have observed in the Renaissance poems, where Lucifer delivers
his military vaunts to his angels alone, to be received, we pre-
sume, by their enthusiastic applause. Satan, in raising his vaunts
to Abdiel, loses much of his heroic stature. We do not see the
experienced general of book 1, who has made his angels rise from
off the burning lake to form perfect ranks before him; we do not
see the leader of book 2 who proposes to visit Chaos alone and
take full upon himself the heroic responsibilities. Instead we see
Satan bullying Abdiel with threats and making absurd claims to
besiege God. Again Milton has limited Satan.

Most of the Renaissance Lucifers depicted in poems describing
the war in Heaven are active leaders who challenge God directly.
Few combine demonic cunning with demonic bravura. Thus
Vondel's Lucifer, who does so, is an important forerunner of
Milton's Satan. He is, first of all, a splendid epic figure; lamenting
God's unjust decree and determining to resist it with the full
power of his own arm, he equals, indeed surpasses, the rhetoric
of the Lucifers before him. But he delivers his speeches to *his
own* coterie of angels—Beelzebub, joined by Belial and Apollyon.
Here is no Lucifer who openly vaunts his intentions. Not until the
very outbreak of war does he take command of that rebellion that
he fostered from the outset. There is no doubt in our minds,
however, that Lucifer is the natural leader, even though his plots
remain unacknowledged in name. It is he who first determines to
resist God's decree. (Beelzebub or Apollyon or Belial may dislike
it, but none shows any sign of holding forth against it.) It is also he
first who suggests that they challenge Michael, the commander-
in-chief of God's armies and the possessor of the key to God's
armories. (Apollyon lags back, fearing war with the Omnipotent.)

Lucifer in private speaks boldly and adventurously as he sets forth his schemes; in public, however, he retains the demeanor of the circumspect and prudent leader. Neither Gabriel nor Michael realizes till late in the poem that he is the author of rebellion.

Both Milton and Vondel stress Lucifer's political cunning. Both dramatize for us—after the archangel has himself determined to revolt—his seduction of his comrade Beelzebub and his subsequent employment of this angel to forward his plot. In *Paradise Lost* Satan directs Beelzebub to move his powers by night, telling "the suggested cause" and casting between "ambiguous words and jealousies, to sound / Or taint integrity" (5.702–704). In *Lucifer* the archangel dispatches his subordinates Apollyon and Belial to stir up the crowd by insinuation and directs Beelzebub to pretend dismay while all the time pressing for insurrection. (Only in Peri's *La guerra angelica* do we find Lucifer using subordinates to do his work for him, and since the subordinates are the allegorical vices Superbia and Invidia, the intention and effect are not the same as in Vondel's drama.) In *Lucifer* the masses of angels, the so-called Luciferists, fully stirred to revolt, drive away their commander Michael, who has attempted to quell them and make them lay down their arms. Now Lucifer at last appears before them. He does not immediately assume command. Indeed, the baton of leadership must be thrust upon him as he pretends hesitancy and caution. Then only does he become the general and then only deliver the words of challenge.

Milton's Satan is similarly indirect. For rather than using exhortation or commands (like Taubmann's or Naogeorgus's archangel), he employs as his basic method the inflammatory question. Are your titles merely titular? Are you now eclipsed in power by God? What new honor and knee-tribute will you pay to God and the Son? Will you submit? Will monarchy be imposed over equals? Will law and edict? Are you not ordained to govern rather than serve? (Of course, the inflammatory question serves Satan well throughout his career in *Paradise Lost,* from the first one he directs to Beelzebub in book 1 to the last he directs to Eve, not to mention the series of inflammatory questions he uses in book 1 to stir his newly wakened angels to action.) Vondel's thrust in *Lucifer* was to illustrate how Lucifer deceived the angels through skillful and deliberate manipulation. Milton also wishes to show this, and he does so first by showing that the crowd that stands before Satan in book 5 has been manipulated by Beelzebub to suspicion and distrust of God. (Unlike Vondel, Milton does not show us the manipulation as it takes place.) Milton's Satan seems at first a straightforward "hero," advocating revolt. But not so. Instead he is the manipulator who undermines the angels' confidence in God's kingdom and leads them to believe they have before them no alternative besides revolt. He is in demeanor like Agamemnon, in tactics like Odysseus. Beneath the appearance of courageous fighter and noble leader is the wily politician. And, outside of Vondel, Milton is the poet who most clearly gives us this impression of Satan.

In book 6 of *Paradise Lost* Satan has his best chance to behave like an epic hero, and at two points in the action he clearly does. The first occurs when, appearing upon the field of battle, brilliantly attired, he issues a general challenge to combat. The second takes place when, preparing to fight Michael alone, he defends "the strife of glory" in which he engages his strength. In so depicting the warring archangel, even momentarily, Milton may be glancing back at those Renaissance poets who granted Lucifer glory in battle. Vondel was certainly one who gives us a splendid description of Lucifer's entry on the field, ringed by troops in sapphire and green:

> Dress'd in a golden coat of mail that shone
> Above his purple tunic, mounted now
> His chariot, with gold wheels, ruby-studded.
> The Lion and fell Dragon were in his team
> In harness all bepearl'd, ready for flight,
> Sprinkled with myriad stars upon their backs,
> And burning for the wild destructive strife,

He bore a battle-axe; his shimmering shield,
In which the morning star was wrought with art,
Hung of his left arm, ready for all hazard.

[Kirkconnell, p. 410]

In't gouden panser, dat, op zijnen wapenrock
Van gloeiend purper blonck, en uitscheen, steegh te wagen,
Met goude wielen, van robijnen dicht beslagen.
De Leeuw, en selle Dracck, ter vlucht gereet, en vlugh,
Met starren overal bezaeit op hunnen rugh,
In't parrele gareel, gespannen voor de wielen,
Verlangden naer den strijt, en vlamden op vernielen.
De heirbijl in de vuist, de scheemrende rondas,
Waer in de morgenstar met kunst gedreven was,
Hing aen den slincken arm, gereet de kans te wagen.

[Vondel, pp. 55–56]

Taubmann similarly presents Lucifer as a formidable epic opponent, armed from head to foot, his terrible helmet on, his cuirass
huge and triple-twilled, rigid with scales (p. 87). Murtola tells us
how sparkling the arrogant angel appears at the head of his dark
and grim troops. Peri first presents the scene in which Lucifer
dons his armor for battle and bestows insignia and weapons on
the allegorical lieutenants who serve him. Then he shows him as
he enters battle, still the splendid epic figure, though captain over
a monstrous horde: Discordia, Rabbia, Ingratitudine, and so
forth. When he speaks to his soldiers, moreover, he is a proud,
bold, and resolute, but nonetheless heroic figure. He spurs them
on, telling them not to be afraid of the enemy and disparaging the
threat Michael and his soldiers offer. Assuring them of victory, he
orders them to the assault.

It is surprising how many poets give Lucifer the opportunity of
making a major battle speech, sometimes several, before he actually engages in arms. Of course they are following epic convention in so doing. But in following convention they permit Lucifer
a good deal of rather impressive heroic flourish. For Lucifer addressing his soldiers does not speak meanly and despicably. In

fact, he sounds little different from any general of epic, who before the battle acknowledges to his soldiers the danger of their
course but urges them to be brave. Acevedo, for example, gives
Lucifer a brief but stirring speech.

> ¡De mi opinion espíritus secuaces!
> Aunque mas peligroso sea el alarde,
> No entre en vuestros ánimos audaces
> Sombra ni rastro de temor cobarde;
> Estad en el propósito tenaces,
> Por mas que el premio que se os debe, tarde;
> Que yo en mi pensamiento voy tan firme,
> Que no puedo, aunque quiera, arrepentirme.
>
> [p. 249]

> O, spirits, followers of my convictions,
> Although my vaunts may be very dangerous,
> Do not let a shade or trace of cowardly fear enter
> Into your hearts. Be tenacious in your purpose,
> However late in coming be the prize due you.
> I in my intent am so firm that I cannot repent,
> Even though I might wish to do so.

Even though Acevedo has told us before the speech that this is
the rebel speaking (thus we should be outraged by his defiance
rather than stirred by his valor), it is the valor that impresses us.

Valvasone similarly gives us a curious mixture of the monster
and the hero. In outer appearance, of course, Lucifer is a monster: a hideous giant with a hundred arms, seven heads, and seven
mouths. And, with his angels likewise transformed, his camp
more closely resembles the pit of hell than the glorious fields of
Heaven. Moreover, since the fury Megara is his chief companion,
this association further emphasizes Lucifer's monstrous qualities.
But, despite all, once Lucifer opens his mouth we hear the voice
of the hero general. Boldly and extravagantly, he promises the
faithful that they will win honor and reward in the coming fight,
for the end of their struggle is the conquest not only of Heaven
but of earth. Crowns and kingdoms upon earth he promises, the

conquest of sea and land, the sun and the moon. All those of earth will come to worship them. Therefore, he urges, take up your arms and do not yield. The opposing side, he insists, is "soft" and unprepared, too unambitious to be equal, too weak, and willing merely to continue to serve God and pray for his favor. Face to face, he vaunts, we will overcome them.

Taubmann's Lucifer also excels in the battle speech. Not once, but repeatedly, do we hear him exhort his angels. On the first occasion he has just received the messenger he had dispatched to God. Hearing that God has refused his terms, he sends the messenger back defiantly and turns to his army. He tells them that the time has come when they must take up their arms.

> Venit summa dies; geritur res maxima, frates.
> Concurrent hodie Rex caeli & Lucifer armis.
> Ingenteis praestate animos, praeclara manebunt
> Praemia victorem.
>
> [p. 85]

> The final day is come; the greatest deed is accomplished,
>   brothers.
> Today, the king of Heaven and Lucifer clash with their armies,
> Exhibit prodigious spirit. The
> Most splendid rewards await the victor.

He next assembles them and drives them forth, and when they stand in arms before him he once more offers encouragement. Go forth, he says, go forth with the hope of future kingdom.

> I decus i nostrum, regni spes una futuri!
> Sentiat has vires belli rudis incola coeli,
> Quidque Draco possit, hodie experiatur in armis.
>
> [p. 88]

> Go forth with my glorious ones, go with a single hope for
>   empire-to-be!
> Let the churlish inhabitant of Heaven feel this strength of battle.
> Whatever the dragon can accomplish, today let him try in arms.

Yet, these are not all. Taubmann twice more gives his Lucifer opportunity to encourage his soldiers-in-arms: once at the end of book 1, after Lucifer has dispatched Satanas to carry out the strategem against the loyal army, once again at the end of book 2, when Lucifer prepares for the final battle with Michael. Having met Michael first and having exchanged challenges, Lucifer turns to his soldiers to assure them of the justice of their cause and to encourage them in the fight now imminent.

> Rerum spes & fortuna mearum,
> O domitor caeli, miles: quod saepè vocasti
> Tempus adest: toties quaesitae copia pugnae
> In manibus vestris. haec lux praestabit honores
> Haec libertatem sceptrumque: haec, judice ferro,
> Pandet, uter melior sit bello; uter arma parârit
> Iustiùs, heic medio posuit Mars omnia campo.

> [p. 104]

> Hope and fortune of my affairs,
> O Lord of Heaven, soldier, because often you have challenged
> The time is now; the occasion of the battle, so often
> Sought out, is in your hands.
> This glory shall win honor;
> This liberty and rule; this with the sword as arbiter
> Shall manifest whichever is better in war,
> Whichever shall have wielded arms more justly.
> At this point war has placed all in the midst of battle.

It is interesting that Milton makes little of the general Satan on the verge of battle. It is perhaps understandable that he has given him no battle speech in book 5; but the omission in book 6 is highly significant. We know from books 1 and 2 that Satan thinks of himself as the superlative leader—not only the great persuader, but the great general. Our first glimpse of him in book 1 was as the general who even in defeat was able to rouse his army. Hearing his voice, his soldiers rise from the burning lake and form perfect ranks before him. The speech he offers them, even in defeat, has kinship with those battle speeches that the aspiring Lucifer of the

Renaissance poems offered in heaven in expectation of victory. For Satan is intent not to yield or to be overcome; he even relishes the thought of future conquest on earth, intent on eternal war, open or understood. In book 6 there is neither a comparable scene nor comparable words. Therefore I think it is quite clear that Milton intends by book 6 to limit severely the kind of heroic expansiveness he had earlier permitted Satan. What he allows in the delusive half-light of Hell he will not allow in the clear sun of Heaven. Satan's heroic moments are notably few, and even those are cut very short. First there is the dramatic entrance, "High in the midst exalted as a God / Th'Apostate in his Sun-bright Chariot sat" (6.99–100), and then the brief magnificence as he strides forth, "tow'ring, arm'd in Adamant and Gold" (6.110). But these descriptions do not herald a scene in which Satan appears to advantage before his army or even delivers an effective challenge to the enemy. Instead, Milton has his brilliant hero advance to be met and repulsed (first verbally, then in arms) by the plain soldier Abdiel. Even his speech to Abdiel lacks a heroic ring; it is grumbling and condescending. He promises to repulse Abdiel and of course fails to do so. He mocks the minstrelsy of Heaven and is met with immediate proof that the disparaged minstrelsy is not to be despised. Thus at the first moment that Milton has lifted up the aspiring warrior-hero he very quickly casts him down.

A similar reversal occurs at two other moments when Renaissance poets have permitted Lucifer to sound and act heroic; at his single combat with Michael and at his defeat. Now poets are by no means unanimous in permitting Lucifer to combat Michael fiercely and heroically before his inevitable defeat. Acevedo and Murtola, for example, render Lucifer instant defeat. The sword of Michael cuts through him and he is overcome. Equally instantaneous is the defeat that poets like Naogeorgus and Mollerus describe, though it is not the surrogate, Michael, but God himself who hurls Lucifer from Heaven. Other poets, however, seem less eager to end their epic battles with the instant capitulation of Lucifer. Therefore they grant him the latitude to behave like an epic hero. Taubmann's Lucifer, as we have seen, is particularly impressive in arms. Taubmann permits him to meet Michael before the battle and engage in an extended sequence of flyting, where he defends the heroic ethic of strength as the highest code.

> An armis
> Venisti, an linquâ mecum certare magistrâ?
> Nequidquam increpitas, aufer terrere minaci
> Garrulitate meos;
>
> [p. 103]
>
> Have you come in arms,
> Do you debate with me what remains of my sovranty?
> To no purpose do you challenge me;
> Cease from threatening my soldiers with menace and prattle.

It seems clear that Taubmann, although he has not finished his epic, intended to conclude it with a heroic single combat between Michael and Lucifer, where the latter is only with difficulty defeated. Both the flyting sequence and the description of open battle in book 3 seem to lead to this. Even Valmarana's Lucifer, though he does not meet Michael in single combat, behaves heroically in defeat. With the help of the *Verbum Dei,* Michael has shattered the resistance of Lucifer's legions, but Lucifer still stands resistant, bearing the full brunt of lightning and still defying God. Although his resistance is vain, although it is swiftly followed by degradation and fall, it is still impressive. Left alone on the field he attains some dignity as a single adversary. Davis Harding has argued that Milton's Satan in his defeat resembles the Virgilian Turnus, who desperately and single-handedly defends his cause even against "Heaven's" will. I argue that the Renaissance Lucifer—Satan's ancestor, so to speak—still more closely resembles Turnus.[20] This is particularly so in *Lucifer* and *Angeleida,* where he chooses to stand when others have fled. In *Angeleida,* he scorns the angels who have faltered:

20. Harding, *Club of Hercules,* pp. 41–51, 100.

Ite, cedete, o fiacchi animi, i'voglio
Restrar qui fermo, & quando il Ciel saetti
Tutto in me sol, ne vincitor, nè vinto
Dal mio proposto mai verrò sospinto.

[2.105]

Go, yield, sluggish spirits. I wish
To remain here resolute, and although I shall see the Heavens
    with arrows
All on me alone, neither conqueror, nor conquered,
Never will I be pushed from my purpose.

Valvasone makes Lucifer not only a valiant but a terrible adversary, ranging the field and upsetting those angels who oppose him, holding fifty shields and fifty weapons before him. Not till he meets Michael is he defeated. In *Lucifer* he is a resourceful captain. When the bow of his half-moon formation breaks, he keeps up his courage and swoops here and there, showing himself "brave and great-hearted still to save the day." By his courage in his chariot, as Vondel tells us, he "give[s] courage to the fainting." He wards off blows and arrows and drives fiercely on in the face of imminent defeat. In his chariot he is a fearsome adversary, for it is drawn by a lion and a dragon. As Lucifer fights with all his might, the lion roars and bites and tears, and the dragon shoots poison from his cleft tongue. In his final assault he attempts to cut down God's banner and to shatter with his battle-ax Michael's adamantine shield. Only in the face of Michael's superior lightnings is he defeated (Act 5).

In *La guerra angelica* as well, Lucifer is a formidable foe who meets defeat only after a sturdy resistance. Having been metamorphosed into a dragon during the battle with Michael, he breathes fire and smoke and lashes his spiked tail. He is a dangerous as well as a persistent adversary, who is with difficulty defeated.

Milton's treatment of Satan is instructive. Milton *does* permit Satan an epic fight, but it is a fight with the angel Michael, not with the hero Son. Moreover, the fight occupies a central rather than a climactic position. Nevertheless, we can clearly see that he has been influenced in his depiction of this fight by the epic battle accorded Michael by Renaissance poets. His description of both adversaries is heroic. As Satan approaches Michael to duel with him, he is the prototype of the epic hero, opposing the loyal archangel with his "rocky Orb / Of tenfold Adamant, his ample Shield" (6.254–255). In his speech to Michael, moreover, he sounds, as Taubmann's and Valvasone's Lucifer had sounded before him, like the epic hero defending the ethic of heroic battle. He turns aside what he calls Michael's threats and calls for deeds to answer words. He exalts war as a strife of glory. Finally he dares Michael to expend his utmost force and vows to stand firm against him. It is his most plainly heroic moment during books 5 and 6, the moment when he most resembles the warrior he claimed to be in recalling the war in books 1 and 2. It is also the moment when he most resembles the Lucifer of the Renaissance tradition. Of course he is defeated, slashed through with Michael's sword, but he has at least stood briefly with "next to Almighty Arm." Milton in granting him this much plainly glances back at the Renaissance tradition. After this brief and splendid moment of angelic duel the war swiftly deteriorates and, what is more significant, Satan never again rises to be an epic opponent. Milton, having briefly highlighted Satan the hero, who in the center of the war meets Michael in an inconclusive duel, denies Satan the heroics of a last stand.

Milton differs from the Renaissance poets in another way as well. At the conclusion of the war, Milton's attention is on the Son rather than on Satan. We taste the Son's victory rather than Satan's defeat. In the Renaissance poems, however, there is a good deal of emphasis, negative though it may be, on the horrors of Satan's defeat and fall. He is allowed to retain central focus, however much poets also accord Michael a glamorous victory. This is particularly the case in that many poets make Satan's fall the occasion of his monstrous metamorphosis.[21] In Valmarana's poem, in Acevedo's, in Vondel's, we see Lucifer and his angels suffer a terrible transformation as they rain from Heaven in the form of sphinxes, chimeras, and geryons. Vondel records the very moment that Lucifer's beauty begins to fade. When he is hurled backward from his chariot, as the frontispiece of Vondel's 1654 edition of the play also shows, his transformation begins. The morning star of his banner fades and his countenance becomes brutish.

Valmarana also records Lucifer's transformation: his beauty is marred, horns spring from his head, and he spontaneously falls as the poet laments his loss. In Valmarana's account Isaiah's influence is particularly strong; Valmarana echoes the words from Isaiah as Lucifer falls, "quomodo de Coeli cecedisti, Lucifer, astris." Even though Valmarana makes us aware that Lucifer deserves his fate, he plays upon our almost inadvertent sympathy for the formerly beautiful angel. He shows us what a humiliating experience his metamorphosis is, how bitterly he reacts to his loss of beauty and honor:

> omnes
> Exuit infelix formosae mentis honores
> Lucifer, & quiquid coelestibus hauserat oris,
> Angelicumque decus furiales vertit in artus;
>
> [pp. 28–29]

> Lucifer, wretched, put off all honor from his glorious being,
> And whatsoever he gathered from the celestial borders.
> His angelic glory he transformed into frenzied power.

Moreover, though Lucifer is expelled from Heaven, it is not without the "last word." Looking about him and shedding vain

---

21. For a fuller account of the background of Satan's metamorphosis see John M. Steadman, "Archangel to Devil: The Background of Satan's Metamorphosis," *Modern Language Quarterly* 21 (1960): 321–335.

tears, he exclaims that he will never give up his fight, even though now he must leave the skies and relinquish the scepter to the tyrant. While strength remains and virtue, he swears to continue his resistance. Of course Valmarana discredits his "heroics." Speaking directly to Lucifer, he tells him to seek Tartarus and his realm there and upbraids him for too little concern for true glory.

> pete tartara, pestis,
> Innocuumque absolue solum, te digna tyranno
> Regna manent. . . . .

[p. 31]

> Seek Tartarus, you plague,
> Set free the harmless earth,
> For a kingdom, worthy a
> Tyrant, awaits you.

But, despite this speech, the poet has accorded the retreating Lucifer some grudging glory. He leaves Heaven humiliated but still the central figure in our interest.

The "Draco" of *La guerra angelica* also proves an interesting figure in defeat. Though finally driven from Heaven by Michael and the force of his vindicating sword, the dragon yet has power to breathe defiance. He flees, but not through fear of Michael. Fate wills it. Yet he will return stronger and be reborn with a hundred heads. Once more he will fight, now directing his anger against God and man. Acevedo's Lucifer also vaunts at the moment of his fall. And he too speaks heroic words. Though the victory may be God's, he says, the glory is theirs.

For many poets, Lucifer's departure from Heaven is not the end of the account. They are intent to show two things: how Heaven reacted to victory and how Hell reacted to defeat. What is significant for our study of Satan is that the poets continue to show Satan as a heroic figure even after his fall to Hell. We must, of course, discount his appearance, for Renaissance poets apparently relished describing the traditional crude devil with horns, multiple heads, scaly feet, and tail. They delighted in showing blood dripping from his mouth and fire issuing from his nostrils. In physical aspect their Satans are worlds removed from Milton's, who in his late metamorphosis becomes ugly and monstrous, but never crude. The Satan of Renaissance epic (while looking monstrous), however, continues to sound heroic in Hell.

Many poets dramatize the woefulness of his circumstances and show him, as Mollerus does, lamenting his eternal damnation.

> Proh tempus miserum, proh lachrymosa dies,
> Proh facinus, quae nos tam caeca superbia coepit,
> Quod summo intulimus tristia bella Deo?
>
> > [n.p.]

> Alas, the wretched time! Alas the day, causing tears!
> Alas, the wickedness all of which blind pride began,
> Because we undertook this sad war against the highest God.

Yet Lucifer is, as the poets show him, capable of more than lament. Naogeorgus's Lucifer begins by regretting the unlucky fight; he and his soldiers were worthy of better fortune and did not deserve to be so conquered. He swiftly rallies and tells his angels to summon up courage and hope for better fortune on earth. Similarly, in *Angeleida* we have a Lucifer who, though defeated, is not without resources and is eagerly looking forward to recouping his fortunes on earth. Turning his attention to the human seed who will in future inhabit this kingdom, he proposes to bend his enterprise in ordering things below. Valvasone's attitude toward his Lucifer is obviously dual. On the one hand he shows us a resilient leader who, speaking nobly to his soldiers, resembles the Satan of book I of *Paradise Lost*. He is a leader who, as in Heaven, still speaks of honor and glory and who is intent on consoling his allies for their loss.

> Perduto habbiamo, o già celesti genti
> Nobili, & belle, hor basso vulgo oscuro:
> Perduto habbiam le vaghe stelle ardenti,

Che nostra Patria da principio furo:
Hora qui ci convien non esser lenti
A fondar nouo regno ampio, & securo:
Perdemmo il ciel, faccia hor lo sdegno nostro
Tremendo a par del Ciel l'infernal chiostro.

[3.9]

We have lost, O formerly celestial race,
Noble and beautiful, now low, obscure commons:
We have lost the beautiful, burning stars,
That was our native land from the beginning;
Now here we come not slowly together,
To found a new empire, ample and secure,
I have lost Heaven; now our
Disdain makes the infernal cloister tremble, equal to Heaven.

But, while permitting him to voice heroic sentiments, Valvasone reminds his readers that Lucifer is less than heroic in appearance and intent. He describes the former prince of Heaven now as a monster who bellows forth words from his seven mouths. Addressing Lucifer directly, he condemns as base the would-be heroic ambitions and assures him that he will gain nothing for his reward but further damnation, eternal pain and fire. These sentiments are not unlike those voiced by the narrator of *Paradise Lost* who, commenting on Satan's resolutions, remarks that they serve "but to bring forth / Infinite goodness . . . but on himself / Treble confusion, wrath and vengeance poured" (1.217–220). But the narrator of *Paradise Lost,* unlike Valvasone, is not dismissing Lucifer from the scene; he is preparing for action to come, action that will include a demonstration of the futility of Satan's previous machinations in Heaven. He is at the beginning, not the end, of his narration. Hence, in his remarks about Lucifer and in his depiction of the newly fallen angel, he resembles the poet-narrators of the *Adam* dramas of the sixteenth and seventeenth centuries as much as he does the poets of celestial battle epics like Valvasone. The situation in which he places his Satan is like that depicted in the *Adam exul* of Grotius, the *Adamo* of

Andreini, the *Adamo caduto* of Salandra, or the *Adam in Bal-lingschap* of Vondel. Milton's Satan, like theirs, first appears on the scene in Hell, newly fallen and still smarting from his defeat. A vigorous leader, resolved to rally his soldiers to new enter-prises, he speaks heroically, defending the "glorious" attempt made in Heaven and encouraging a new attempt on earth. Like Valvasone's Lucifer, the Satan of the *Adam* drama recalls, some-times poignantly, sometimes boastfully, his former attempt on Heaven. Andreini's and Salandra's devils glorify their great feats in arms, which "caused the pale face of Heaven to twitch in fear" (*L'Adamo,* 1.3,) or boast how by sheer will they "could have blotted out Michael and all his host and Heaven too" (*Adamo caduto,* 2.1).[22] Milton's Satan speaks in a similar vein. He is more reserved, more ironic, more indirect than his predecessors, more prone to speak of a fight not inglorious than to glorify directly past exploits. But his intent is similar—to raise his allies to new enter-prises by recalling the glory of the old ones.

> O Myriads of immortal Spirits, O powers
> Matchless, but with the Almighty, and that strife
> Was not inglorious, though th' event was dire....
>
> [1.622–624]

Milton's Satan in book 1 is a conventional general in defeat that the Renaissance both reviled and glorified. For the Renaissance in making Satan an epic figure perforce made readers grant him grudging admiration. In book 1 at least, Milton is content to grant him that same grudging admiration, to permit him glory-

---

22. Other Renaissance Satans are also boasters. Cowley describes in *Davideis* how Satan boasted that he took noble arms against God's tyranny and fought so valiantly that he deserved triumph rather than defeat:
> There was a *Day*! oh might I see't again
> Though he had fierce *Flames* to thrust us in!
>
> [Kirkconnell, *Celestial Cycle,* p. 422]

Fletcher's Satan also glorifies his military past:
> But me, O never let me, spirits, forget
> That glorious day when I your standard bore....
>
> [Kirkconnell,*Celestial Cycle,* p. 276]

mongering speeches, to show him splendid even in defeat. But Milton has looked not once, but twice, at Satan's fall and defeat. In book 1 Satan falls with flaming glory and Milton raises the Isaiahan lament. In book 1 we are indulged (by Satan at least) in the pathos of lost glory, and we hear Satan boast never to yield and not to be overcome. We are in the world that Renaissance epic had bequeathed to Milton. And we hear the poet-narrator, like other poet-narrators before him, repudiate Satan and his empty vaunting while permitting him to sound the cause of glory.

In book 6 we look at Satan's defeat from another perspective, and there we see clearly that the glory of battle was a Satanic illusion. For Satan did not stand heroically against the loyal sons of Heaven. In truth, even in the so-called heroic warfare of the first day, he suffered repulse by Abdiel and check by Michael in a single crushing blow. On the second day his heroics degenerated to "gamesome mood." The last words we hear him utter in book 6 are not rousing encouragements to his army, not stirring promises to return despite defeat, but the devilish derision he directs to the loyal angels who stand before him offering traditional epic war. As Milton looks at Satan in book 6, he grants him not one scrap of honor either as a soldier or as a general. Instead, Milton strips him of the traditional "honors" that poets before him had allowed. Satan does not even attempt a last duel against the Son (surrogate in *Paradise Lost* for the conqueror Michael); he does not stand resistant while his soldiers flee; he offers no heroic words before he is forced to quit Heaven. And his fall to Hell is not glorious. He is driven with his angels in mass, like a herd of goats and timorous flocks. How far is this from the military defeat Vondel and Valmarana granted him. How far from his flaming retreat as a dragon in Peri's drama. Only in Hell does Milton permit Satan to seem heroic. In Heaven he is defeated unheroically and falls, unnamed and unnoted, in the rout driven before the Son.

CHAPTER 7

The Son of God and
the Strife of Glory

For thee I have ordain'd it, and thus far
Have suffer'd, that the Glory may be thine
Of ending this great War, since none but Thou
Can end it.

[6.700–703]

The last day of the war in Heaven, from the dawning of that third sacred morn to the triumphal return to the throne of bliss, belongs completely and unequivocally to the Son of God. He both ends the physical war with his appearance (for in the face of the Son's chariot all military resistance ceases) and resolves the complex theological, moral, and political issues the war had raised. He is the supreme warrior (as the Renaissance Michael before him had been), the representative of God's omnipotence (having had the virtue, grace, and power of the Father transfused into him), and an ideal figure of personal heroism realized.

Most striking, of course, to readers of *Paradise Lost* is that the Son takes on himself the role of battle hero, exacting that victory that scriptural authority (Rev. 12: 7–9) and Renaissance poetic convention had given to Michael. We have seen in previous chapters that those writers who did not accord God's omnipotent arm or his lightning sole power to rout Satan entrusted this responsibility to Michael. From the medieval period on, poets had portrayed Michael as the hero who, in the words of *Die Altdeutsche Genesis,* "lifted up his right hand and hit the Devil such a blow that Heaven broke under him" (p. 518).

In poems before *Paradise Lost* the Son of God had played little

235

part in the war. It is true that some poets (like Taubmann, Valmarana, or Heywood) use as a device to motivate Lucifer's rebellion the prediction that the Son as Word Incarnate will exalt men over the angels.[1] It is also true that some Renaissance theologians felt that envy of the Son's future kingdom motivated Lucifer in his original revolt. But the Son as a personal adversary to Lucifer, as the soldier who in Heaven single-handedly routed the aspiring archangel, is of little significance before *Paradise Lost*. The only important appearances of the Son in this capacity had been in Dracontius's fifth-century *Carmen de Deo* and in Rupert of Deutz's twelfth-century *De victoria Verbi Dei*. In the Renaissance Valmarana also portrays the Son as a military figure who, bearing a magnificent sword, inspires Michael and his angels to a victory that without him they could not have won. But, so far as I can tell, no other poet of the Renaissance besides Milton has so unequivocally made the Son of God a hero who in Heaven wins complete victory over Satan.

What is interesting, moreover, in Milton's portrayal of the Son is that Milton has modeled the hero Son both on traditional Renaissance figures of Christ and on figures of the warring archangel Michael who was victor over Lucifer.[2] Physically, the Son is very like the Renaissance Michael: a radiant figure whose victory over Lucifer is spiritual as well as military, an ultimate hero of faith. In many ways the Son of God in *Paradise Lost* takes on, as he assumes the role the Renaissance Michael had played, the gar-

---

1. A little-known Spanish work, *De los 9 nombres de Cristo*, by José de Sigüenza (1544?–1606), also makes Lucifer revolt against God because of hate and envy of Christ, to whom the princedoms of the world were to be given. See Helen D. Goode, "The Unknown *De los 9 Nombres de Cristo* of José de Sigüenza," *Papers on Language and Literature* 12, (spring 1976): 129–131

2. Christ as soldier of God appears in Christian tradition throughout the Middle Ages and the Renaissance as the hero who defeated Satan on the cross (see the *Dream of the Rood*, for example), as the leader of the Church Militant, and as the conqueror who will come in the clouds to defeat Satan at the end of time. When Revelation 12 is read as a forecast of the end of things. Michael not uncommonly (he who is like God) is interpreted as Christ. But when Revelation 12 is read as a description of Satan's expulsion from Heaven at the beginning of time, Michael then is almost universally taken to be the archangel.

ments, so to speak, of the warring archangel. It is useful then to begin this study of the Son of God with a closer look at the Renaissance Michael.

I

The Renaissance Michael is visually splendid: poets describe his blond hair and rosy complexion, his armor, shining with gold and diamond.[3] Painters corroborate these descriptions by portraying Michael as a handsome courtly figure adorned with jewels, embroidered garments, and shining armor.[4] Prominent in both painting and poetry is the military demeanor of Michael, in full armor with sword at his side or in his hand. Both the title page of Valmarana's *Daemonomachiae* and the frontispiece to the chapter on Lucifer's rebellion in Heywood's *Hierarchie of the blessed Angells* depict the victorious Michael brandishing the sword. This sword is described by Taubmann as adorned with yellow jasper. The prominence of the sword in these portraits of Michael prefigures, of course, its use in the war, where sometimes (as in Acevedo's and Murtola's poems) with a single stroke it effects the victory. At any rate, arms and armor are the characterizing parts of Michael's portrait; he is never described without them. Indeed, their splendor and strength (as in Taubmann's description of his shining breastplate and scaly bronze cuirass) are his splendor and strength. Important scenes in both Peri's *La guerra angelica* and Vondel's *Lucifer* show Michael arming for battle. In the latter play Michael's arming prepares us for his victory.

3. Gasparo Murtola, *Della creatione del mundo,* canto 1, stanza 64 (Venice, 1608), p. 22; Alonso de Acevedo, "Dia primero," *De la creacion del mundo,* in *Biblioteca de Autores Españoles* (Madrid, 1864), 29 (vol. 2): 250.

4. See plates 4–29, 47–51 in Roland Mushat Frye, *Milton's Imagery and the Visual Arts* (Princeton: Princeton University Press, 1978), for illustrations of Michael. Pietro Perugino's and Piero della Francesca's altarpieces of Michael (National Gallery, London) are particularly impressive: Piero della Francesca (plate 18).

Michaël:

> Uriël, schiltknaep flux, men breng' den blixem hier,
> Mijn harnas, helm, en schilt. breng herwaert Godts banier.
> Men blaze de bazuin. te wapen, flux te wapen.
> Ghy Maghten, Troonen, wat getrou is ...
>
> . . . .

Gabriël:

> Dit harnas past zoo braef, alwaer't u aengeschapen.
> Hier komt de veltbanier, waer in Godts naem em wapen
> U toestraelt, en de zon in top u heil belooft.
>
> . . . .
>
> Schep moedt, Vorst Michaël: ghy zult Godts oorlogh voeren.

Michael:

> Swift Uriel, my Squire, fetch my lightning,
> Harness and shield and helmet, and God's banner!
> Now let the trump be blown! To arms, to arms!
> Come, all ye Thrones and Powers that are true ...
>
> . . . .

Gabriel:

> This harness fits as bravely on thy limbs
> As if created with thee. Here's the flag,
> In which God's name and weapon shine upon thee,
> And a Sun rampant promises success.
>
> . . . .
>
> Courage, Prince Michael. Thou shalt lead His battle.[5]

> [4.53–68]

Milton's Son inherits some of his military splendor from the Renaissance Michael. He, like Michael, accepts God's commission and arms for battle, girding on, as God tells him, his sword upon his puissant thigh, grasping his bow to him and "Quiver with three-bolted Thunder stor'd," (6.764), putting on his radiant armor. He becomes thus the perfect figure of the soldier absolute; but with the Urim of the priest upon his breastplate he is much more. In the Renaissance Michael soldiership, though lit with radiant spirit, shone forth; in the Son soldiership is subordinated to spirit.

5. Kirkconnell, *Celestial Cycle,* p. 400; Vondel, pp. 43–44.

Clearly, however, Renaissance poets intend to present Michael as a hero of faith, the defender of God, who can function (as only the Son functions in *Paradise Lost*) as a surrogate for God. It is notable in poems like *Angeleida* and *La guerra angelica* that Michael is closer to the Father than any other angel. Standing by the throne of God in intimate colloquy with the Almighty, his joyous faith contrasts with Lucifer's perfidy. In *Angeleida* God addresses him directly, appointing him not only commander of the celestial armies, but supreme warrior commissioned specially to seek out Lucifer in combat. In reply to God's commands, Michael proclaims how glorious it is to fight beneath God's standard and promises to exact vengeance for God.[6] His words resemble those of Milton's Son, who asserts that he always seeks to glorify the Father (6.726–729).

Still more suggestive of *Paradise Lost* are the colloquies of Michael and God in *La battaglia celeste tra Michele e Lucifero* and in *La guerra angelica,* for in both these poems Michael prostrates himself before the Father, who transfers *all power* to him. In *La guerra angelica,* God expressly says that he has reserved for Michael the honor of driving from Heaven "questa perversa peste." His own power, God declares, he has conferred on Michael that he might possess scepter and eternal empire over his "crude adversary." Moreover, God commands that at the war's end Michael repair the damage done in Heaven.[7]

While it is true, of course, that God in *Paradise Lost* also confers power on Michael and dispatches him to battle, he does so only in a formal and ceremonial way. For the Son God reserves the intimate transfer of authority. In the Son God confides, as he has not confided in Michael, setting forth his great plan to end the war. For the Son is not dispatched as a general to head armies but is sent as "the" chosen warrior (like the Renaissance Michael before him) to end the war, to reestablish peace, and to repair Heaven. Further, Milton has carefully differentiated the Son's

6. Valvasone, *Angeleida,* canto I, stanzas 121–132, pp. 21–23.
7. Peri, *La guerra angelica,* pp. 84–85. Also see Alfano, *La battaglia celeste tra Michele e Lucifero,* pp. 45–46.

role from the role he permits to his own Michael. During the first two days of the war, Michael is commanding general, noble and heroic, but limited in success; but on the third day he yields his place as central figure so that the Son may become the hero and achieve unqualified success.

Even as loyal spokesman for God, Milton's Michael wields smaller sway. This has been a leading role for him in sixteenth- and seventeenth-century poems and dramas, where he is frequently given the opportunity to answer Lucifer directly. For example, in Thomas Heywood's *The Hierarchie of the blessed Angells* (1635), Michael, upon hearing Lucifer's boast that he will exalt his throne above God's, immediately replies.

> Why what is he,
> That like the Lord our God aspires to be?
> In vaine, *ô Lucifer*, thou striv'st t'assay,
> That we thine innovations should obey;
> Who know, As God doth purpose, be, it must;
> He cannot will, but what is good and iust;
> Therefore, with us, That God and Man adore,
> Or in this place thou shalt be found no more.
>
> [p. 340]

Similarly, in Mollerus's *De creatione et angelorun lapsu carmen* Michael appears right at the outset to challenge Lucifer's blasphemous words and at the same time to attempt to dissuade him from a rebellion that is clearly futile. To revolt from a Creator who is the source of honor, hope, and safety, he points out (sounding a note Milton's Abdiel is to sound), is to revolt from reason itself. In Valmarana's *Daemonomachiae*, Michael urges that there is no true honor and good apart from God and demands that Lucifer uphold the faith that he as *magister* of Heaven has plighted (pp. 25–26). As the champion of good, Michael in Vondel's *Lucifer* upbraids the assembled band of Lucifer's followers, offering to mediate any dispute but warning that violence will be punished. All, he declares, except those who fight under his banner, war against God.[8] In battle, Michael further upholds his de-

---

8. Kirkconnell, *Celestial Cycle*, pp. 392–394; Vondel, *Lucifer*, pp. 34–37.

fense of God. In Taubmann's, Valvasone's and Alfano's poems, Michael meets Lucifer on the battlefield and, like a proper classical warrior, before engaging him in combat exchanges words with him. His words, particularly in Valvasone's poem, closely resemble those of Milton's Michael, for he denounces Lucifer as a traitor and demands that he quit Heaven.

In *Paradise Lost* Michael is only one of the spokesmen for God. Not Michael, but Abdiel, first rises to answer Lucifer's charges, to refute his likes, and to decry his presumptuous challenge of God. Abdiel too first meets Satan on the battlefield and, adding deeds to words, repulses him with a mighty blow. To the humblest of angels, rather than to the highest, Milton has assigned this role of responding champion, and in so doing he again parts company with earlier poets who had so characterized Michael.

Throughout book 6 of *Paradise Lost* Michael, though prominent among the angels, acts a more limited part in the war than does the Michael of Valvasone or Taubmann or Alfano. It is true that he, as in the Renaissance poems, leads forth his angels, draws the line of battle, bids the martial trumpet sound, and directs the course of battle. But whereas Milton summarily tells us that Michael so acts, Renaissance poets usually describe him in action. And whereas Milton reports the words of the angel Michael only once, they repeatedly record his speeches. Valmarana, for example, permits Michael a long speech encouraging his allies, a match to the speech wherein Lucifer had encouraged his. Michael tells his angels that it is their responsibility to punish Lucifer and so avenge God.

> Nunc tempus, nunc summa rei, nunc terminus aeui
> Currentis, quicquid portendunt saecula....
> Ergo agite, & dominum fidi ulciscamur amantum....
>
> [p. 26]

> Now is the time, now the pitch of action, now the limit of his age
>   run,
> Whatever the ages portend....

Therefore, come and let us avenge our loving master with
dedication. . . .

As the title tells us, Alfano in *La battaglia celeste tra Michele e
Lucifero* centers his work on the warring archangel, throughout
reporting the speeches of Michael as he defends God's cause, first
before God himself, then to his soldiers, and finally to Lucifer.
The last speech specifically concerns Lucifer's lost honor, for
Michael sees Lucifer as a fellow soldier who has forfeited his
faith. He, the faithful warrior, challenges the faithless to a final
contest.[9] In *Bellum angelicum* Michael also has many speeches in
which he shows himself preeminent as leader of the angels and
hero of the epic. In the first, he tells God he is his soldier, prepared to draw the battle line and seek Draco in arms, indeed to
pursue war with all possible expediency. In the next, he appears
before his army assembled for battle; he himself, sword in hand,
denounces the evil of Lucifer and urges his angels to the mighty
work before them. "Let us go," he says, "into the frenzy of
battle, and though the way is hard, let us not give in to fear and
despair. Our commission," he continues, "is just, and we must
execute it with justice. The dragon incites this war, but ours will
be the victory." The angels reply stoutly: "Go, Michael; we will
follow; we delay no longer."[10] Now Taubmann describes Michael
and his army marching in pursuit of the enemy: Michael in the
midst of his soldiers stands out, head and shoulders, like a god.
Eminent as a strategist as well as a soldier, Michael succeeds in
eluding the ambush of Satanas, trapping him instead, and awaits
the approach of Lucifer with his reinforcements. To the soldiers
trapped with Satanas he cries, "Come forth, earthworms! Now is
the time to perform deeds!" To his own army he gives the order
to stand and prepare for battle.[11] Michael's final speech and his
most impressive moment occurs after Lucifer (or Draco, the Ser-

9. Alfano, *Battaglia celeste*, pp. 40–41, 45–46, 47–48.
10. Taubmann, *Bellum angelicum*, pp. 95–97.
11. Taubmann, *Bellum angelicum*, pp. 100–101.

pent, as he is called) advances on the field to meet him. A formal debate ensues in which Michael, God's champion, once more attempts to dissuade the rebel from his cause, "What hope," he asks, "can you entertain, having raised this battle against the immutable law of God and the universe?" As Draco stands adamant, Michael promises to meet him and dispatch him to Tartarus. What follow are yet two more battle speeches: the first, Draco to his angels, the second, Michael to his.

> Ne miles, ne verba time violenta Draconis:
> Caussa jubet melior casus sperare secundos:
> Nusquam abero vobis; hâc spe praesumite pugnam.
> Ipse ego vim belli excipiam, solusque ruenti
> Objiciam telo caput, atque in me omnia vertam.
>
> [p. 105]

> Fear neither the soldiery nor the violent words of the Serpent
> Our better cause bids us hope for a better outcome;
> On no occasion will I be absent
> From you; with this expectation, take up the fight.
> I myself will undertake the fierceness of battle, and alone
> I shall strike off his head with my weapon hurled;
> On me everything depends.

Throughout his epic Taubmann has focused on the heroic Michael; he leaves us on the last page of this unfinished work with the glimpse of Michael fighting valiantly in the midst of his soldiers.

This kind of generalship has little place in *Paradise Lost*. To his commander-in-chief Michael, Milton has offered few opportunities for exultation.[12] Underplaying the victory of the first day, he takes us to the rebel rather than the loyal camp after the first day of battle. Moreover, though Michael might congratulate himself on wounding and repulsing Satan, he could not claim to have

---

12. In both *Paradise Lost* and *De doctrina*, Milton describes Michael as the head of the celestial armies and treats him with respect. See *Christian Doctrine*, 1.9, in *Complete Prose Works of John Milton* (New Haven: Yale University Press, 1973), 6:347.

chased him from Heaven. With stalemate established on the second day, Michael and his angels are displaced from their central
position in the action. But the Son does not take over Michael's
generalship or become a supersoldier to fight against Satan. He
cannot be thought to bring reinforcements to the loyal army, as
the Renaissance Michael, in Taubmann's epic actually did. Further, despite his armor, arms, and chariot, he cannot truly be
thought of as a soldier who like the Renaissance Michael engaged
Lucifer in a classical duel or a dragon encounter. As the Son
advances in his living chariot, no epic adversary stands before
him; no dragon flames in the night. Therefore, though Milton may
have modeled his Son on the Renaissance Michael (the Son does
resemble Michael in physical demeanor and in dramatic circumstance), he must when he comes to describe the final scene of
conquest depart from the traditions of the Renaissance poem.

It is not, of course, that the victory of the Renaissance Michael
over Lucifer lacks spiritual significance. In all the Renaissance
poems I have considered, Michael is clearly the representative of
right. He overwhelms Lucifer, sometimes as in Acevedo's *Creacion del mundo,* with a single blow.[13] He is lit with humility and
zeal, and he is inspired, as poets like Alfano or Valvasone tell us,
by faith and love of God.[14] But in the last analysis Michael's war
with Satan is a physical war, won by a soldierly angel who possesses an invincible sword—invicible, of course, in all poems but
Paradise Lost. In works like *Angeleida,* where Michael faces a
monstrous opponent, or in *La guerra angelica* or *La battaglia
celeste,* where Lucifer has been transformed into a dragon, it is
plain force and courage and not a little superior expertise in arms
that wins the day for Michael. Few poets permit Michael's
spiritual eminence to go unassisted by his military prowess. And
of those poets, it is only those such as Heywood who are determined to write a *psychomachia* and to limit the battle to "the two
motions of the Will and Minde" (p. 342). In Heywood's *Hierar-*

13. Acevedo, "Dia Primero," p. 250.
14. See, for example, Alfano, *Battaglia celeste,* p. 52.

chie it takes no more than Michael's humility and zeal to defeat Lucifer's insolence and spleen. Valvasone and Vondel, however, show Michael rising to full spiritual eminence only at the final moment of Lucifer's defeat. In *Angeleida* Michael dazzles his adversary with his sunlike brilliance, eclipsing his light and making faint his strength (2.122); in *Lucifer* he becomes almost godlike, shining as though ringed by suns and so overcoming the fading "Morning Star" (act 5). And in moments such as these, indeed, the Renaissance Michael seems to differ little from Milton's victorious Son. Yet, however brilliant these moments of spiritual transcendence, Michael remains in most Renaissance poems God's superhero, not the "Effulgence of His Glory," but a warrior modeled on such classical battle heroes as Achilles and Hector and Diomedes, like them possessed of superhuman strength and divinely endowed in soldiership.

In the aftermath of the battle (as the Renaissance poems describe it), moreover, Michael reaps the rewards of his superior soldiership. Milton is once more indebted to his predecessors who first described, many of them with lavish detail, the victorious celebrations in Heaven that follow Satan's defeat. Michael's triumph in Heaven, though different in some essential ways from the Son's, is a model for it. In the victory scenes, as in the duel that preceded them, Michael acts a double role, part conquering general, part saint. On the one hand, the poets are rhapsodic about the spiritual victory. In *Angeleida* heavenly flowers bloom, filling the air with delicious odors; in Murtola's *Della creatione del mondo* (an account where the descriptions of the aftermath of the war are longer by far than those of the preceding action), Heaven shines resplendently. In *La guerra angelica* Michael, presenting himself at God's throne, is proclaimed God's minister and given authority over the lucent spheres of Heaven.[15] Yet, even as the poets celebrate the superb spiritual victory of this greatest of angels, we are unmistakably reminded of a pomp with

15. Valvasone *Angeleida*, 3.57, p. 55; Murtola, *Creatione* (stanzas 77–96), pp. 27–32; Peri, *Guerra angelica*, pp. 113–114.

very military overtones. What we see is in fact a Roman triumph. Trumpets sound, palms are waved, the loyal angels march like well-drilled classical soldiers. Earthly comparisons abound, though raised to heavenly superlatives. The pomp in Heaven is compared with that of France and Rome, and Michael, welcomed as the greatest of heroes, is said to surpass those earthly generals who reward their soldiers with gold and silver.[16] His martial prowess is unabashedly praised, with his courage, daring, and skill. Once more his formidable armor is described, once more his invincible sword is raised before us. The choruses of angels that ring out to greet this warrior praise the force of his arm that effected Lucifer's defeat.[17] He himself delivers victory speeches wherein he exults in his conquest of the archfiend, and in Peri's play he presents his trophies to God as evidence that he has overcome his rival. The commendatory sonnet with which Valvasone ends his epic also celebrates a very martial victor.

> Eccelso Heroe, Campion invitto, & Santo
> De l'impero diuin, per cui pigliasti
> L'alta contesa, e'l reo Dragon cacciasti
> De l'auree stelle debellato, & franto. . . .

> Highest hero, invincible champion, and saint
> Of the divine empire, for which
> You have fought the high contest,
> And have chased the wicked dragon
> From the golden stars, subdued and crushed. . . .[18]

16. Murtola, *Creatione* (stanza 83), p. 29.
17. See Peri, *Guerra angelica,* act 5, scene 2:

O glorioso Duce,	O glorious leader,
O celeste Guerriero,	O celestial warrior,
C'hai troue al fier Dragon'	Who has discovered the impious
l'empio pensiero.	thought of the proud dragon.

See also Vondel, *Lucifer,* act 5:

Gezegent zy de Helt,	Blest be that hero most
Die't goddeloos gewelt,	Who all the godless host
En zijn maght, en zijn kracht,	With standard and with power
en zijn standert	and with might
Ter neder heeft gevelt.	Hath cast down from their boast!
[Vondel, p.61]	[Kirkconnell, *Celestial Cycle,* p. 41]

18. Valvasone, *Angeleida,* p. 64.

In these final proceedings, Michael the general outshines Michael the saint; force outweighs faith. But Milton's celebrations for the Son, though like in kind to those of the Renaissance poems, are different, as we shall see, in intent.

Thus Milton, though decisively influenced by those poems in which Michael appears as hero of the war in Heaven, takes an independent way in depicting both his own Michael and his Son. To Michael, he has accorded the same place as leader of the angels as the Renaissance poets did, but he has sharply restricted his achievements both as military and as spiritual leader. He has permitted him fine moments, but he never lets him become the transcendent figure that the Renaissance Michael so often is. Transcendent, of course, is precisely what the Son in *Paradise Lost* becomes, assuming command when Michael and his angels become deadlocked against Satan, but becoming more than champion and general. Like the Renaissance Michael, however, the Son is an agent personally selected by God who, unswerving in his purpose, comes to fulfill God's will. So in a sense Milton retains for the Son what had also been the heart of Michael's role in the Renaissance epics and dramas: that of loyal servant.

2

Even though the charisma of the military Michael persists in Milton's portrait of the Son of God in book 6, even though the love and obedience of the angel have their correspondence in filial love and service, these qualities are tempered and transformed as they appear in the special person of the Son, Messiah and king. Further, the victory the Son attains is quite different from that attained by the angel appointed to defeat Satan. For Milton, in creating the final scenes of book 6, had in mind to do more than merely bring Satan to defeat by a divine agent. He ends the war with the person whose promotion to kingship had in a sense provoked the war, so demonstrating to the recalcitrant rebels the truth and righteousness of that kingship, as they are now compelled to bow in defeat to their sovereign. Moreover, Milton has conceived of this scene of triumph at the end of book 6 both as a counterpart to that scene in book 3 where the Son's offered sacrifice provokes jubilee in Heaven and as a counterpart to the final victory over the dragon on earth, alluded to first in book 3 and to be yet more fully dramatized by the prophetic scenes in book 12. Hence, though the Son's victory over Satan is modeled on the victory of the Michael of Renaissance drama and epic and retains much of the flavor of this "type" of victory; yet it is much more. With the Son's victory Milton furthers his characterization of the Son, introduced first in book 3; he ends the war where it began (with the enthroned Messiah); and he looks ahead in his epic and in history to two more victories of the Son (at his Resurrection and at the world's end). In so doing he reminds us not only that the victor in book 6 is the supreme soldier, as was the conquering Michael (whom we have expected to see in this role), but that he is also the divine Logos of book 3 (Word, wisdom, and effectual might of God the Father); Christ rising from the dead, having spoiled (like the conqueror the Renaissance often thought him to be) principalities and powers and nailed his enemies to the cross; and finally the conquering Christ of the book of Revelation, come in the clouds attended by his thousands and ten thousands of saints. What Milton has given us is rich in implication for books 5 and 6 and richer still for the whole epic.

To understand fully this dramatic appearance of the Son in book 6, it is necessary to consider not only, as we have done, the poetical background, but also the theological. In the theological background it is important to include both the conception of the victor Son as it appears in seventeenth-century theology and most particularly in the writings on Revelation, and also the concept of the Son Milton has begun to develop in book 3 of *Paradise Lost* and the yet fuller conception he included in his theological treatise *De doctrina Christiana*. In turning to seventeenth-century commentary on Revelation I undertake a foray into theological background, as I have done in previous chapters. I feel I do the same with respect to *De doctrina Christiana*, with the added conviction that Milton's own theological treatise is likely to be more pertinent to *Paradise Lost* than are treatises of others, however contemporary with him. Since Maurice Kelley's close application of *De doctrina* to *Paradise Lost*, however, resistance has arisen to reading the treatise as a gloss on the poem and to identifying the nontrinitarian Son therein with the "trinitarian" Son of *Paradise Lost*. While admitting that poetry is different from theology and that epic poems tend to be more conservative than nonconformist treatises, I cannot help feeling that there is much in *De doctrina* to complement and even enrich one's understanding of *Paradise Lost,* and particularly of the character of the Son as drawn by Milton.[19]

Had we never known the Son until books 5 and 6, his appearances there might be frankly enigmatic. In book 5 he appears once only, and then not as the resplendent king crowned upon God's holy hill (we witness the coronation indirectly) but as the private spectator to Satan's rebellion, speaking ironically of that rebellion in reply to God's laughter. Defense of his monarchy (until late in book 6) the Son leaves to others: to Abdiel and Michael, who rise admirably to argue and contest his case, both true heroic speakers of words and doers of deeds. In Heaven of book 5, we know the Son "sitting in bliss imbosom'd by the Father" (5.597), only as a second-person cipher for the Father who perfectly but merely echoes God. This is why book 3 is important as a prologue to book 6, for the Son of book 3 is far more than an echo of the Father and so foreshadows the Son of book 6, who also proves to be his own person. The functions of the Son in book 3 and book 6 are complementary. If we look carefully, we see that many concerns of the two books are also complementary, for in each God is faced with the problem of sin (Adam's and Satan's—Milton links and then differentiates them in book 3), and in each the Son becomes the force by which the problem is solved, offering himself in book 3 as sacrifice for Adam, in book 6 as punisher of Satan.

19. Among those who take up the problem of the relationship of *De doctrina Christiana* to *Paradise Lost* are B. Rajan (*"Paradise Lost" and the Seventeenth Century Reader* [London, 1947], pp. 22–38) and C. A. Patrides, in *Bright Essence: Studies in Milton's Theology* (Salt Lake City, 1971), pp. 71–77, 165–178.

Clearly, in books 3 and 6 Milton saw the Son serving as agent for the Father. It becomes pertinent then—indeed, it becomes mandatory—to ask, What kind of agent? Is he merely the "radiant image" of the Father's glory, as he is first introduced in book 3, the only begotten Son by whom and through whom the Father is expressed to the rest of creation? Or is he also, as Irene Samuel has asserted, an "independent being" who "speaks his own mind, not what he thinks another would like to hear."[20] In *De doctrina Christiana* Milton makes much of the fact that although the Son is divine, closer than any other to the Father in that he was first generated by the Father as Son and became the agent through which the Father made the rest of creation, he is nevertheless separate from the Father, an independent being. Generated in time (albeit heavenly time), he is not, like the Father, eternal and inoriginate. Distinct in essence from the Father and sharing only so much of the Father's substance as the Father chose to give, he is lesser than the Father or subordinate to him. Yet, though he possesses a separate and subordinate nature, he can become one with the Father and can even be equal to him as the Father chooses to bestow equality—through gift, not by necessity (God cannot be constrained by necessity). Further, the Son can be one with the Father in mind, in will, in act. This, Milton stresses in *De doctrina Christiana,* is the real union between Father and Son, not, as orthodox trinitarians urge, the union of substance and essence, but the union and communion of mind.

> How, then, are they one? The Son alone can tell us this, and he does. Firstly, they are one in that they speak and act as one. He explains himself [59] to this effect in the same chapter, after the Jews have misunderstood his statement: x. 38: *believe in my works so that you may know and believe that the Father is in me and I in him.* Similarly xiv. 10: *do you not believe that I am in the Father*

20. I am indebted to Professor Irene Samuel for her discussion of the council in Heaven: "The Dialogue in Heaven: A Reconsideration of *Paradise Lost,* III, 1–417," *PMLA* 72 (1957): 601–611, reprinted in *Milton: Modern Essays in Criticism,* ed. Arthur E. Barker (New York, 1965), pp. 233–245.

*and the Father in me? I myself am not the source of the words which
I speak to you; but the Father who dwells in me, he performs the
works.* Here it is evident that Christ distinguishes the Father from
the whole of his own being. However, he does say that the Father
dwells in him, though this does not mean that their essence is one,
only that their communion is extremely close. Secondly, he declares that he and the Father are one in the same way as we are one
with him: that is, not in essence but in love, in communion, in
agreement, in charity, in spirit, and finally in glory. [*Complete
Prose Works*, 6.220]

Throughout *Paradise Lost* and most especially in books 3 and
6, it is the oneness of mind, heart, and spirit that Milton emphasizes in Son and Father. But this union of mind and intimacy
of heart comes about, Milton shows us, not because the Son is
inseparable from the Father and can only echo him, but because
the Son chooses to bring his mind and heart to service and in so
choosing demonstrates to other beings (angels and ultimately
man) how they may also come to union. In both book 3 and book
6, we see a Son who discriminates and acts as a separate being,
who is "by Merit more than Birthright Son of God" (3.309), a
dynamic being whose love and service are freely given. This freedom to give, to love, to serve, to act could not exist if the Son of
Paradise Lost were not, like the Son Milton described in *De
doctrina,* independent. For were he like the Son of orthodox
trinitarianism, inseparable from God in substance and essence,
indeed cosubstantial and coequal with him, what we observe in
books 3 and 6 would be a ritual dialogue, not a trial of merit and
service.[21]

21. For further discussion of this problem, see my article "The Dramatic Func-
tion of the Son in *Paradise Lost:* A commentary on Milton's 'Trinitarianism,' "
JEGP 66 (January 1967): 45–58. I do not attempt to solve, however, the problem of
the source of Milton's subordinationalism, attributed by professors Hunter and
Patrides to Milton's study of the early church fathers (*Bright Essence: Studies in
Milton's Theology* [Salt Lake City, 1971]) or by Maurice Kelley (*This Great
Argument* [Princeton, 1941]) to the influence of Arius. For I believe that Milton
was an independent theological thinker who developed ideas from a variety of
sources, following none exclusively, and redeveloped and reshaped such ideas as
his own. See my review of *Bright Essence* (*JEGP* 72 [January 1973]: 128–132).

The Son in *Paradise Lost* is the finest example of creaturely heroism; that he appears so at the conclusion of the war in Heaven, an episode where we have many opportunities to observe false and true heroism, is not without significance. Like the loyal angels, he illustrates the free service of Heaven that Raphael defines for us at the beginning of the narrative ("freely we serve / Because we freely love," 5.538–539) and that Abdiel and Michael also exemplify. We should remember that Milton thinks of the Son in *Paradise Lost* not only as the "Begotten Son, Divine Similitude," but also as the highest and the first being in the scale of creation. So he designates him in book 3, line 383, "of all Creation first," employing the same terms he uses in *De doctrina*, the first of created things (*rerum creatarum primum fuisse*).[22] The Son thus has in a sense a dual nature from the beginning, for he encompasses in himself both the creaturely and the creatorial. As creature, he recognizes and rejoices in his derivation from God. In book 3 he affirms the "life" in himself that God has given him to possess forever: "by thee I live" (3.244). In book 6 he speaks of the joy of being part of that "All" that is God (6.732–733). In book 3 this knowledge of himself as God's creation and his trust in God enable him to offer to save mankind. In book 6 his willingness to be creaturely and subordinate to God contrasts sharply with Satan's unwillingness to do so. For Satan not only has refused to serve God's commands, but even refuses to acknowledge his derivation from the Creator. The Son chooses to serve God, to obey—indeed, he so delights in obedience and in the willingness to fulfill God's will that he terms it his "glory," "exaltation," and "whole delight." It is significant that Milton shows us a Son in book 6 who *chooses* to obey and by this choice saves Heaven from the pollution of evil that Satan has brought to it. The choice to serve in book 6 is perhaps not so dramatic as it is in book 3, but it is no less significant. The Son is the only one who

---

22. See the original Latin of *De doctrina Christiana* in the Columbia edition of *The Complete Works of John Milton* (New York, 1931–1938), 14:180–181.

can end the war; if he declines to do so, it will go on forever. (The words are God's: "since none but Thou / Can end it" [6. 702 – 703].) The situation is deliberately made a parallel to book 3, where none but the Son offers salvation for man. Again the words are God's: "O thou in Heav'n and Earth the only peace / Found out for mankind under wrath" (3.274–275). In each case we are presented with a being—true, the highest being in the hierarchy—but still a being, separate from God in person and essence, who chooses to obey the will of God. And he chooses to do so not because, like the Son of trinitarian orthodoxy, he must, being joined with God in all ways (substantially, essentially, in-originately one with him, sharing his omniscience, omnipresence, and omnipotence by nature), but because he so elects. In book 3, guided by faith and love and trust in God, not informed by innate omniscience, he chooses to fulfill God's will and to save man, even though it may mean death to him. That he will succeed not only in saving man but in rising and triumphing over death he knows only intuitively, for he trusts that the God who gave him life will preserve that life and lead him triumphantly back to Him. In book 6 the trial is less obviously dangerous, but it is still a trial. And here the Son responds to a direct injunction. He is commanded to take on God's omnipotence and to manifest by it his deserved right. Here he must do two things: fulfill God's will and by showing himself worthy heir vindicate God's word. This obedient fulfillment, this "divine" manifestation, Milton clearly thinks of as parallel to the mission of obedience to earth that, similarly, a "third sacred morn" will bring to full accomplishment. Finally, both book 3 and book 6 stress the joy of obedience fulfilled. In book 3 the Son describes his reentry into Heaven, having triumphed over death and harrowed Hell. In Heaven no cloud of anger remains; peace is assured, with reconcilement and joy entire. In book 6 the Son promises to return to the Father, resigning those powers he has assumed, content "that thou in me well pleas'd, declar'st thy will / Fulfill'd" (6.728–729). In both instances we see both the joy of re-union with God and the satisfaction of having served and having obeyed. If the angel Raphael has chosen to emphasize the contrary lesson—the terrible example of disobedience—let us not overlook that a more compelling and positive example is also available to the creature: the joy of obedience. For the Son acts here that creaturely role that the Renaissance Michael had acted elsewhere; and Milton, though he here confers that role on the being who is the highest and first of creation, nonetheless shows us that it is one all creation can and should emulate.

Although the Son's obedience and love and willingness to serve are wholly subject to emulation, his act is not. None but he can take on God's omnipotence, none but he can rescue Heaven and expel the unrighteous. From the time he ascends into the chariot to the time he returns to God's throne, there is something transcendent about the Son that can be accounted for only by recognizing the operation of the divine within his being. In an earlier chapter we considered how the arrival of the chariot symbolized the operation of divine providence within the lives of men. Certainly this is so. But the chariot itself, as it carries the resplendent Son enthroned, symbolizes much more. It is the vision of divine glory.

Glory has been a key word in the war from the beginning. When Satan uses the word, as he does in asserting to Michael that he means to win "the strife of Glory," it is clear that he uses it almost interchangeably with the Homeric *kudos* or *kleos,* meaning by it the old heroic ideal of inspired battle courage. That the Son dismisses that concept is made apparent when he challenges the rebels to try his "battle valor":

> That they may have thir wish, to try with mee
> In Battle which the stronger proves, they all,
> Or I alone against them, since by strength
> They measure all, of other excellence
> Not emulous, nor care whom them excels;
> Nor other strife with them do I voutsafe.

[6.818–823]

254

This is almost a parody of the heroic "single" combat, the Son single against the entire rebel army.[23] Yet the point the Son makes is a serious one. Battle strength can provide no true standard for excellence or glory. It can only provide a standard for strength, and if this is one's measure for all, then to be defeated by superstrength proves the only standard one can respond to. Therefore the Son proposes no higher combat with the rebels than strength to strength. That his "war-making" proves more is another matter—that he is not merely a Hector, though adorned with Hector's epithet, that he is more than the supersoldier Michael whom Milton wisely allows to stand aside at this point lest the real values of battle for "glory" be obscured.

From the beginning it is clear that the Son understood that the real issue between him and Satan was a "matter of Glory." In retrospect we understand this as we reread book 5, lines 735–742.

> Mighty Father, thou thy foes
> Justly hast in derision, and secure
> Laugh'st at thir vain designs and tumults vain,
> Matter to mee of Glory, whom thir hate
> Illustrates, when they see all Regal Power
> Giv'n me to quell thir pride, and in event
> Know whether I be dext'rous to subdue
> Thy Rebels, or be found the worst in Heav'n.

What we read in context as ironic jeering becomes, as we move to the end of book 6, the prophecy of the Son's glorious appearance in his chariot. The key word here is "illustrates"; the hate of the rebels illustrates or makes glorious the Son, that is, provides him the opportunity for true glory, or illuminates him gloriously.

---

23. John M. Steadman, *Epic and Tragic Structure in "Paradise Lost"* (Chicago, 1976), traces the classical parallel of this scene to the pursuit, single-handed, of Hector by Achilles, who has commanded the army to refrain from combat. Using Castelvetro's and Minturno's Renaissance commentaries on the scene, Steadman asserts that Milton is attempting, as the critics urge, to enhance the element of the marvelous in epic when he pits the Son alone against an entire army (pp. 110–112).

But what is glory? Clearly, it is a term closely connected with God and with the Son as he is image of God, that is, as he expresses God. In book 3 the Son is introduced as the "radiant image of [God's] Glory" (3.63). Glory, then, is a quality the Son possesses not of himself, but of God. When the Son is seen most glorious (3.139–140), it is because all the Father shines in him substantially expressed; on the Son expecially the "effulgence of [God's] Glory abides" (3.387–388); and in him only the quality of love abounds more than glory (3.312). Yet glory is not a quality exclusive to God or the Son. Glory shines in the angels as the Son creates them and crowns them with glory, and to their glory he names their hierarchies: "Thrones, Dominations, Princedoms, Virtues, Powers" (5.839–840). Clearly, glory is part of the divine, born in a creature as he derives from God. In Hell, though dazzling order and splendor and even courage survive, glory is extinct. The ranks of fallen angels, assembled before Satan in book 1, shine in all but this: "yet faithful how they stood, / Thir Glory wither'd" (1.611–612).

For both God and the Son, the Son undertakes the battle so that he might win glory. Empson, taking glory simply as the Homeric *kudos,* sees the Son "winning his spurs."[24] But this is to respond to glory as Satan did. The Son wins glory not by taking part in the war, but by ending it.

> For thee I have ordain'd it, and thus far
> Have suffer'd, that the Glory may be thine
> Of ending this great War....
>
> [6.700–702]

Further, the Son's glory derives not from conquering his adversary, Satan, but from pleasing God by fulfilling his will. In the truest sense the Son's glory in battle is only this: the illumination *within him* of God's divinity. Herein lies the meaning of his ascent into the chariot and the revelation of that chariot to rebel and loyalist alike.

24. Empson, *Milton's God,* pp. 95–97.

Curiously enough, though we think of the Son's chariot as a battle chariot, it is so only in the limited sense that it carries him (as chariots carried heroes) to the battlefield. As Milton shows us in book 7, the chariot is not restricted to battle. Indeed, "Ezekiel's" chariot, on which the chariot of book 6 is based, is not a battle chariot; in fact, it is not a chariot at all except in the symbolic sense of container or conveyance of divinity. For the chariot of Ezekiel was interpreted by most seventeenth-century exegetes as simply a vision of the divinity or, most specifically, of the Son of God as divinity when he was to come in the last days. Often, as we note in David Pareus's commentary on Revelation, the vision of Ezekiel was thought one with John's vision of the beasts in Revelation.[25] It was an epiphany of the glory of God in the Son. Peter Sterry in one place calls the chariot of Ezekiel the appearance of "our Saviour as He descends in a Divine Glory," in another the revelation of the "Glories in the Kingdom of the Spirit, the Mystical Person of Christ." Sterry thinks specifically of this vision as one to come in the last days "when these Cloudes, which now are upon us, shall open themselves" and "Jesus Christ with a Traine of Gloryes" shall descend and "alight amidst us."[26] Now it is true that Christ in his Second Coming descends to judge the world (and Pareus or Sterry or other commentators as they describe the event to come never forget this). Yet the chariot per se is not, despite its whirlwind, clouds, and fire—those more terrifying aspects that Milton has retained ("fierce Effusion," "smoke and bickering flame, and sparkles dire," 6.765–766)—merely a vision of judgment. And this is important, for though it is to roll over "Shields and Helms, and helmed heads"(6.840), we must not think of it, as has G. Wilson

25. David Pareus, *A Commentary upon the Divine Revelation of the Apostle and Evangelist Iohn*, trans. Elias Arnold (Amsterdam, 1644), pp. 91–92.

26. See especially the following sermons of Sterry: *The Clouds in Which Christ Comes* (London, 1648), pp. 15–35; *The Coming Forth of Christ in the Power of His Death* (London, 1650), Epistle Dedicatory and pp. 26–43; also the following collections: *The Discourse of the Freedom of the Will* (London, 1675), pp. 79–82, 97; *The Rise, Race, and Royalty of the Kingdom of God in the Soul of Man* (London, 1683), pp. 206, 278–279, 421–422.

Knight, and some critics since him, as the ultimate weapon of war.[27] That it becomes so for the rebel angels means only that, blinded to true glory, they can see it as nothing else.

When God proclaimed the kingship of the Son in book 5, he was proclaiming in truth the mystical unity of all creation under this very special being. Ironically, of course, the proclamation to union resulted in the first breach of union, as Satan withdrew from the throne of God, leaving it "unworship't, unobeyed." When the Son comes in book 6, it is to manifest that union proclaimed earlier by the Father and now to be brought to realization. In mounting the chariot, the Son initiates union. Peter Sterry's commentaries upon the vision of Ezekiel are once more pertinent to our investigation, for Sterry viewed the chariot as symbol for the new creation. It is the "Image, in which he [Christ] shall appear at the last Day, as a New Creator and a New Creation, making all things New; as the most Entire, most Naked Image of the Invisible God, in all his most Pure and most Invisible Glories; as the First-born of the whole Creation."[28] In his act of coming, Christ in the chariot (like Christ as rider of the white horse in Revelation 6) is a prince who shows himself to his subjects and receives homage, then gathers them to himself in "One Spirit of Beauty and Immortality."[29] For, as he re-creates, the Son also unifies all under his headship. His chariot, in which all parts work as one, is itself a symbol of the unifying re-creation.

> The Glory of the holy Angels make the New Earth; the Horses, and the Wheels in the Chariot of the great King. The Wheels, the Visible Part of the Creation, the Wheels are made of Angelical Glory: But they are the Angels of *Service* in a New Spiritual Glory. The Invisible Things of the Creation, the Living Creatures in the Chariot

---

27. G. Wilson Knight, *Chariot of Wrath* (London, 1942), p. 158: "Messiah's God-empowered chariot is a transcendental conception deriving from Old Testament prophecy, but also incorporating and driving to the limit Milton's habitual fascination with the military and the mechanical. It is at once a super-tank and a super-bomber."
28. Sterry, *Rise, Race, and Royalty,* pp. 421–422.
29. Sterry, *Clouds in Which Christ Comes,* pp. 15–24, 17.

are the Angels of the Throne in the Glory of the Kingdom; of the Coronation, and Marriage-day.[30]

For David Pareus the vision of the chariot is confirmation of Christ's glory, and honor, and power. Christ as the creator of all things assumes his rightful power over all.

The celebration of all power is due to the creator and governour of all things: As this from the act of creation he assumes as proper unto himselfe.[31]

Hence, as we read the final passages of book 6, we should keep in mind that the vision of the chariot symbolized for the seventeenth-century mind the key to the divinity of Christ. So, when the Son mounts the chariot, he reveals to enemies and friends alike the meaning of his divinity. What we see foremost in Milton's chariot is power, union, and majesty. The chariot rushes forth of itself, undrawn; its power, as the power of the Son, is in its own being. Thick flames flash everywhere, "careering Fires between." The bow and quiver, hung beside him "with three-bolted Thunder stor'd," or Victory, sitting eagle-winged (6.762–764), are figures for immense power, held and reserved (power to be used only at half-strength, for the Son's main purpose is to reveal, not employ, the resources of his divinity). As power is revealed, so is union. One spirit rules the chariot, though its configuration is manifold. The four cherubic shapes that compose and convey it each have four faces and bodies that are set as with stars, and wings that are set with eyes, and set with eyes are the wheels also. In these many parts, all intricately linked and interinvolved, is a single watchfulness of which the eyes, as Pareus commented, are the symbol, denoting "full and perfect light or knowledge."[32] In the midst of the chariot is that emblem of pure serene majesty or glory, the sapphire throne, upon a crystal fir-

30. Sterry, *Rise, Race, and Royalty,* pp. 421–422.
31. Pareus, *Commentary,* pp. 93–94.
32. Ibid., p. 93.

mament, inlaid with amber and all the colors of the rainbow. And on that throne sits the Son himself, whose only "armor" is the radiant Urim, that divinely wrought celestial breastplate that marks once more his eminence in spiritual authority.[33]

The effect of the Son is threefold: joy to the faithful, grief to his enemies, and renewal to all Heaven. The loyal angels rejoice in the Son's appearance and accept him as their savior. The rebels, except for their hardening, might do the same, for the Son comes in majesty to be received. Only as he is rejected does he reject and punish. For the sight of him is *glorious,* and he seeks to gather all to his glory, all to himself, as Sterry would have said, into "One Spirit of Beauty and Immortality." Milton's comment is terse: "They hard'n'd more by what might most reclaim" (6.791). To see the Son in glory is to be moved by joy and love and desire for union, if one's spirit can yet be so moved. But the rebel angels are spiritless, drained by their own choice of that in them which was angelic and heavenly. Raphael wonders at such perverseness. For at the sight of the Son's glory the rebels, empty of joy, become filled with envy. This, not their fall, is their true tragedy. Obdurate, obsessed with hate, they form their last line of resistance against the Son. And he punishes them as they have already punished themselves; such is his doom or judgment upon them—that as in their hearts they have become "Godless," so too they now must be removed from God. The rage they have turned against the Son now is deflected upon themselves. The will of the Father, which they have resisted, that will that honored the Son before them, becomes the instrument of their undoing.

33. The Urim designates the Son in his priestly (rather than his kingly or prophetic) role, a reminder that he comes to mediate as well as to judge. Hence we should note that the Son's coming in book 6 reveals him in those three roles he is to exercise in his final coming: prophet, priest, king. Peter Sterry, *The Teachings of Christ in the Soule* (London, 1648), is particularly instructive in the relevance of these three roles in Christ's Second Coming (pp. 6–9). He remarks that "one of the Principall works of the Priest" is to teach "the Knowledge of God." The prophet (prophētēs) "foretell[s] things to come" and "*tell*[s] *forth* the Hidden truths of God." In the final scenes in book 6, the Son teaches and foretells truths to rebel and loyal angels alike.

"Kingdom and Power and Glory" appertain, as the Son says, to the Father; these the rebels have desired for themselves and could even now have, if they could receive the Son who has come before their eyes possessed of all three. He has come to gather. His effect on the physical Heaven *has been* just this. Responding to him, recognizing his headship, the uprooted hills retire to their places; Heaven renews his wonted face; hill and valley smile with fresh flowers. Deliberately, Milton has made the physical environment respond as a living organism, indeed, as a responsive creature, a being who hears and moves, reacts and smiles. Hills and valleys the Son gathers to himself, and they smile and renew, in his glory, their own glory. The rebels, though spectators to all this, refuse to bloom, but before his renewing presence wither; before his living spirit fall spiritless. To them alone the blaze of his glory is a destroying and afflicting fire or plague.[34] They now are uprooted by the force of the Son, who by contrary force has placed the uprooted hills once more in order.[35]

The description of the rout of the rebel angels is, of course, terrible. But we must remember that what Milton is portraying here is primarily the terror-struck consciousness of the rebels. As Homer in the *Iliad*, book 18, shows us Achilles, his head ringed in fire, shouting his terrible war cry, as the opponent the Trojans fear and flee before, so Milton shows us the Son as the rebels react to him: thunder in his hand, his chariot glaring lightning, a sight more monstrous than the gap of the wasteful deep into which they hurl themselves. To the attendant loyal angels his "Almighty Acts" are wondrous; to the disburdened Heaven they are cause for rejoicing and reparation. With the opening of Heaven to disgorge the rebels and the close of Hell upon them, all terror, horror, pain, and woe are silenced.

34. See Pareus, *Commentary,* p. 147. "This joy of the Saintes, as I even now said, is opposed to the howling of the ungodly under the plagues: *Mountaines fall on us.*"

35. See Anne T. Barbeau's discussion of the restoration of Heaven in "Satan's Envy of the Son and the Third Day of the War," *Papers on Language and Literature* 13 (1977): 362–371.

In his passage of return in the triumphal chariot, sole victor, the Son at first suggests a martial victor like the Renaissance Michael. The palms that shade him can be the palms of a Roman triumph or the palms of Jerusalem that laud the earthly Jesus' brief kingly glory. But Milton has taught us too much about true heroism and glory, both here and in book 3, for us to suppose that the Son is merely exulting in "martial" or in "kingly" triumph. The glory of the Son is not in his triumphal progress, but in his return to the Father. As the Son has gone forth to be received by his creatures, he now returns to be received by the Father—to be received now as *worthy*. Because we have already shared in the vision of book 3, we know that all worthiness, all merit, resides not in high deeds of triumph but in simple, good, and loving service. From such service as the Son has just rendered and will once again render when he fights and conquers on the cross, and finally also when at the world's end he conquers Satan eternally, comes hope. Because of the Son, Heaven has been restored; because of the Son earth may be also. The return of the Son in triumph is symbol for the return of order, joy, peace, and love, for those "golden days" prophesied in book 3, "fruitful of golden deeds, / With Joy and Love triumphing, and fair Truth" (3.337–338). In these final days glory will become bliss; the Son now is received into both by the Father, "who into Glory him receiv'd, / Where now he sits at the right hand of bliss" (6.891–892). Bliss is achieved through perfect union with the Father, a union also possible for all creatures through the Son. The narrative of the war in Heaven begins and ends at the throne of God—begins with the proclamation of union, ends with its realization. Glorious as this union appears, it is but emblem and prophecy of the full union yet to be accomplished, a union foretold in book 3, line 341, by God himself, on that day when "regal Sceptre" shall be laid by and "God shall be All in All." In book 6 the prophecy is repeated by the Son, who promises to lay aside sceptre and power and to join all creation through himself to God "in the end / Thou shalt be All in All, and I in thee / For ever, and in mee all whom thou lov'st'' (6.731–733). This, then, is the ultimate aim of the Son's heroism, as he rescues Heaven, as he goes to earth incarnate and returns resurrected, and also finally as he judges and redeems earth in the final days to join it to Heaven.

We have in the Son a new kind of hero, who contrasts both with the Homeric hero who fights for *kudos* and the ''angelic'' hero who strives for divine victory. While scorning neither glory nor victory, the Son's final goals transcend both. Distinguished by the joy of willing service and the light of spiritual illumination, the Son strives to bring salvation and union and so to dispel the darkness of ''dubious Battle on the Plains of Heav'n.''

Paradise Lost and
Satan's Vain Attempt

with ambitious aim
Against the Throne and Monarchy of God
Rais'd impious War in Heav'n and Battle proud
With vain attempt.

[1.41–44]

The whole of *Paradise Lost* resounds with the repercussions of Satan's vain attempt against God. Had there been no war, not only Satan's but man's history would have been different. The events of the poem from Satan's regrouping of his angels in Hell to his expedition to earth and success there against man and even to the future history of man (foretold by Michael) lie in the shadow of a war, technically over and done with, whose effects continue to be felt, as Adam and Eve go down in defeat before Satan's "cold war" strategy and war itself is reborn, first in the conflicting elements and then in the human societies before and after the flood. War reaches out from the center and touches every part of Milton's epic; its fiery afterglow and looming shadow are cast over the landscape of the epic that might seem removed from its influence. As the Trojan war dominates the epics the *Aeneid* and the *Odyssey* (which only recount episodes from it), so the war in Heaven dominates *Paradise Lost*. So important did Milton consider the war that he placed it at the very center of his poem. He did not make it a mere backdrop to the story of Adam and Eve, a prologue, as it so often is in hexaemeral poems, told in tandem with the account of Creation and then dismissed from the stage. Altering his earlier plan (conceived when he still envisioned *Paradise Lost* as a drama) to recount the war in a choral piece, he gave it epic form and prominence.[1] He built toward it in the earlier books of the poem, then used its dramatic lessons to interplay with and inform later episodes. That his concept of the war in Heaven differed in many ways from the concepts that both poetical and theological traditions had fostered made it all the easier to use the episode freely in the poem. The war could thus be both a commentary on the genesis of evil and a prophecy of the course evil would take in the fallen world. It could be a dramatization of the heroic values Satan inspired and a critique of those same values. And it could be, still more importantly, a revelation of divine principles and purpose. Coming at the poem's center, the war became an episode that could look both ways: back on the events that set the poem in motion in books 1 and 2 and forward both to the climaxes in book 9 and to prophetic sections of books 11 and 12, which take the reader to the apocalypse, where the problems, so to speak, begun with Satan's defection from God finally will be resolved. Hence, for *Paradise Lost* the war in Heaven is much more than the simple historical event told to enlighten Adam and Eve, to explain the cause of Satan's desire for revenge. It is in the largest sense the genesis of ''all our woe'' and the promise of our ultimate restoration and the return of Eden.

I

The war in Heaven concludes the first half of *Paradise Lost*— concludes its, while in terms of plot, by the end of book 6 it brings the narrative to precisely the point where it began in book 1: the fall of the rebel angels. Yet, while we have come full circle in terms of time, we have not done so in terms of place; for in book 6 we are in Heaven, rejoicing with the victors, not in Hell bemoaning loss with the vanquished, as in book 1. With this radical

---

1. See Allan H. Gilbert, *On the Composition of Paradise Lost* (Chapel Hill, N.C., 1947), pp. 11-19.

change in perspective, we have the opportunity to pause for a moment and look back on where we have been: to reassess our experiences of Heaven and of Hell.

The reassessment of Hell is important, for Hell, despite its fearsome fire and darkness, has proclaimed itself a noble society, virtuous and free. Having survived the dire change of place, Hell boasts itself true Heaven and claims its leaders are yet princes of Heaven. With the experience of Heaven in books 3 and 5 and the narrative in book 6 of the exploits of Satan and his angels, we now have the chance to assess that claim. Is Satan a glorious leader, who has suffered defeat but is still able to rally his soldiers bravely and to undertake a heroic and dangerous mission? Does Hell mirror Heaven in order and discipline and retain, though darkened, the splendor of that celestial place? Books 1 and 2 both affirm and deny—affirm the splendor of Hell as Pandemonium rises in magnificence, order, and discipline with the impetus of "angelic" courage and resourcefulness but deny that such order necessarily is angelic. Indeed, the narrator warns against too ready admiration of Hell's magnificence and furnishes, with the catalog of demonic gods, more than a few hints that Hell's virtues are generic to Hell. Yet there is no positive refutation of the Satanic claim that the heroism and splendor of Hell are heavenly in origin, that the angels, though fallen, retain their native virtue and order. It seems possible that Milton, like his predecessors in the Renaissance epic and drama, permits Satan to retain in Hell some vestiges of his heavenly self and that he portrays those vestiges by investing Satan with the discipline of a classical hero. We have observed how Tasso and Valvasone and Vida endow Lucifer with noble manners and speech as they remind us that this devil, now before us, was once an angel. So, in books 1 and 2 of *Paradise Lost*, it might appear that the classical decorum of Satan and his angels is a reminder of their heavenly state.

Milton, however, considers not once, but twice Satan's military establishment, and he considers Satan's orders in Heaven only after he has already reviewed the ranks of Hell. Herein he differs from other Renaissance poets who either view one (not both) of the Satanic societies or else view both chronologically, so that Hell is described *after,* not *before* Heaven. But Milton comes to the description of the society of Heaven only after he has first shown us Hell and let us witness the claim that Hell makes of Heaven. So we have the opportunity to compare the orders of Hell with the orders of angels we see grouped in prelapsarian splendor about God (at the beginning of the account in book 5) or with the orders of angels Satan withdraws to the North. We note first that Satan's orders in Hell bear only superficial resemblance to the prelapsarian orders of God. Satan has attempted to make Hell resemble Heaven by centering himself in Hell, as God is central in Heaven, through arranging his angels about him in a circle and by dispensing from his raised throne orders and degrees that he proclaims are identical with Heaven's. In the overall organization under hierarchs, in the vastness of numbers, in the general array of angels under splendid banners and standards, it is true, Heaven's host and Hell's are similar. In Heaven, however (5.582–594), no brazen trumpets summon to assembly as in Hell (1.531–567); no spears are borne, "a Forest huge," or "serried Shields in thick array," nor do "thronging Helms" appear. In book 5 angels assemble in ranks, but in book 1 angels arise as soldiers who move like Spartan hoplites or Homeric warriors "in perfect *Phalanx* to the *Dorian* mood / Of Flutes and soft Recorders" (1.550–551). In prewar Heaven music sounds to lead the mystical song and dance about God's throne; in Hell music sounds to move the march of soldiers and to raise them to battle, as it raised "to highth of noblest temper Heroes old / Arming to Battle, and instead of rage / Deliberate valor breath'd" (1.552–554). On closer inspection Hell's assembly is more like the assembly in the *Iliad,* book 2, than the assembly in prewar Heaven.

Once war has begun, of course, all this changes. Loyal and rebel angels alike assume military orders, bear classical arms, march to the sound of instrumental harmony, and wage antique battle. But, having shown us these arms and this conduct and discipline of war first in Hell, Milton tells us tacitly that they are not "native" to Heaven. In the Heaven of book 5, the banners that waved recorded acts of zeal and love—holy memorials, not acts of combat and heroic rage. The banners of Heaven could hardly have recorded deeds of battle when war before Satan's war was unknown.[2] The loyal angels, even when they must do battle, are not eager soldiers like the rebels, striving to immortalize their deeds of combat. Raphael's own record bears this out, for he memorializes above all others that act Abdiel performed without spear or sword. Though there is hierarchy in Heaven, it is not a military hierarchy but an ecclesiastical one—everything in Heaven is centered on and arranged about God.

When Satan withdraws his angels to the North and regroups them about himself, he alters Heaven's prime principle of order and creates a military code of service to take the place of service to God. He permits his angels to believe that the military code is identical to that code God first ordained and, when fallen to Hell, he rejoices that the military code that existed in Heaven may be revived in Hell, exulting with his compeers Moloch and Belial that so long as Doric discipline survives, so long as heroic council yet is possible, even so long does "heavenly" order abide in Hell. Thus, cleverly, Satan has made that heroic code that he himself created when he resolved on war, and not the centrality of God, the essential of "Heaven." Book 6 shows us clearly that the heroic manners of the fallen angels were not vestiges of their "angelic" nature but marks of their lapsed state. Military discipline and classical decorum, the characteristics of Homeric warfare—all those qualities of the heroic life that Satan and his angels glory in and revive in Hell—come into existence with

2. Merritt Hughes is one of the few critics I know of who has raised the question whether there had been previous conflicts in Heaven: "Have there been past conflicts in Heaven which ended in acts of oblivion so perfect that Michael is unconscious of them? Does he regard the memorials of their acts of zeal and love as tributes to nothing but their generous conclusions in peace and perfect harmony?" Merritt Y. Hughes, "Merit in *Paradise Lost*," *Huntington Library Quarterly* 31 (November 1967): 17.

Satanic war. Satan marshals the first soldiers, puts weapons at their disposal, and leads them to attack, founding the first military society as he fathers war. But, as we see Satan rally his soldiers to arms at the end of book 5, we are experiencing this for a second time. And we judge him more critically. How much less splendid is the rally to arms in Heaven (in secret and under cover of night) than the assemblage that "first" took place in Hell! How much less fervid the furious dispatch to war, and how quickly does the glorious promise of Hell fade, as Doric discipline and heroic vaunting come to nothing, as bitter carnage, riot, and foul disorder succeed. The battle we see before us in book 6 uncovers the ugliness and shame that Hell's heroic manners had sought to hide. Satan's generalship is exposed, for he is unsuccessful both as a single warrior and as a leader, checked in his encounters with Abdiel and Michael and thwarted in his attempted cannon strategy. Was Satan in Hell making up for what he did not accomplish rather than living up to what he did? The courage he displayed in Hell appears in Heaven as desperate warmongering rather than valor; it is clear that Satan would rather destroy Heaven than give up his battle. Father of war and the war society of Heaven, Satan translates to Hell not the native values of Heaven, but those heroic values he himself created in Heaven in order to wage heroic war—values, incidentally, that he will also translate to earth when he infects Greece, Asia, and Egypt with his war mania.

Both book 1 and book 6—whether describing Hell's military machine or Heaven's—resound with earthly premonition. Hell's soldiers are equipped with the arms and armor of classical warriors; Heaven's soldiers fall to the fight like those "Homerically" trained but are able to adapt their strategies of war to the latest modern machinery, the cannons of the second day, or to retreat to the most primitive weapons—missile warfare, with the missiles the very rocks and hills of Heaven. What does this foreshadowing of earth mean? The description and similes of Hell offer the first hints, but it is not until book 6 that Raphael clarifies for us the

relationship between Satan's war society and the war societies to
come on earth. In Hell, when Satan's soldiers are compared to
the cavalry of Pharaoh or the Spartan militia, we stand in doubt
whether the similes do more than extol the precision of Satan's
armies by likening them to armies that we, as earthly readers,
may recognize and admire. When Milton in an impressive sequence at the end of book I (lines 573–589) tells us that Satan's
reassembled army is vaster than all the armies that will war on
earth (the giants that fought against Zeus, the heroes of Thebes
and Troy, the knights of Charlemagne and Arthur), is he doing
more than numbering the extent of arms? Only in retrospect do
we realize that Milton is commenting not only on the likeness of
the armies of earth to the armies of Hell, but on their genealogy.
Satan's armies resemble those of Sparta or Mycenae or Thebes or
Egypt because Satan is father to these armies as he is father to
those of Hell. So Raphael will tell Adam and Eve obliquely in
book 6 when he comments upon Satan's invention of the cannon. Should mischief abound on earth, war and the machines of
war will come to plague the sons of men; the mischief Satan
raised in Heaven will come to earth, and with it all the arms and
machines of destruction. So, when Milton in book I compares
Satan's army to those of earth, he is preparing his readers in two
ways: first, for the two-day warfare in Heaven when Satan will
run the gamut from the noble contest of heroes (with their classical or medieval chivalry) to the primitive ravaging of "giants"
and "gods," and, second, for the revelation that this warfare in
Heaven "predicts" warfare on earth.

Looking back on the simile in book I after we have experienced
the warfare in Heaven, we note how Milton has reversed the
order of warfare listed in the simile. For in book I he begins with
primitive ravaging (the Titans and the giants in their struggle with
the gods), but in book 6 he holds this upheaval till last. In Heaven
we progress from heroic contests to modern strategy only to fall
back at last upon primitive, hand-to-hand upheaval (though of the
most dangerous sort). War ends, Milton seems to say, where it

begins: in primitive destruction. Hence the sequence of the war in Heaven serves in many ways to judge the "heroic" society of Hell. In Hell Milton permits the splendid rally to arms, the glorious outpouring of soldiers, who seem arrayed only to triumph. Later, in Heaven, when the Son brings Satan's armies to judgment, he is also judging implicitly the rally in Hell. For in Heaven Satan's armies rise only to come to defeat, only to show the futility of even the most splendid rally to arms. The judgment of the Son in book 6 upon Satan's war is judgment both of the warmongering of Hell and of all war. Unlike the poets who preceded him, Milton is not content merely to bring Satan to defeat in Heaven; he must also bring to defeat the ethics of power that moved him to war and show how those ethics continue to move earth to seek Satanic warfare.

How severe is Milton's judgment on Satan's "heroic" does not become apparent until books 9 and 10, when Satan's heroic enterprises come to a climax. Books 1 and 2 of *Paradise Lost* have taught us that the war in Heaven was only the first phase of Satan's warfaring. Dismissed from Heaven, Satan continues to "fight," rallies his army, and then sets out for earth as a single "heroic" spy. (Diomedes' and Odysseus's spy mission in the *Iliad,* book 10, is not more cold-blooded.) So in book 9, when Satan is about to turn his spy mission to final "combat," Milton prefaces the account with recollections of the climaxes of such epics as the *Iliad* and the *Aeneid,* placing in heroic context an enterprise that appears far from heroic. Can the seduction of a weak and gullible woman compare with the wrath of Achilles, pursuing Hector about the walls of Troy, or the rage of Turnus at "Lavinia disespous'd," or the revenge of Neptune or Juno on Ulysses or Aeneas? Satan himself, the erstwhile heroic protagonist whom we saw in duel with Michael or pursued like Hector by Achilles, regrets that he must divest himself of his former soldiership. Descending into the serpent, he bitterly remarks: "O foul descent! that I who erst contended / With Gods to sit the highest, am now constrain'd / Into a Beast" (9.163–165). His awareness in book 9 that he does not play the epic hero when he seduces Eve does not, however, deter him in book 10 from exulting like a hero in his victory: both when he meets Sin and Death in Chaos and is enthusiastically received by them and when he prepares for his hero's reception in Hell.

The final scenes in Hell are set against a would-be heroic background, for these scenes belong by tradition not to the aftermath of Satan's victory on earth, but to the aftermath of his defeat in Heaven. Milton has withheld until book 10 the metamorphosis of Satan from angel to dragon that other poets had shown at the beginning or at the end of the battle in Heaven. Peri, Valvasone, and others had transformed Satan as the battle began in order to make him the most fearful of adversaries, a hundred-armed giant or the dragon of Revelation. Vondel and some others had waited until Satan's defeat to effect his transformation, turning him from angel to devil as he yields to Michael and falls from Heaven. But no other poet I know of defers the transformation until after Satan's seduction of Eve and his return to Hell, thus making the metamorphosis punishment not only for his crime in Heaven, but for all subsequent crimes and, further, an ironically appropriate punishment for having assumed the form of a serpent to achieve his victory over Eve.

In delaying the metamorphosis till book 10, Milton avoids the pitfalls of either making Satan merely a monster as he wars in Heaven or exciting a false pathos in the loss of angelic beauty with his loss of angelic place. At the end of book 6 or the beginning of book 1, the cruel and sudden metamorphosis might have seemed to proceed from divine vindictiveness rather than Satanic crime (there is already pathos in book 1 in the loss of angelic splendor Satan has suffered). By delaying the metamorphosis till book 10, Milton has time to show that the outer transformation merely reflects the inner change.

In books 1 and 2 and still more persistently in book 6 there have been portents of the coming metamorphosis. Satan's children, Sin and Death, unveil to their reluctant father the deformed side of his nature; Sin, herself once a beautiful goddess, now serpentine and hideous, predicts what Satan is to be. The monsters that abound in the vestibules and farthest reaches of Hell, the "*Gorgons* and *Hydras* and *Chimeras* dire" (2.628), shadow forth the transformations that await Satan's angels. In book 6 there are further hints of monstrosity: Satan's angels wage war not like spirits of light, but like the sons of Earth. Before they fall they are herded like swine or goats; not till book 10, however, do they assume these beastlike forms. In book 9 Satan, in order to destroy man, chooses the shape of the serpent and so, unwittingly, his own future shape. With the serpent he is judged at the beginning of book 10, and his metamorphosis merely carries out that judgment:

> down he fell
> A monstrous Serpent on his Belly prone,
> Reluctant, but in vain: a greater power
> Now rul'd him, punisht in the shape he sinn'd,
> According to his doom....
>
> [10.513–517]

This metamorphosis is a final comment upon the heroic Satan who with ambitious aim raised war in Heaven against the throne and monarchy of God. Satan in book 10 has come from victory, not defeat, a victory he invests with all the would-be martial glamour he was unable (we know) to achieve in Heaven. Gloating over the credulous woman he has gulled, he resembles that Satan who in Heaven gloated and made game (with his compeer Belial) at the loyal angels' bewilderment before the cannons. Just as then, his ironic laughter sets him up for one more ironic reversal. The metamorphosis comes not merely to humiliate Satan in his moment of triumph, but to put that triumph into perspective. For the first time since he warred in Heaven and met with the greater power of the Son, Satan is made to bow and recognize his limitations and God's authority. But, whereas in Heaven his defeat was a collective rout with his angels, he now faces a lone and personal humiliation. Denied glorious and single eminence in Heaven, driven to Hell, where he singly vaunts that lost heroism, Satan now achieves his moment of ''recognition.''

Book 10 closes then the account of Satan where it ought to have begun: with his metamorphosis in Hell. Outwardly now, Satan resembles the monstrosity that rages within. In visage like a hero, battleworn but brave, Satan first appeared in Hell, so departed to earth, and so hoped to return. Imitating in his adventures the hero Son, Satan hoped to find in Hell a glorious reception like that which always awaits the Son, most prominently when he returned from conquest of the warring rebels. All, Satan hopes, will assemble to him and listen to the account of his generalship. But Satan's return to the throne in Pandemonium is not like the Son's return to bliss; not triumph awaits him, but judgment. Book 10 carries out the sentence the Son pronounces implicitly on Satan *and* his angels. Satan is transformed and his angels are herded once more, but now like serpents. The dire change that overtakes all is a last ironic commentary on that society that pronounced itself unchanged, though in Hell.

2

If books 5 and 6 help put in perspective the experience of Hell, they also deepen immeasurably our understanding of Heaven. With 415 lines in book 3 that tell of the council in Heaven, they constitute the major sources of our information about God's realm and are in themselves the longest continuous narrative of Heaven. (After book 6, only in brief passages do we soar with the poet into the Heaven of Heavens.) The vision of Heaven in books 5 and 6 is important not only for what we learn of God and the Son, but for its portrayal of that society of angels who stood firm in their loyalty to God. Since the focus in *Paradise Lost* is so often upon those who did not or who will not stand firm, not without significance is the description of those who did. In describing the loyal angels, books 5 and 6 complement book 3, for both sections of *Paradise Lost* show the angels in orders, in book 5 standing about God in prewar splendor in their "Orbs / Of circuit inexpressible" (5.594–595) and in book 3 reassembled "thick as stars" (3.61). Book 5 reveals the society of Heaven before Satan challenged it, and book 3 shows us that Heaven's angels have withstood the challenge and returned to prelapsarian unity and service.

What is important in books 3 and 5 is the enthusiastic and unreserved response of the loyal angels to God. In neither book do they hold center stage, except briefly, but their presence is continuously felt. For, if God in Heaven initiates thought and decree, it is the angels in their response that make such thought or decree felt. It is they in whom it sounds and echoes, they who in response make song ring throughout Heaven. God's decree may be grand and beautiful, but unless it is rejoiced in by the angels, it is in a sense without meaning. Hence those passages that describe the response of the angels to God are significant. In book 3 the decree of God that man shall find grace produces in the angels a sense of new joy; the Son's offer to save man makes the angels exult and fills their songs with new melody. In book 5, while Satan is silent and grieves at the announcement of the Son's elevation, the angels join in song and dance. Though the war breaks into their dance and ruins the harmony of song, the peace that comes at the end of book 6 makes Heaven resound once more with song.

In Milton's theology, the servants of God are not empty reflectors of the divine image but creative agents who support God dynamically and who second and further his decrees. With the Son, who names himself and acts the role of the "chiefest of servants," the angels define for us how faith transforms itself to action. They are models and exemplars for man—and, with the Son, they may even mediate between God and man. To create and to judge man, God sends his chief servant, the Son, his Word, wisdom, and effectual might; but to educate and to mediate he sends the angels Raphael and Michael, who know and have proved what service is, to teach Adam and Eve. Raphael's account of the war in Heaven is a testimony of service—as is Michael's later narrative. From God comes the directive to each angel to enlighten and instruct Adam, but from the angel's own experience and faith comes the shape and content of the narrative. What Raphael speaks, moreover, reflects not only the experience of the war, but his knowledge of God's further design to save man and his knowledge (through God's revelation) of the machinations of Satan in Hell.

Hence, when Raphael narrates how the angels stand joyously about God, both at the beginning and at the end of the war, how they hymn the Son as savior and hero when he returns to God, his narration looks back on and interprets scenes we, as readers, have experienced. The angels' jubilee at the end of the war echoes their jubilee in book 3 at the prospect of man's coming salvation, while at the same time it contrasts with the devils' glee in Hell at the prospect of man's coming seduction and fall. Books 3 and 2 had presented contrasts between the service of God's angels and Satan's devils. In book 2 the devils, cheered at Satan's proposal to go to earth, bend toward him with ''awful reverence prone'' (2.478), anticipating the angels' reverence in book 3 before the thrones of God and Messiah. But their joy, though compared to sun after shower, is tempered with gloom and cannot match the unclouded joy of Heaven. Freedom they find irksome and choice sad, and they disband to wander perplexed or to raise song in praise of those deeds that led to their own destruction. The angels, in contrast, wreathe garlands for their hair and disband only to band once more for charming symphony or sacred song; taking the harps (not the arms) that hang at their sides, they measure their time in joy, not irksomeness.

Their joy looks forward to the joy of the loyal angels in books 5 and 6, where the contrast between loyal and rebel angels, implied earlier, is more fully developed. Again the actions of the two groups define their spirit: the rebels scatter from God's throne after they hear the decree honoring the Son—scatter as they once more shall at the end of the war when they flee from Messiah. The

loyal angels gather to God's throne, when news of Satan's uprising causes them to assemble before God; likewise at the end of
the war, the loyal angels assemble to witness the acts of Messiah
and to hymn his praise. This victory song that concludes
Raphael's narrative of the war recalls dramatically the anthem of
book 3, in praise of the Son, that we have already heard, though
of course the former must "precede" it and be model for it. Both
describe the Son as God's true heir ("Son, Heir, Lord . . . Worthiest to reign" [6.887–888]; "Begotten Son, Divine Similitude"
[3.384]), and both celebrate his victory over Satan, though the
hymn in book 3 joins praise of the victor Son to praise of man's
savior. The two songs echo one another as perfect complements
and contrast with those epic hymns of the devils in book 2, who
sound only their own and not another's praise.

The echoing songs of books 3 and 6 have another lesson to
teach, however, for in Heaven song is always about to be renewed, as the angels renew their service to God. And in this
antiphon of the angels, the love of God and the victory of good
over evil are continuously celebrated. In book 6 the angels resume their anthem to celebrate a moment when heavenly love has
won and hellish hate has been defeated, as God's great sentence
in book 3 (line 298) promises eternally. So this hymn at the end of
book 6 serves to punctuate and bind together the first half of
Paradise Lost. It comments upon the songs of Heaven in book 3
and the songs of Hell in book 2 and so, like the entire episode of
the war in Heaven, it looks back on the preceding action in the
poem. Defining as it does the way of the loyal angel and contrasting it with the way of the rebel, it defines and contrasts by implication the ways of Heaven and Hell, judging the first, and with it
Satan, while justifying the second and God.

3

For the second part of *Paradise Lost* there are earthly lessons
to be gleaned from the war in Heaven. In books 4 and 5 and still
more resolutely in book 7, Milton turns to earth, and what the

intervening narrative in books 5 and 6 shadows forth of earth and for earth proves of great importance. Raphael's primary purpose in recounting Satan's history, we must remember, is to warn Adam and Eve that Satan is about to translate to earth the evil that has sprung in Heaven. (That Raphael's narrative also teaches other lessons is but an indication of the richness of Milton's epic method.) As readers, then, we must ask ourselves first how the account of evil's genesis may assist Adam and Eve in warding off evil from Eden. Evil, as we know, has already entered the garden and posed for the human couple the puzzle of its origin in Eve's dream. That puzzle Raphael will not unravel, for he comes neither to lecture nor to sermonize, but to provide Adam and Eve with information and lessons they must interpret for themselves. He merely tells them the full account of Satan's disobedience and urges them to obey. How the knowledge of Satan's fall may assist them in warding off their own falls, he leaves them in their own wisdom to discern.

For both Adam and Eve there are particular lessons to learn from Raphael's narrative: for Eve, lessons that point backward to her encounter with Satan in her dream and forward to her encounter with the serpent. Indirectly, Raphael instructs her on who her seducer is and how he may be resisted. Can she, who in her sleep heard the voice of Satan tempting, "Why sleep'st thou, Eve" (5:38), not hear (in Raphael's account) the same accents at Beelzebub's ear, "Sleepst thou, Companion dear" (5.673)? Can she not see in the splendid angel who drew the starry flock, alluring them with his countenance while cheating them with his lies, the angel of her dream in his prelapsarian beauty? Can she not discern, further, the likeness between the seductive oratory Satan uses before his angels and the seductive words of her dream? In the dream the angel challenges the edict against the apple; in Raphael's narrative Satan challenges God's edict to obey the Son. In the dream he encourages her to assert her privilege as human being; in Heaven Satan urges the angels to claim their native rights. In her dream Eve sees the angel grasp the apple; in

Raphael's account Satan tries to grasp all power in Heaven. The analogies are here, and even if Eve does not draw them directly, she is still being led by Raphael to approach new experiences critically, not to be swayed, as were Satan's angels, by comely promises and by attempts to discredit God's word.

Raphael's account provides Eve not only with illustration of the Satanic subtlety she must resist, but also with a practical example to guide her on specifically how to resist it. Abdiel, one of the humble and inferior angels, can be a compelling example to Eve, the humbler or lesser of the human pair, for he shows Eve how to apply strength and reason against an enemy. Against the company of angels and against Eve at the tree, Satan will employ similar tactics. He will attempt to persuade the creature that God is undermining his status, which the creature himself must defend by himself elevating it. So doing, he will undermine the creature's trust in and love for God. He tells the angels that they are threatened with knee-tribute, yet unpaid; Eve he tells that she and Adam are insecure in their lordship if rigid law and command exist above them. Implying that God is a threatener, rather than the Father of good, Satan urges that the creature is free of responsibility to him. So he urges him to break the bond by breaking the law, suggesting that this act will be proof of dauntless courage.

Eve does not know that when she listens to Satan's words in book 5 she is previewing her own seduction. She might, however—had she so chosen—have been previewing her own success, if she had followed the example of Abdiel and taken his answers to Satan for her answers to the serpent. When the serpent questioned the justice of God's decree, she then could have, like Abdiel, risen to the defense of God's justice. Abdiel showed her that the justice of the decree cannot be separated from the justice of the God who made it: "Can'st thou with impious obloquy condemn / The just Decree of God, pronounc't and sworn" (5.813–814). God's justness, for Abdiel, is synonymous with his goodness, and of his goodness the angels have abundant evidence: "Yet by experience taught we know how good, / And of our good, and of our dignity / How provident he is" (5.826–828). This defense of God's justice is important, for it could have prompted Eve to her own affirmation of God's justice when, in book 9, Satan as serpent attempts to undermine God's authority with an argument analogous to the one used in book 5. The serpent urges that God's prohibition of the tree implies an unjust God, whose decrees are to be resisted: "God therefore cannot hurt ye and be just; / Not just, not God; not fear'd then, nor obey'd" (9.700–701). As he tempted the angels, he tempts Eve to disregard a decree of God by suggesting that the decree is contradictory and unjust. Eve now has the opportunity to act as Abdiel did or to act like Satan's angels: to assent to Satan's logic, which traduces a God to whom she owes much, or to resist. She knows that God's decree is a symbol of his authority, "Sole Daughter of his voice," and therefore just; so she tells the serpent. She knows, moreover, the goodness of God and his providence in exalting her happy state. Did God not turn her from the fruitless vision of the lake to the fruitful embraces of Adam? Did he not give her and Adam this abundant paradise, raising them from the dust? Should his command not then rather urge than inhibit their future happiness? Abdiel is ready, in similar circumstances, to affirm that God's decree to obey the Son can only result in the angels' continued happiness, exalted and united under one head. How readily might Eve have affirmed God's just prohibition and turned from the tree. How easily might she have learned from the lowly angel, who like her had stood before the tempter.

Often it is observed that circumstances seem to conspire against Eve, that she, the weaker, is tempted alone by a being superior to her, who has disguised himself to appear innocuous.[3] Certainly this is so. But, though alone in treacherous circumstances, Eve is not defenseless. Only by disobedience to God's

3. I have taken up the question of "circumstance" and Eve's responsibility for her fall in my article "Eve and the Doctrine of Responsibility in *Paradise Lost*," *PMLA* 88 (January 1973): 69–78.

command may she fall, and she has been taught by example the consequences of disobedience and likewise the rewards of obedience. Before her are Satan and Abdiel: both heard a command of God, but one left it unworshipped, unadored, the other, "than whom none with more zeal ador'd / The Deity, and divine commands obey'd," stood firm (5.805–806). If Eve, like Satan, fails, it is because her faith falters and her love cools, not because she lacks reason or example. For Raphael's narrative has taught us that an individual may obey, whatever the circumstances, if his heart is lit with love for God. Abdiel faces his trial alone and succeeds, winning the favor of God and acceptance into the full company of saints. For Eve there is no progress of the soul, no just meed in Heaven, no welcome into the company of saints, but the judgment of God rather than his approbation. On earth the drama of confrontation, which Abdiel acted triumphantly, is reenacted with fatal consequences. Thus this brief episode that Raphael relates not only serves to illuminate the kind of service God's creatures may choose, it testifies how Eve's encounter with Satan might have been different. Free will can have its triumphs as well as its tragedies.

4

No one in *Paradise Lost* escapes trial, for, as Adam himself observes, "Trial will come unsought" (9.366). Inevitably the quality of one's faith will be tested in circumstances that define its weakness or its strength. And trial will be suited exactly to the individual to be tried. For that reason Adam's trial will necessarily be different from Eve's or from Abdiel's. Instead, he will be confronted with a dilemma not unlike that faced by the highest of the angels, Michael or Gabriel: how to keep faith in a seemingly impossible situation. Michael and Gabriel have expected to meet Satan face to face and defeat him in battle, but they soon learn that their fortitude and virtue count for little against Satan, who may be bested in one battle, but who still and ever, as the father of war, calls the turns of war. So, after success on the first day, they meet with humiliation on the second and then violence and upheaval that hold them at stalemate. Not prowess of arm is being tried but the resilience of spirit. Will they think God has deserted them when they see their enemy ever stronger and the easy victory even more distant? Will they not weary in a fight that could prove endless? Will they not in bitterness turn from service to a God who has delivered them to hopeless battle? Have they not cause to cry out that all is lost?

In his expectations, Adam is not very different from the loyal angels; he thinks to do battle with Satan directly. He tells Eve (at the beginning of book 9) that he expects "first on [him] th' assault shall light" (9.305). The opportunity for heroic contest never comes, however. Adam's expectations are violently reversed, for instead of facing Satan he faces Eve, who has already eaten of the fruit. Satan has determined the terms of contest. Like the loyal angels, Adam confronts a situation he has not created and cannot control. He sees a world gone to wrack and cries out:

> How art thou lost, how on a sudden lost,
> . . . .
> some cursed fraud
> Of Enemy hath beguil'd thee, yet unknown,
> And me with thee hath ruin'd.
> [9.900, 904–906]

Adam had thought to master Satan, arm to arm, but Satan has outwitted him and turned events to his disadvantage. Like the angels, he now finds, without knowing how or why, that the strife has turned against him. Eve is apparently lost, and with her his world of sweetness and delight. He no more recognizes this wild Eden than the angels their Heaven torn with battle. So, in desperate circumstances the quality of Adam's faith is to be tested. Will he, like those angels he saw embattled against Satan, strive on, even though the strife seems hopeless, the situation remediless? Facing apparent defeat, can he, like them, keep heart? Will he think that God has deserted his creature? The lesson of the war in Heaven is that God *does* keep faith with those who keep faith with him. The loyal angels who abide by God despite the fury of their Satanic adversaries see the apparently hopeless war reversed, see the Messiah come to rescue.

If we doubt that the second day's battle offers the loyal angels a crisis in faith comparable to the one Adam experiences in book 9, we need only consider how carefully Milton from book 3 on has invited comparison between the angels' situation and man's. In book 3, when God first raises the question of man's coming test, he places man's transgression of obedience in the context of the recent test of the angels, the "Ethereal Powers / And Spirits, both them who stood and them who fail'd" (3.100–101). To both man and angels, free will was given; among the angels some prove their "true allegiance, constant Faith or Love" (3.104) and some do not. For Milton, the proof of service rests not only in the loyal angels' abiding with God and forming his army, but in their continued loyalty amid severe trial and adversity. The single angel Abdiel proved his faith not only in dissenting from the rest, in fleeing their company, but in repudiating their lies before he fled. True heroism for Milton does not come cheaply. Accordingly, Milton's loyal angels face what no other company of loyalists (in Renaissance epic and drama) had endured, the difficult and discouraging battle of the second day, where endless warfare appears a not impossible eventuality. Milton deliberately drives them to the test. Only after the test is their service confirmed when Messiah appears, for what Messiah commends in their warfare is its faithfulness. From beginning to end (even when, we might add, the outcome was most dubious) these angels have been faithful, "fearless in [God's] righteous Cause" (6.804). Accordingly, after Eve faces her Abdiel-like crisis, where her zeal and love for God are assailed by Satanic lies, Adam's faith and constant love are besieged by doubts and dark dilemmas. When Adam forsakes his maker, we must see his act in context; the loyal saints of Heaven do not forsake their God, the loyal saints of earth (the battling Christians, who are prefigured in the angels) will not forsake theirs. For all, Messiah stands ready to rescue.

It is particularly important in book 9 to remember that Messiah is the rescuer to whom Adam should look. (We, as readers, already know that Messiah is the one who—despite man's revolt—will rescue Adam, Eve, and all their faithless progeny.) We must not forget that Adam knows Messiah—knows him as the "God" who walked in the garden, who gave him Eve in the first place and solved the dilemma of his loneliness. Will this God, who could turn bone to flesh, take away his "last best gift"? Raphael's testimony suggests that he will not—that for the sinless, rescue is not only imminent, but certain. Can Adam forget that the Son came in book 6 to succor the angels and to restore Heaven? Will this Son not restore Paradise for one who, like the faithful angels, stands true?

Like Eve, Adam has two ways before him: the way of Satan and the way of Messiah. He chooses the former, turning from God and repeating the devil's primal disloyalty. For, like Satan, he chooses self above God, or chooses that portion of self we may call Sin; for Eve, no longer daughter of God and man, is Sin, daughter of Satan. The allegory of book 2 assumes in Eden this ugly reality. Eve, accepting the fruit of pride and tempting Adam, no longer is the emanation of God and man, but the emanation of Satan. Adam, moreover, in turning to her, does not cleave to his erstwhile lovely wife (though he may deceive himself and some unsuspecting readers into supposing that he does); he cleaves to sin and self-interest. He who might have chosen the heroic fortitude of the angels parodies with his act the saving grace of Messiah and chooses the way of Satan, stained with primal ingratitude and disobedience. Ironically, once more, we see reenacted on earth the sin born in Heaven.

Adam's actions, however, have still more ironic contexts. Although, like Satan, he turns disloyally from God, rejecting his goodness and despairing of his mercy ("But past who can recall, or done undo? / Not God Omnipotent, nor Fate," 9.926–927),

Adam in his dilemma seems to resemble the Son far more than Satan. The Son it was in book 3 (150–166) who, foreseeing man lost, pleaded his case, arguing that God should not destroy his creature, loved so late, or permit the adversary to obtain his end and frustrate God's. It is no accident that Adam's words to Eve, upon seeing her fallen, echo those of the Son.

> How can I think that God, Creator wise,
> Thought threat'ning, will in earnest so destroy
> Us his prime creatures, dignifi'd so high,
>
> . . . .
> so God shall uncreate,
> Be frustrate, do, undo, and labor lose,
>
> . . . .
> yet would be loath
> Us to abolish, lest the Adversary
> Triumph. . . .
>
> [9.938–940, 943–944, 946–948]

But the resemblance of Adam's words to Christ's points up, as happens so often in *Paradise Lost,* a difference rather than a similarity. Christ argues with God in order to resolve the strife of mercy and justice he has discerned in God; Adam argues merely to evade God's justice. Christ offers to die *for* man in order that man might ultimately be reunited with God; Adam in dying *with* Eve merely effects the total separation of man from God. Hence Adam's glorious trial of exceeding love is the parody of the true act of sacrifice. Adam, perhaps, cannot be expected to rise to that "unexampl'd love" the Son manifests (before which even the angels of Heaven stood mute), to die *for* Eve, emulating *truly* the great savior; but he may be expected to abide, loyal, in his love of God. Loyalty is the lesson Raphael has taught. To those who remain loyal, God's miracle can happen. Raphael, who has witnessed this miracle and knows Messiah not only as his own and the angels' savior but as man's as well, has taught Adam lessons that might sustain his faith and keep him from despair. The Son of Raphael's narrative perpetually reminds us that God stands to his creatures as Father, a father it is joy to obey, to whom Adam may turn in adversity. And the Son himself is that savior who will rise for Adam on a third sacred morn to grant him the victory he now disdains.

Hence it appears that Milton has placed Adam's act in context with the Son's, so that we may clearly differentiate the two. At the same time, he has led us to connect Adam's act with Satan's and, albeit reluctantly, to recognize that Adam's "sacrifice" for Eve is an impulse for separate good that, like Satan's, causes his defection from God. Many poets before Milton had linked Satan's fall and Adam's, had shown how Satan's disobedience was precursor to Adam's: both turn in ingratitude against their maker. Thus, it is to be expected that Satan's revolt should resound with intimations of Adam's and Eve's: first fall shadows forth universal fall. For Satan, for Eve, for Adam, sin begins when the creature resolves to separate himself from his Creator: in this Milton follows the tradition of theologians who first described Satan's intellective sin. The monologues of Eve and Adam, in which each singly resolves to renounce his Creator's word for his own separate good, have therefore more than a few echoes of the attitudes Satan assumed when in book 5 he first justified his revolt to Beelzebub. Successful dramatists and epic writers from the medieval playwrights or the author of *Genesis B* on had shown how Satan's prideful aspirations had laid down the pattern for man's. Singly, angel or man consents to evil.

But Milton, having transposed the chronology of the war in Heaven from introduction to midpoint in the story of Adam and having made the human couple themselves hear the account of Satan's revolt, has created effects far more complex than those designed by earlier hexaemeral writers. Not only has Milton introduced Adam and Eve to the being "who envies now [their] state, / Who now is plotting how he may seduce / [Them] also from obedience" (6.900–902); not only has he shown them the dangers and subtleties of Satanic seduction, he has also offered them inspiring models for loyal behavior in Abdiel, in Michael, and in Raphael, the narrator-guide, who himself has freely stood because he freely loved. So Milton had made the account of the beginning of evil in Heaven one that points directly to its recurrence in Eden. Moreover, those two incidents of his account in which he departs from Renaissance tradition, in which he freely invents or changes the narrative, are the ones that most insistently point ahead. The trial of Abdiel has unavoidable implications for the trial of Eve; the dilemma of Michael has unavoidable lessons for Adam. By making the war a compelling exemplum of faithful service, Milton has, above every poet before him, shown us that Adam's and Eve's sad choices were far from inevitable.

5

The lessons of Raphael's narrative do not fade with the fall of the man and woman for whom they were first designed. What we have learned in books 5 and 6 about sin's origin and progress can and should be applied throughout *Paradise Lost*—most particularly in the final books. What Raphael, the first visiting angel, tells as history is intimately related to what the second, sterner angel, Michael, tells as prophecy. The two angels are not dissimilar: both have been witnesses to and participators in the great events of angelic history. Both know how evil began and both know (though God's revelation of the events in universal history) that it will ultimately be conquered on earth as in Heaven. Moreover, what Raphael tells of evil's rise in Heaven has implications not only for its first eruption in Eden, but for all future eruptions on earth. Satan's rebellion, as the first event in the so-called celestial cycle, has direct relation to all events that follow throughout time, even until the end of time itself. Evil will recur on earth, much as it began in Heaven, as creature separates himself from his Creator. Men, like angels, will grow corrupt when one infects many with his pride, and war as an institution will rear its head once more as a result of communal ambition.

Milton and his age understood that history must be read looking forward as well as backward—sacred history most particularly so. So, as we have seen, they read the story of the war in Heaven in chapter 12 of Revelation as the past account of Satan's struggle against Michael, which resulted in his expulsion from Heaven; as the ever-continuing account of godly men's struggle against the forces of Satan in this world; and as the prophecy of that last battle of the saints against the dragon. Hence in book 6 Milton makes his angel Raphael as much a prophet, as he recounts the first war of Satan, as he has made the seer Michael as he recounts all events since Satan's and Adam's fall.

Sin, as Milton makes clear in book 6, as well as in books 10, 11, and 12, cannot and will not be contained. Its effects are felt first in the sinners themselves, then in everything that surrounds them. Satan stains the lovely landscape of Heaven with war and war machines; Heaven is overcast by darkness, then ablaze with fire; hills and valleys are disfigured as angels attack the landscape. In Eden, at the moment of sin earth feels the wound; then ruin spreads visibly, as it had in Heaven. Conflict breaks out among the animals, and the elements of nature are divided against themselves. Extremes of cold and heat arise, and warring winds rage.

> These changes in the Heav'ns, though slow, produc'd
> Like change on Sea and Land, sideral blast,
> Vapor, and Mist, and Exhalation hot,
> Corrupt and Pestilent: Now from the North
> of *Norumbega,* and the *Samoed* shore
> Bursting their brazen Dungeon, arm'd with ice
> And snow and hail and stormy gust and flaw,
> *Boreas* and *Caecias* and *Argestes* loud
> And *Thrascias* rend the Woods and Seas upturn;
> With adverse blast upturns them from the South
> *Notus* and *Afer* black with thundrous Clouds
> From *Serraliona;* thwart of these as fierce
> Forth rush the *Levant* and *Ponent* Winds
> *Eurus* and *Zephir* with thir lateral noise,
> *Sirocco,* and *Libecchio.*
>
> [10.692–706]

What we saw during the war in Heaven has predicted these changes we now see on earth. Indeed, Milton has for earthly application adapted from the poets who preceded him one of the most common metaphors for ethereal battle: the war of the winds. Renaissance poets had depicted in the rage of the winds the fierce passion with which celestial spirits warred against one another. Now Milton, with his description of the winds' rising violence, shows how the very elements of earth respond to the birth of discord in the human heart. Sin in Heaven or on earth cannot be contained: the universe quakes in response.

The visions of the world-to-be in books 11 and 12 also testify how sin spreads its outrage. Throughout the social structure, Adam now sees the repercussions of that sin born in Heaven and translated by him to earth. Envy will rise anew in Cain and divide him from his brother, as Satan's envy divided him from Messiah. Then violence will erupt: murder on earth, war in Heaven—for everywhere Sin, as we know, breeds Death. As Satan's envy has its counterpart on earth, so does his guile. The fair atheists who allure the sons of God with their beauty and charm are called daughters of men (of Cain), but, like Eve after her fall, they may be named daughters of Satan. His graceful, easy persuasiveness may be seen in their seductive manners; his false beauty undid one-third of the angels, theirs undid the righteous descendants of Seth. In Heaven or on earth, the ways of sin are pleasant, but the consequences are dire. From the angels' easy yielding to Satan rises the destructive war in Heaven. From the unwise coupling of the sons of God with the daughters of men comes that race of warriors that turns earth into an armed camp. Prodigious men of strength are born who order society according to those heroic principles Satan first established in Heaven. The trumpets, banners, and clarions of war, first lifted in Heaven, now reappear on earth, and the grim face of war once more shows itself. Adam, beholding the scenes of carnage, stands amazed, apparently having forgotten both Raphael's account of the war in Heaven and his prophecy that war or the engines of war might be reinvented by men, should evil abound on earth.

Milton, however, hopes that his reader has not forgotten, for his descriptions of the warfare on earth contain more than a few recollections of war in Heaven. Like book 6, book 11 traces the rise, progress, and full heat of battle. At the beginning men exercise in arms, "part wield[ing] their arms, part curb[ing] the foaming Steed, / Single or in Array of Battle rang'd / Both Horse and Foot, nor idly must'ring stood" (11.643–645). Thence proceeds the conduct of battle: one foraging army disrupts the meadows and pasturing flocks, another lays siege to a city with "Battery, Scale, and Mine" (11.646–656). The defenders in opposition, protecting the wall, hurl "Dart and Jav'lin, Stones and sulphurous Fire" (11.658). A council of war, in which elders and warriors mix and harangues are heard, fails to dissuade any from battle but does produce one man of middle years, who "rising, eminent / In wise deport" spoke much "of Right and Wrong, / Of Justice, of Religion, Truth and Peace, / And Judgment from above" and who from the violent hands of those disapproving his words must be snatched by Heaven itself (11.664–671). Now violence erupts everywhere and no refuge is to be found; sword-law reigns.

Whereas singly and collectively there is nothing remarkable about this panorama of battle (its model could have been the *Iliad* or any other classical epic poem), in overall effect and in individual detail there are clear echoes of book 6. In book 6 we are told how war commences with armies eager to display their military expertise: leaders are practiced "when to advance, or stand, or turn the sway / Of Battle, open when, and when to close / The ridges of grim War" (6.234–236). In Heaven, as on earth, "fiery Darts in flaming volleys" fly through the air (6.213); "foaming Steeds" are reined (6.391); and a pastoral landscape is torn and ravaged. And at the end, in Heaven as on earth, violence erupts everywhere and sword-law reigns. Even in the depiction of the lonely dissenter to war, who preaches right and warns against judgment, there is an obvious parallel between Abdiel and Enoch.

When Raphael chose to liken heavenly to earthly form in telling his account of the war in Heaven, he not only presented pictures convenient for earthly apprehension, but also shadowed forth visions of a future to come.[4] Hence, when war in book 11 makes its first appearance on earth, Milton calls to mind with indirect reference and echo the panorama of war in Heaven.

Book 11 also shares with book 6 a resounding indictment of war as an institution. Throughout book 6 there is amazement at, distaste for, and finally rejection of war. Raphael at first wonders that "Angel should with Angel war, / And in fierce hosting meet, who wont to meet / So oft in Festivals of joy and love / Unanimous, as sons of one great Sire" (6.92–95). Michael scorns the "Acts of hateful strife, hateful to all" (6.264), and Messiah rejects the entire ethic of heroic warfare: "since by strength / They measure all, of other excellence / Not emulous" (6.820–822). Book 11 picks up and develops these themes. Adam shares Raphael's amazement that brother should war with brother; he condemns war as the multiplication "ten thousandfold" of the sin of "him who slew / His Brother" (11.677–679). Michael develops Messiah's indictment of "heroic" virtue, crying out against those societies where "Might only shall be admir'd, / And Valor and Heroic Virtue call'd; / To overcome in Battle, and subdue / Nations . . . shall be held the highest pitch / Of human Glory" (11.689–694). Book 11 presents, in fact, the most complete critique in *Paradise Lost* of the classical heroic ethic, the same ethic that in books 1 and 2 moved Satan to regroup his army in Hell and that in book 6 moved him, to begin with, to seek "glory" against God. In books 1 and 2 Satan clings to the notion that battle-courage (the courage never to submit or yield) is a value that can survive defeat. In book 6 Satan's notion of battle-glory,

---

4. Critics differ in interpreting Raphael's meaning, some preferring to read his shadowing forth as Milton's attempt at accommodation, others to read it as foreshadowing. I believe it is both. For a provocative discussion of critical opinion on this point, see Leland Ryken, *The Apocalyptic Vision in "Paradise Lost"* (Ithaca, N.Y.: Cornell University Press, 1970), pp. 12–32.

the idea that might is right, fades before the true glory of the Son. In book 11 Satanic "battle-glory," as manifest in the giants of old, seems pure parody. How far from the giant angels of book 1, retaining somewhat their heavenly splendor, are these giants, merely huge of limb, who delight in "infinite man-slaughter" and who love to style themselves "great Conquerors, / Patrons of Mankind, Gods, and Sons of Gods," but who, as Michael names them, are "Destroyers rightlier call'd and Plagues of men" (11.695–697). In them the Titans of Hesiodic fable are recalled, or the Giants, sons of Earth, who in the various classical theogonies or gigantomachiae did prodigious deeds on earth. In thèm, too, Satan's giant angels and their mighty deeds of war are reduced to earthly scale.

Book 11, with its companion book 12, not only offers a critique of war, but shows that war is, in final measure, futile and endless, being governed by cycle. Peace succeeds war, corrupting what war wasted, and then in time "civil broils" or "hostile deeds" arise until, come full circle, war breaks out once more. As the war in Heaven demonstrated, violence meets with repulse, only to rise to new assault. Warfare in itself, the angels learned, is unending (only in God's time and with God's word can it end). The three days' warfare in Heaven shadows forth eternal war on earth: war ends only to begin again. For a time the flood sweeps away the heroic societies of earth with their glory-seeking war and luxurious peace; but the new world, which at first brings forth paternal rule and fraternal equity, at last gives birth to a new warmonger.

Satan, the first tyrant of Heaven, the first emperor of Hell, is progenitor of the tyrants who seize power on earth. First there is Nimrod, who with "proud ambitious heart... will arrogate Dominion undeserv'd / Over his brethren, and quite dispossess / Concord and law of Nature from the Earth," oppressing with "War and hostile snare such as refuse / Subjection to his Empire tyrannous" (12.25–32). Nimrod's subjugation of his brothers, his violence to the concord of the earth, his abuse of nature and reason—all these recall the Satanic originals. Adam and Michael in book 12 deplore what Abdiel and the angels did in book 6: that equal should assert lordship over equal and that those formerly free should willingly serve a tyrant. Satan in Heaven rejects right Reason for his guide, Messiah (his worthier) as his king, and having first enslaved his own good judgment, then enslaves those below him. So observes Abdiel:

> This is servitude,
> To serve th' unwise, or him who hath rebell'd
> Against his worthier, as thine now serve thee,
> Thyself not free, but to thyself enthralled. . . .
>
> [6.178–181]

Michael's observations in book 12 about the ways of tyranny on earth are analogous: Man refuses right reason for his law and so loses liberty, which "always with right Reason dwells / Twinn'd" (12.84–85):

> Reason in man obscur'd, or not obey'd,
> Immediately inordinate desires
> And upstart Passions catch the Government
> From Reason, and to servitude reduce
> Man till then free.
>
> [12.86–90]

As a consequence, tyranny comes into existence as a judgment upon man's permitting unworthy powers to assume the lordship over his reason; thus he loses his outward liberty also.

In Pharaoh, Milton presents another type of Satanic tyrant, a portrayal for which he has prepared us since book 1, when he described the devils in flight over Hell like the locusts hanging "o'er the Realm of impious *Pharaoh*" (1.342) or when he likened the fallen angels to the sedge upon the Red Sea when Pharaoh's Memphian Chivalry was overthrown (1.304–311). Satan stands to Pharaoh as father to son, a son who exhibits particularly his progenitor's lawlessness and frenzy. Some critics have seen in Satan's relentless fury against the loyal saints of Heaven foreshadowing of Pharaoh's persecution of God's chosen people on earth. Correspondingly, some suggest that the Son of God who infixes plagues in the souls of the rebels, as he drives them from Heaven, is like the God of Israel who drove plagues among the resisting Egyptians.[5] Thus, in book 12, when Milton casts Pharaoh's pursuit of the Israelites and his drowning at the Red Sea in terms of battle and defeat, we recognize the connection between this latter-day Lucifer and his original. Pharaoh in his blindness persecutes the Israelites, pursuing vain war, as Satan originally in Heaven opposed God's will and raised war against him. Yet all the strength of Pharaoh's warfaring comes to nothing. As Christ tames the dragon-Satan, God, having wounded the river-dragon, Pharaoh, with ten wounds, humbles and destroys him at last, troubling "all his Host / And craz[ing] thir Chariot wheels" (12.209–210).

> *Moses* once more his potent Rod extends
> Over the Sea; the Sea his Rod obeys;
> On thir imbattl'd ranks the Waves return,
> And overwhelm thir War....
>
> [12.211–214]

Pharaoh and his army, drowned in the hostile waves, recall all too clearly Satan and his army weltering in the waves of the fiery lake.

With these portraits of Nimrod and Pharaoh, Milton is developing political paradigms that have far-reaching implications. Milton expects us to see in Nimrod or Pharaoh particular tyrants whom we can readily connect with the archetypal tyrant, Satan. But he also expects us, as we did with the war in Heaven, to look ahead

5. Several critics make this point. See, for example, Lawry, *Shadow of Heaven*, p. 211. The most sustained comparison of the warring angels and the warring Israelites occurs in Jason Rosenblatt's article, "Structural Unity and Temporal Concordance: The War in Heaven in *Paradise Lost*," *PMLA* 87 (1972); 31–41. Michael Lieb in an unpublished paper, "Milton and Holy War," further evaluates the wars of the Israelites in the Old Testament as background to the war in Heaven.

and perceive a general pattern. The lessons Raphael or Michael teach are not for Adam alone, but for all people to come. Milton did not write without specific applications for his own age: when he discussed the tyrants of the Old Testament in *The Tenure of Kings and Magistrates* or *Eikonoklastes*, he expected his readers to discern in the corruptions and abuses of the past other abuses closer at hand. The poet of *Paradise Lost* expects no less. Through Raphael's and Michael's narratives, he shows how Satan makes tyranny rise in Heaven, how he establishes it in Hell, and how from Hell he produces the line of tyrants that brings forth now a Nimrod, now a Pharaoh, now a Charles. Hence he permits his readers to apply what Raphael has said of Satan, or Michael of Nimrod or Pharaoh, to the contemporary political scene. The struggle in Heaven between Satan and the warring saints or the persecution of the Israelites by Pharaoh can shadow forth events in seventeenth-century England: the struggle between Charles and the saints, the battling soldiers of the Commonwealth. Yet not this moment alone but many throughout history are also suggested by Raphael's and Michael's narratives. Milton wrote not political allegory, but epic.

Throughout books 11 and 12, Adam witnesses with increasing dismay the spread of evil in ever-widening circles; even with the advent of the Messiah evil will not be conquered. The earth will labor on, indifferent to good, benign to ill, groaning under its immense burden of sin—it is a dismal picture. From the beginning the poem has promised better: to recount not only man's first disobedience and all the woe consequent upon loss of Eden, but also the promise of that greater man who is to restore us and regain the blissful seat. The themes of restoration and regain should not be forgotten in the last books, no matter how pervasive seems the plague of disobedience, death, and woe throughout the human race. Milton has taken care to balance in these last books the emergence of deliverers of man with those destroyers of man. Moreover, with these deliverers he always looks forward to the great deliverer Son who will exemplify in the highest the faith and obedience of the faithful men who went before him: Abraham, Joseph, Moses, Joshua. The Son's devotion to God is figured in Abraham; his kingliness and authority in Joseph; his mediation in Moses, who bears his high office in figure (12.240–241); and finally, in Joshua, his generalship and his future combat with Satan.

> But *Joshua,* whom the Gentiles *Jesus* call,
> His Name and Office bearing, who shall quell
> The adversary Serpent, and bring back
> Through the world's wilderness long wander'd man
> Safe to eternal Paradise of rest....
>
> [12.310–314]

That *Paradise Lost* should return at the end to the theme of deliverance fulfills not only the promise of the poem's proem, but also the great promise that the center books dramatize. The Son who came to deliver the angels, who drove his antagonist Satan from Heaven with his rebel angels, who restored the empyrean and created earth, must come to conquer Satan on earth, to redeem man, and to restore Eden. If the war in Heaven predicted the translation of evil to earth and its spread throughout human society, it must accordingly predict also its eventual downfall. Books 11 and 12 bring forth both good and evil, destruction and re-creation. Book 11 concludes with a flood that both destroys and makes possible new creation, illustrating the pattern the center books set.

Oppression and vice may threaten to engulf all, but good will rise in opposition and creation resurge. Not for long may destruction undo the works of creation, for "to create," as book 7 proclaims, "is greater than created to destroy" (7.606–607). As earth smiles in renewal after the flood, Milton tacitly repeats this theme. Like the flood, the war in Heaven caused the end of one order but established the way for the creation of another: Heaven was renewed by the Son and earth brought into being. Book 11 presents us with a parallel moment: God has brought to an end one day in order to begin another. Having purged earth, like Heaven, of wantonness and pride, he raises creation from one man. Noah in book 11 is father and governor of the race, sprung newborn after destruction; as with Adam in book 7, God demonstrates through him his ability to repair detriment, to bring in a moment another world into being, and to create "out of one man a Race / Of men innumerable" (7.154–156).

Like book 7, book 11 closes with a great rhapsody to creation after destruction, fruitfulness after waste, new covenant after spent sin. With its token of the olive branch and convenant of the rainbow, book 11 celebrates the beginning of a new order while recollecting the genesis of the old. The earth's reemergence from the flood in book 11 is like its first emergence into being from the creative waters. In book 7, the mountains first appear, then the hills, then the bare earth with "verdure clad" (7.285–315); in book 11 the process is repeated as the ark becomes fixed upon "some high mountain," then waits until "now the tops of Hills as Rocks appear," and finally the dry land, "Green Tree or ground whereon his foot may light" (11.850–852, 857–862). Although the conclusion of book 11 is in a sense an afterimage of the first Creation, it is also a vision of the last. The rainbow, "betok'ning peace from God and Cov'nant new," dawns over Noah like the new day in Heaven over the angels awaiting the Son, that day which itself betokened the final day on earth for the saints in expectation of the fire that will purge and renew "both Heav'n and Earth, wherein the just shall dwell" (11.901). Milton does not miss the opportunity, as Noah begins his regime on earth, to look long into the future to a happier beginning when the final regime of the Son will guarantee the covenant of the rainbow.

6

How often throughout *Paradise Lost* does the promise of the new Heaven and earth (made possible through the Son's triumph over evil) come to comfort and reassure. The narrator, the angelic messengers, the Son, and God himself repeatedly predict, before Eden's golden days are past, that they will return, and so thematically *Paradise Lost,* as it moves to the fulfillment of Man's sin and his expulsion from Eden, offers the assurance of the alleviation of sin and restoration. Not, however, until the end of book 12 is the promise—first pronounced in book 3 by God or figuratively enacted in book 6—delivered to Adam as he is introduced to the Son as that "greater man" who is to "restore us, and regain the blissful Seat." The presentation of the Son in book 12, moreover, is carefully designed to emphasize his role as the victor over Satan and the restorer of Paradise. The angelic narrator dwells not upon the life of Jesus, but upon his triumphant death and victory over Sin, Death, and Satan, those enemies whom the Son had expelled from Heaven in book 6 and who in book 9 themselves won victory over Adam and Eve.[6] Thus, the narration in book 12 of the Son's earthly career has particular significance in recalling two previous climaxes in the poem: the victory in book 6 of the Son over Satan, and the victory in book 9 of Satan over Adam and Eve.

The victory of the Son on the cross over Satan, Sin, and Death is the second of the three great contests the hero Son wages throughout history, the first having been before the beginning of earthly time and the last at the end of time. Toward this second contest the narrator has moved us since the beginning of the poem. In book 2 he alludes distantly to it, remarking, when Death and Satan first meet as foes: "so matcht they stood; / For never but once more was either like / To meet so great a foe" (2.720–722). In book 3 the Son himself looks forward to his great battle with Satan, Sin, and Death:

6. The presentation of the Crucifixion in book 12 has been a problem for some critics. John Carey, for example (*Milton* [London, 1969], pp. 88–89), sees it as a major blemish in the poem and argues that it is "horribly unlike the gospel accounts," where Christ appears as forgiving, rather than vindictive.

Death his death's wound shall then receive, and stoop
Inglorious. . . .
I through the ample Air in Triumph high
Shall lead Hell Captive maugre Hell, and show
The powers of darkness bound. . . .

[3.252–256]

At the same time as the Son predicts his victory over Death, the angels in book 3 recall, significantly, his subduing of the warring angels. In book 8 Sin and Death, her black attendant, wait in the shadows, ready for surprise and conquest, which, assured by Satan in book 9, in book 10 they assume. Breaking from Hell's gate, they make their way through Chaos and meet Satan, risen bright from earth in triumph. It is to check the conquest of Satan and the power of Sin and Death that the Son comes to earth, and it is upon this confrontation that Milton places his emphasis. He strips from his account of Jesus all that will draw attention away from the meeting of the Son with his adversaries. He introduces Messiah as one dispossessed of right, proclaimed by Heaven but denied by earth; son of the Power most High, king, but unable to ascend his throne until he has dispossessed Satan. For his reign upon earth is to be, as it was in Heaven, without end, without bound.

he shall ascend
The Throne hereditary, and bound his Reign
With earth's wide bounds, his glory with the Heav'ns.

[12.369–371]

In this overall plan, into which Milton introduces and reintroduces the figure of the Son as present, past, and future antagonist of Satan, book 6 has special importance. For in book 6 alone the victory of the Son over Satan and his cohorts is granted full dramatic development. Not just an incident prophesied or briefly recollected, it is a scene that occupies the dramatic climax at the center of the poem. As such, it has great importance for the ending of the entire epic. For at the end of book 12 Milton takes us back to the climax of book 6, as he begins his narration of the victory *on earth* of the Son against Satan and his allies, now not rebellious angels joined with him against the Son, but his own inner evils, his children Sin and Death, allegorized into mighty warring opponents. In connecting the Son's victory in Heaven with his victory on earth against Satan and Satanic enemies, Milton is developing, as I observed in chapter 2, the speculation of Renaissance theologians that the enmity of Christ and Satan manifest on earth had originated in Heaven, that the contest for kingship in the world had begun as contest for the kingdom of Heaven. The emphases of Milton's brief account of the Son in book 12 are, strangely enough, exactly those of his earlier account in books 5 and 6. In both he tells first of Satan's denying kingship to the Son. In Heaven, Satan withdraws from the Son's kingdom and sets up his own kingdom in the North in opposition, attempting to deprive the Son of his right. On earth he has succeeded in dispossessing the Son of his kingdom: Messiah is born denied his right. The two-day war in which Satan offers contest to the faithful is in many ways like the history of earth up till the birth of Christ. The faithful struggle on without their general, now here, now there winning victory against Satan, but never totally repulsing him. Their plight is like the plight of the angels, beset with Satan's legions while the Son is withheld from the fight. In darkness they struggle, a darkness that does not lift until that third day's dawn, which so clearly prefigures the Resurrection.

In book 12, as in book 6, Christ comes to relieve the oppressed and to win the victory over Satan; but, in each circumstance, he does not come or act exactly as anticipated. Adam, like the loyal angels, expects the Son to act as a great military leader, who will duel gloriously with Satan. A Michael, made wise by his experiences in the war in Heaven, cautions Adam against expecting too literal a fight.

Dream not of thir fight,
As of a Duel, or the local wounds
Of head or heel: not therefore joins the Son
Manhood to Godhead, with more strength to foil
Thy enemy. . . .

[12.386–390]

Christ will not wage a physical war, nor will his victory be one of arms; his victory will be *of the spirit*. In obedience and love he will put down disobedience and so put down Satan.

Not by destroying *Satan,* but his works
In thee and in thy Seed; nor can this be,
But by fulfilling that which thou didst want,
Obedience to the Law of God, impos'd
On penalty of death, and suffering death
. . . .
The Law of God exact he shall fulfill
Both by obedience and by love, though love
Alone fulfil the Law. . . .

[12.394–398, 402–404]

In book 6 the Son, though splendid in his chariot and accompanied by ten thousand thousand angels on either side, exacts a spiritual victory. He comes, obedient to his Father's word, to cast out disobedience. In book 12, alone and defenseless, he is the same in purpose: he casts out in mankind the works of Satanic disobedience while obeying the law of God.[7]

On earth or in Heaven, the Son acts to fulfill the word of God and thereby successfully completes the trial set before him. His earthly trial involves endurance of "reproachful life" and "hated death," condemnation to the cross by his own nation—in short,

7. B. Rajan's comment on Christ's earthly and heavenly battles is instructive: "Christ's triumph in Heaven is poised against His triumph on the cross. The one is shown in the panoply of military conquest, the other as a battle waged and won in the mind, which, while less spectacular, is in no way less effective" (*"Paradise Lost" and the Seventeenth Century Reader,* p. 49).

submission to the oppressive law man's sin has made him subject to. Exerting that courage to submit, to yield, to be overcome, the Son restrains himself from acting; the erstwhile conqueror of Heaven is captured and bowed beneath enemies until death frees him to act once more. Then, turning upon the enemies that have afflicted him, Sin and Death, he nails them to the cross, thus freeing himself and mankind.

> But to the Cross he nails thy Enemies,
> The Law that is against thee, and the sins
> Of all mankind, with him there crucifi'd.
>
> [12.415–417]

In a stunning reversal, the conquered becomes the conqueror, the conquerors the conquered. The reversal is not unprecedented, however: at the end of the second day's combat in Heaven, the Son effects a similar one. Creation has been brought to wrack, darkness covers all; then out of the darkness the Son rises, as he is to rise in future time from the dark of the grave. With a sudden blaze the Son mounts the chariot and the "third sacred morn" begins to shine in Heaven, presaging the "third dawning light" foretold in book 12 and the reappearance of the Son armed in power.

> Death over him no power
> Shall long usurp; ere the third dawning light
> Return, the Stars of Morn shall see him rise
> Out of his grave, fresh as the dawning light....
>
> [12.420–423]

In rising from earth, Christ puts on majesty and beauty and assumes the kingship denied him, just as in book 6 he mounted the throne of the chariot to demonstrate his kingly authority.

Consistently, throughout *Paradise Lost,* the Resurrection of the Son has been described in terms suited to military victory. As the Son himself first spoke of future rising in book 3, he compared

his liberation from the grave to the act of conquest performed by a
great hero.

> Under his gloomy power I shall not long
> Lie vanquisht; thou has giv'n me to possess
> Life in myself forever, by thee I live,
> Though now to Death I yield . . .
> . . . .
> But I shall rise Victorious, and subdue
> My vanquisher. . . .
>
> [3.242–245, 250–251]

This description, of course, perfectly looks forward to the conquering Son of book 6, whose rising upon his enemies so implicitly suggests the later conquest over Death. But we must keep
in mind that, however martial the Son may appear, however
much he enacts the role of supreme soldier and hero, he comes to
thwart spiritual, not physical, enemies. Unlike any other soldier,
he casts out death and confers life. The life of Heaven he restores
by doing away with the death-dealing forces of Satan, the life of
earth by conquering those same enemies the sin of Adam and Eve
has granted victory on earth.

The Son is the giver of life. Endowed by the Father "to possess
/ Life in [himself] for ever" (3.243–244), he can lay down "life for
life," and can yield to Death, assured by faith that God will rescue him from the grave. Because of this faith in the life God has
given him, he can confer life on others, can rescue from Death
those who have proved "faithless." For Milton, as for all Christians, the death at the first tree is inextricably connected with that
at the second. Adam and Eve give up their life in Eden by means
of that first fatal tree, which seems to promise a life beyond life
but instead confers death. Faithless, deluded by Satanic lies,
either directly or indirectly, they turn from the soldier Christ,
who can confer life and shield them from death, and become the
prey of the conquering Sin and Death. At the second tree, therefore, Christ must do battle with Sin and Death, must win back for

Adam and Eve and all mankind the right to life. Metaphorically, then, throughout *Paradise Lost* the Son is the soldier who fights for life. Against Sin and Death, Satan's two main arms, against Satan, that Homerically perfect hero, whose courage is set on never submitting or yielding, never being overcome, the Son is the godly perfect foil. The Son's soldiership can never be measured in human terms, as can Satan's, for in his acts, he is Godlike. So Michael, attempting to explain to Adam the significance of the Son's fight on the cross, says: "this God-like act / Annuls thy doom" (12.427–428). Truly, throughout *Paradise Lost,* all the Son's acts are Godlike, for in all his acts he is creator, casting out the forces that destroy life and restoring it. His soldierly victory on the cross brings life and hence should be read as a corollary to the life-restoring triumph in Heaven.

In a different way the Son's rout of Satan after the Resurrection completes the action of book 6, for in book 12 we find the personal confrontation of the Son and Satan that did not occur at the end of book 6. There the Son merely expelled Satan with his cohorts in one company. But in book 12 Satan's humiliation is described. Dragging him in chains through the air, where Satan had once exulted in triumph with his children Sin and Death, the Son leaves him confounded there,to await at the world's end his final dissolution, also at the hands of the Son. But Milton only alludes to that final victory. We have tasted Satan's humiliation; it is more significant now to experience the Son's return.

Glorious as are the victories of the Son, still more glorious are his returns in triumph to his Father. Throughout *Paradise Lost* Milton portrays the two in tandem. The Son goes forth, armed with God's power, to conquer, to create, to redeem, to judge; a king in full array, he departs from the almighty throne only to return with still more pomp to resume his place in bliss on completion of God's behests. These departures and returns are bright moments in *Paradise Lost,* whether foreseen prophetically by the Father, the Son, or Michael or narrated dramatically by Raphael. In book 3 the Son describes his future reentry into Heaven, after his Resurrection and victory in the air over Satan: with his redeemed, he shall return to see the face of God, "wherein no cloud / Of anger shall remain, but peace assur'd, / And reconcilement" and "Joy entire" (3.262–265). In book 7 Raphael narrates the "bright pomp" of the Son's return to the Father after the sixth day of Creation: "up to the Heav'n of Heav'ns, his high abode" he rides and sits him down "with his great Father" (7.553, 587–588). In book 12 Michael tells of two returns, one after the Resurrection, when "to the Heav'n of Heav'ns he shall ascend / With victory, triumphing through the air" (12.451–452), the other "when the world's dissolution shall be ripe" and the Son, having judged the faithful and the unfaithful dead, shall return with the faithful and "receive them into bliss" (12.459–462). These visions of going and returning are interlocked; each suggests or looks back on the others timelessly as it holds and affirms its own moment in time.

Central to all the passages that describe the Son's departure from and return to the Father, however, is the great passage at the end of book 6—by far the longest and most detailed—wherein God confers all power on the Son and sends him forth and then, after the completion of his mission, welcomes him back into glory. This passage describes fully its own moment in time: the conquest of Satan in Heaven and the renewal of God's empyreal realm; it also suggests the conquests and renewals prophesied in books 3 and 12. The apocalyptic import of the Son's dispatch and return must not be underestimated. The return to the Father in book 6 with the saints of the loyal army looks to the return at the world's end when he shall reenter Heaven with the gathered saints of earth. The drama of book 6 is inextricably connected with the prophecies of books 3 and 12.

To the vision of Eden restored, of course, the poem moves steadily from the proem on. Before and after the fall, God promises that the golden days of Eden will return, that a new Heaven and earth will be established. God's own words in book 3, assuring that realm ("see golden days, fruitful of golden deeds, / With

Joy and Love triumphing, and fair Truth,'' 3.337–338), are paraphrased by Michael when he delivers the promise to Adam in book 12 (''New Heaven, new Earth, Ages of endless date / Founded in righteousness and peace and love, / To bring forth fruits Joy and eternal Bliss,'' 12.549–551). These prophecies, though beautiful, are distant, cloudy images and dreams of a future that is to be—enigmas still dark. They foretell a sunrise that has not yet occurred, depict a Christ who is to come in the clouds. But the distant hero of the Second Coming is that same Son of book 6, whom we have known face to face through Raphael's account, whom we have seen mount his splendid chariot, whose salvation was intimately and dramatically real. Moreover, the Son in book 6 performs there, and only there, the conquest of evil and the regeneration of good he is yet to perform on earth. The visions of earth are the truth of Heaven.

Paradise Lost concludes as Adam and Eve make their solitary way through Eden, the consequences of their disobedience all too vividly portrayed in that eastern gate, lit with dreadful faces and fiery arms. Half of the sentence in the proem has been fulfilled—they know the mortal taste of the fruit, the desolation of a lost Eden, the woes of a world-to-be. Before them is the world, choice of rest, and a providence to guide them. The second half of that sentence may yet be fulfilled, as the accounts of both angelic teachers have assured. The prophecy of Michael is the promise for the future, the narrative of Raphael the assurance from the past. In recounting the Son's victory, Raphael foretold for Adam and Eve a triumph they could not yet share. But his assurance that the Son had put down evil in Heaven and had restored it to its golden state was to become the pledge that the same Son (known now as the greater man of the poem's proem and the revealed savior) would once more triumph and restore the golden days—''for then the Earth / Shall all be Paradise, far happier place / Than this of *Eden,* and far happier days'' (12.463–465).

Index

Index

Index

315

The War in Heaven

Designed by Richard E. Rosenbaum.
Composed by The Composing Room of Michigan, Inc.
in 10 point Times Roman V.I.P., 3 points leaded,
with display lines in Times Roman.
Printed offset by Thomson/Shore, Inc. on
Warren's Number 66 Antique Offset, 50 pound basis
Bound by John H. Dekker & Sons, Inc.
in Holliston book cloth.

Library of Congress Cataloging in Publication Data

Revard, Stella Purce.
  The war in heaven.

  Includes index.
  1. Milton, John, 1608–1674. Paradise lost. 2. Milton, John, 1608–
  1674—Political and social views. 3. Great Britain—Politics and
  government—1603–1714. 4. Devil in literature. 5. War in literature.
  I. Title.
  PR3562.R4   821'.4   79-23297

  ISBN 0-8014-1138-6